THE MEMOIR OF NAJATI SIDQI

MODERN MIDDLE EAST LITERATURES IN TRANSLATION
Series Editor: *Dena Afrasiabi*

Other books in this series include:
Seviyye Talip
Ibn Arabi's Small Death
Poetic Justice: an Anthology of Contemporary Moroccan Poetry

THE MEMOIR OF NAJATI SIDQI

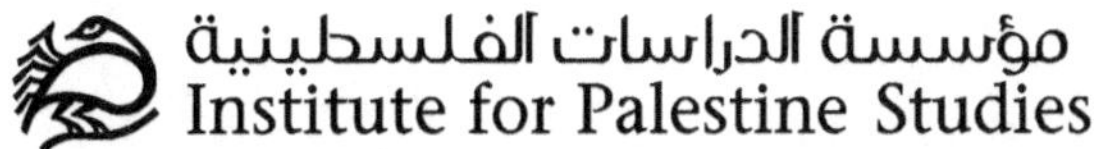

Printed in the United States of America.

Cover design by Saffron Kaplan
Book design and production by Allen Griffith of Eye 4 Design

Library of Congress Control Number: 2025944104
ISBN: 9781477333228

CONTENTS

ACKNOWLEDGEMENTS

This translation began as an undergraduate research project at Boston University growing out of Margaret Litvin's "Arabic Translation & Interpreting" course. We are grateful to the BU Undergraduate Research Opportunities Program (UROP), which generously funded Gideon Gordon's work in Spring 2023 and Anas Farhan's work in Spring and Summer 2023; we also thank Associate Dean of Humanities Alice Tseng and the Humanities Research Fund. Litvin's 2021-22 Radcliffe Fellowship offered time and a receptive community to research the Sidqi family. Fellowships from the BU NEH Humanities Professorship (2023), the Foreign Language & Area Studies program (2023-24), and the Center for Arabic Study Abroad (2024-25) helped hone Gordon's Arabic language and translation skills.

As Sidqi's grandson Marwan Zeibak notes in his preface, many scholars before us have been drawn to Najati Sidqi's legacy. Our first debt is to Palestinian poet-scholar Hanna Abu Hanna (1928-2022), whose editing work left us an excellent source text. For information, documents, and conversations that helped us contextualize Sidqi and figure out details large and small, we thank historians and filmmakers Marc Almodóvar, Joel Beinin, Musa Budeiri, Abigail Jacobson, Masha Kirasirova, Nieves Paradela, Amal Ramsis, Salim Tamari, Sana Tannoury-Karam, and Yair Wallach. We are grateful to the Institute for Palestine Studies and especially to IPS head librarian Hala Zeinelabidin, who graciously facilitated access to Sidqi's archive in Beirut during a summer 2023 research trip. Other archival sources came from Paris, where we thank the staff of the Pierrefitte National Archive for sharing relevant files from the Fonds de Moscou, a treasure trove of French police reports on Comintern activism. Materials from the Russian State Archive of Socio-Political History in Moscow (RGASPI) were kindly obtained by Andrei Nesterov. Michelle Ramiz, also on a BU UROP fellowship, helped decipher Najati and Lotka's handwritten Russian correspondence. Sari Shrayteh provided research assistance in Beirut.

We thank Tarek al-Ariss for suggesting the University of Texas Press, an ideal home for this book. The text benefited from the generous feedback of Orit Bashkin and William Granara (who have revealed their identities as our peer reviewers) and from Dena Afrasiabi's attentive editing and Allen Griffith's layout wizardry. We thank Saffie Kaplan at the UT Center for Middle East Studies for designing a cover that captures Sidqi's enthusiasm for new cities and sights. Cartographer Bill Nelson helped visualize the extent of Sidqi's travels. Sarahh Scher provided an excellent index. Joel Beinin read the text for accuracy and kindly contributed an informative, timely foreword.

Above all, through every stage of this project from concept to publication, we have appreciated the keen interest and good suggestions of the Sidqi family: Najati and Lotka's son Said Sidki in Brazil, their daughter Hind Sidki Zeibak in Athens, their grandson Marwan Zeibak in London, and the Sidqis' great-granddaughter Alina Papikian in Moscow, as well as members of the Dafni extended family in Israel. These relatives have generously shared photographs, letters, official documents, recollections, and thoughts, and we are grateful for their trust. It has been a huge honor to make Najati's story available to his descendants who do not read Arabic.

Our own families have also been wonderful. We are grateful for the support and patience of Ken, Henry, and Esther Garden; Jennifer, Stacy, Samuel, and Jacob Gordon; and Alfadino, Mazlina, Anis, Deena, Rayyan, and Imtinan.

Finally, we three are grateful to each other for making this project the pleasant collaboration it has been. Begun as an experiment, this translation has kept us company for 30 months, sparking some good transatlantic conversations about ideology, travel, heroism, and hats. Now it can keep you company as well. We hope you enjoy it as much as we have.

PREFACE

Marwan Zeibak

The path to publishing my grandfather's memoir in English has been a journey of many decades. My grandfather wrote the book in two phases—beginning in 1958 and completing it in early 1976. He did so at the behest of my mother and uncle, who believed that this incredibly tumultuous period of his life, which was shaped by some of the most consequential events of the twentieth century, needed to be documented. Only a few months after finishing it, in April 1976, he carried a copy of the manuscript by hand to Athens as he fled the Lebanese Civil War.

Years after his death in 1979, the manuscript was tracked down by the Palestinian writer and poet Hanna Abu Hanna, who edited it and had it published by the Institute of Palestine Studies in 2001. Now, more than twenty years later, it is being published in English for the first time. For our family, this is a triumph, not only because it allows the memoir to reach a wider international audience, but also because, on a deeply personal level, it means that my siblings and cousins and I—most of whom are not fluent in Arabic—are finally able to read our grandfather's words. In his own voice we're able to hear about his daring travels, clandestine missions, and encounters with some of the more colorful revolutionaries of the time.

That a new wave of scholars has taken interest in my grandfather's work is a testament to the enduring nature of his political and literary legacy.

The principles he championed remain more relevant than ever in today's geopolitical climate. Our family sincerely hopes that readers will appreciate the unique historical value of this text. Additionally, we would like to share three personal reflections as we revisit—or, for many of us, read for the first time—my grandfather's memoir, many years after it was originally written.

The first reflection is that many readers will notice what isn't said in my grandfather's memoir as much as what is. My grandfather was a private and protective person, and he chose to focus his memoir only on his political journey, which was the first phase of his intellectual life. However, Margaret Litvin and Gideon Gordon's introduction does a beautiful job of shining a light on the nameless and faceless "shadows that underlie" his account. This is a reference to my grandmother, Lotka, and my aunt, Dawlat—they were at the center of my grandfather's life during this period, despite their absence in his memoir. This book is dedicated to these two formidable women, whose extraordinary courage in the face of terrible injustice is an inspiration, and whose stories we believe also deserve to be told.

The second reflection is that preserving Palestinian history has never been more crucial, especially at a time when the near-total erasure of Palestinian identity and society is taking place. In this moment, it is essential that we amplify the voices of the victims of the ongoing genocide and tell the stories of those who came before us—particularly those that challenge colonial narratives and distorted portrayals of Palestinian society. Despite being born into two different, often conflicting cultures, my grandparents enjoyed a loving fifty-year marriage built on their shared commitment to political justice and human rights for all. Now, more than ever, their message must be shared.

The third reflection is that liberation struggles around the world are interconnected and rely on each other to thrive. My grandfather put this lofty idea into action through his involvement in the Spanish Civil War, declaring that his goal was to liberate the Arab world by combating fascism in Europe. He further exemplified this moral stance when he publicly condemned the

Molotov-Ribbentrop Pact. In doing so, my grandfather prioritized morality over party loyalty, at great personal cost, recognizing that at the heart of Nazism was racism, which both thrived on and further fueled the extreme oppression of the "other."

Examining the modern-day Palestinian rights movement, it is evident that the strongest sources of international support are emerging from those communities and groups that understand that the struggles of oppressed people everywhere are intertwined, our fates interdependent, and that "nobody is free until everybody is free."

As a final note, our family would like to extend a deep and heartfelt thank you to all those who have kept my grandparents' legacy alive over the years through their tireless scholarship, research, and documentation. There are many, and we are grateful.

FOREWORD

Joel Beinin

Only a small number of firsthand texts by Palestinian Arabs record their experiences confronting the Zionist colonial settlement project and British imperial rule in British Mandate Palestine. Even fewer such texts are available in English. Najati Sidqi's memoirs are valuable for this reason alone. Some might discount their significance because Sidqi was a member of the Palestine Communist Party (PCP), which was on the political margins of both the Jewish and Arab communities—but as this book shows, marginal and even politically homeless voices can offer insights that more mainstream nationalist perspectives render invisible.

Under the British Mandate, coalitions led by urban notables and large landowners dominated Palestinian Arab politics. The Arab Executive, comprised of Muslim and Christian notables, was established in 1920 and led by Musa Kazim al-Husayni, whom the British had recently deposed as mayor of Jerusalem. Shortly thereafter, Musa Kazim's distant relative, al-Hajj Amin al-Husayni, accepted a British appointment as Grand Mufti of Jerusalem. Al-Hajj Amin also served as president of the British-established Supreme Muslim Council. By the 1930s two major factions emerged. The *majlisiyya* (Councilites) followed Amin al-Husayni, while Mayor Raghib al-Nashashibi, from a rival Jerusalemite family, led the *mu'aridun* (Opposition).

The PCP had no confidence in the politics of notables or any of the coalitions they led. It believed that Arab and Jewish workers, supported by the Arab peasantry, were the only force that could defeat Zionism and British imperialism and overturn the regressive social order dominated by the notables. It understood the Palestinian national movement as a component of the global struggle against imperialism with many international allies, not only in other Arab countries but also as far away as the Soviet Union and Republican Spain.

That strategy has been judged harshly because it failed, magnified by the derailment of 20th-century socialism and by the Soviet Union's conceptual dogmatism and multiple crimes. Perhaps a longer-term historical perspective might reconsider that judgement in the light of the failure (to date) of any other strategy.

Communism emerged in Palestine as a movement of a small group of radicalized Ashkenazi Jews who had recently arrived in Palestine as Zionist settlers. Inspired by the 1917 Bolshevik Revolution, they sought to align themselves with the Communist International (Comintern) established in 1919 under the leadership of the Communist Party of the Soviet Union. Najati Sidqi was one of the first Arab recruits to the PCP. He joined the party soon after the Comintern accepted the PCP's application for membership in March 1924.

Four months later, Karl Radek, the head of the Comintern's Eastern Section, wrote to the Third PCP Congress, "Until now, the party was composed of immigrant Jews. In the future, it must become a party of Arab workers to which Jews can belong who have acclimated and rooted themselves in the Palestinian conditions, people who know Arabic." This would have been a formidable task even if the worldwide upsurge of socialist and anti-imperialist movements anticipated by the Comintern after World War I had succeeded. However, following the defeat of revolutionary movements in Germany, Italy, Iran, China, and elsewhere, implementing this directive was beyond the capacity of a small, new political formation comprised overwhelmingly of Russian- and Yiddish-speaking Jews, some of whom were not yet fluent in Hebrew, let alone Arabic. Nonetheless, internationalist discipline required the PCP to accept the Comintern line.

Sidqi was well positioned to recount the PCP's internal struggles in its efforts to Arabize and its ideological and strategic debates over how the party should relate to the conservative leadership of the Palestinian Arab nationalist movement. But he chose to tell a different story. We learn much more about his experiences as one of about a dozen Arabs and five Jews the PCP sent to Moscow for political education at the Comintern's Communist University of Toilers of the East (KUTV) between 1925 and 1930, his work as a journalist for *al-Sharq al-'Arabi* in Paris in 1933-36, and his work to defend the Spanish Republic during the Spanish Civil War of 1936-39 than about the PCP's trajectory and his role in it.

Sidqi offers fascinating details about his life as a student in Moscow in 1925-28. His capsule summaries of the KUTV curriculum suggest a rigid and dogmatic Marxism poorly informed about the specific conditions of countries of the global South. Sidqi is obliquely critical of Stalinism, especially Stalin's dismissive assessment of the revolutionary capacity of the nationalist movements of colonized peoples which often impeded the progress of Arab communism, and the suppression of political debate among KUTV students. He encounters, but doesn't seem to have much understanding of, the early sexual politics of the Russian revolution. His discussion of the relationships of the foreign KUTV students with young Russian women doesn't seem notably different than what might be expected of students in a bourgeois university. Sidqi also tells us about the conditions of life in Moscow in the post-World War I and post-Russian Civil War era and the popular pride in modernizing accomplishments like the construction of the Moscow metro.

Within a year after Sidqi returned to Palestine, the 1929 Buraq Uprising (known in British and Zionist parlance as the Western Wall Disturbances) erupted. During the week of August 23-29, 1929, Arabs killed 133 Jews and injured between 198 and 339 others. British Mandate police and Jews killed 116 Arabs, including 20 who died in revenge attacks by Jews or indiscriminate British police gunfire, and wounded at least 232. According to the report of the British Government's Commission on the Palestine Disturbances of August 1929 (the Shaw Commission), the Arab attacks on Jews in Jerusalem, Hebron, Safed, and a score of other localities were a response to increasing tensions over communal rights at the Western Wall, the retaining wall of the Second Temple known as al-Buraq Wall in the Muslim tradition. On August 15, right-wing Zionists had demonstrated at the Western Wall, chanting "the Wall is ours," and raised the Zionist flag. The Shaw Commission's report also noted the broader context: "the Arab feeling of animosity and hostility towards the Jews consequent upon the disappointment of their political and national aspirations and fear for their economic future" and fears that Jewish immigrants constituted "a menace to their livelihood [and] a possible overlord of the future."

Sidqi tells us that the PCP Central Committee debated how to define the Buraq Uprising: was it a sectarian massacre or a nationalist revolt? He reports that many Jewish party members considered it a massacre. But the Central Committee decided "that it was a nationalist uprising that had no connection to outbreaks of incidents of sectarian violence like the murder of the Sheikh of the Jaffa mosque and his family, the massacre of students in a Talmud school in Khalil [Hebron], or other anomalous incidents uncharacteristic of uprisings." This is a partial and misleading account. It is unclear if Sidqi was fully aware of the scope of the contentious debate and the issues at stake or if, writing in 1976, he was circumspect due to residual communist loyalty or to protect his daughter Dawlieh, who still lived in the Soviet Union.

The local party leadership, still overwhelmingly Jewish, initially judged the 1929 events to be akin to a pogrom. The Comintern ordered the PCP to revise its evaluation and to understand the events as a nationalist uprising.

The Comintern's determination was not based on firsthand investigation but derived from its analysis of the three stages of global post-World War I history: a first period of revolutionary anti-capitalist upheavals that included the victory of the Bolshevik revolution; a second period of capitalist consolidation during most of the 1920s; and a third period of renewed radicalization and revolutionary activity from 1928 on. If this schema was correct, then whatever excesses may have been committed by the Palestinian Arabs who rose up in August 1929 could be considered the collateral damage of a revolutionary movement.

Oddly, for a political movement that prided itself on having a dialectical analysis of history, neither the PCP nor the Comintern seemed to consider the possibility that the Buraq Uprising could be both: a sectarian riot whose Jewish victims were predominantly ultra-Orthodox non-Zionists, and simultaneously an anti-colonial uprising motivated, as the Shaw Commission suggested, by Palestinian Arab anxieties about Zionist designs on a Muslim holy site as well as concerns about the political and economic future of Palestinian Arabs. Revolts against settler colonialism have frequently entailed indigenous peoples brutally attacking civilians, whether unorganized, as in the case of the Buraq Uprising, or organized, as in native American tribes' opposition to the colonization of North America or the 1956-57 Battle of Algiers.

The Comintern abandoned its erroneous periodization of world history after Hitler came to power in 1933. This cleared the way for the shift to the policy of a popular front against fascism formally adopted at the 7th Congress of the Comintern in 1935, too late to confront the rise of fascism in Germany.

A second factor in the Comintern's instruction to the PCP to revise its understanding of the Buraq Uprising was the party's failure to implement the Comintern's Arabization directive earlier in the 1920s. Sidqi relates that the Jewish party leaders were reluctant to share the leadership with Arab members whom they considered less well-trained theoretically. Sending Arab members to study in Moscow was meant to prepare them for party leadership. But Sidqi was one of only four of the Palestinian Arabs sent to study in Moscow who returned to Palestine to become PCP leaders.

Sidqi was elevated to the PCP Central Committee in the aftermath of the Buraq Uprising. He does not explicitly say that this was part of the effort to implement the Comintern's Arabization directive. But it seems likely. Even after his elevation to the party Central Committee he seems to have had a weak appreciation of the scope of action of the international communist movement.

Sidqi was surprised that the Central Committee convened to discuss the impending 1931 Profintern (Red International of Labor Unions) conference, and he sounds even more surprised that he was selected as one of the party's two delegates to the conference. Readers of his memoir may be caught off guard too, because Sidqi has told us nothing about his trade union work that would explain his selection. The only relevant information he supplies is that he directed the party's work in Haifa, the center of both Arab and Jewish trade unionism, and was in touch with two Lebanese railway worker activists and with Sheikh 'Izz al-Din al-Qassam, who attracted many port workers to the Istiqlal mosque where he served as imam. The party's trade union work was not very successful at this point, so it is possible that there was simply little of note to report.

Another site on which Sidqi focuses more than on communist activity in Palestine is the Spanish Civil War of 1936-39. Sidqi was one of five Arab members of the PCP who served on the republican side during that war. The others were with the International Brigades: Naguib Youssef, Fawzy Sabri al-Nabulsi, Malih al-Kharruf, and 'Ali 'Abd al-Khaliq, who died fighting for the Spanish Republic.

A fictionalized version of 'Abd al-Khaliq's life is the subject of Hussein Yassin's Arabic novel, *'Ali: The Story of an Honorable Man*, which was long-listed for the 2018 International Prize for Arabic fiction. In that novel, Yassin quotes a sentence from Sidqi's memoir in which he introduces himself to a squad of republican militiamen who stopped him on the street shortly after he arrived in Barcelona to ask why he wasn't enrolled in their ranks. "I am an Arab volunteer who has come to defend the Arabs' freedom on the Madrid front! I have come to defend Damascus in Guadalajara, Jerusalem in Cordoba, Baghdad in Toledo, Cairo in Andalusia, and Tétouan in Burgos," he proclaims. Here we see some of Sidqi's literary flair and his appreciation of the link between the pan-Arab struggles against western colonial powers (France, Britain, Spain) and the defense of democracy against fascism in Spain. He elegantly presents his internationalist outlook as rooted in Arab anti-imperialist struggles.

Sidqi is not shy about acknowledging racism in the communist milieu. Just as he noted the anti-Black racism among Muscovites when he was a student, he relates that communist officials in Paris were angered by his criticism of "the colonialist tendencies of some leaders of both the French and Spanish communist parties," his call to Arabize the Communist Party of Algeria, and his reproach of the Spanish Communist Party leaders for their indifference to the Moroccan colonial question. The Communist Party of France did not support Algerian independence until after French President Charles de Gaulle declared his willingness to accept Algerian self-determination in late 1959.

After his time in France and Spain, Sidqi was sent to Damascus to work with the Communist Party of Syria under the leadership of Khalid Bakdash. There he broke with the international communist movement by denouncing the August 21, 1939, Molotov-Ribbentrop Pact between Hitler and Stalin. His book *al-Taqalid al-islamiyya wa'l-mabadi' al-naziyya: hal tattafiqan?* (Islamic Traditions and Nazi Principles: Are They Compatible?) argues that racism was the most important element in Nazi ideology that rendered it incompatible with Islam. It is an important statement in opposition to Palestinian and other Arab nationalists who flirted with or were outright collaborators with fascism simply because the Axis was fighting against the British and French empires.

Sidqi's book also criticizes the nominally liberal Egyptian Wafd's limited willingness to support the British war effort, arguing that it was in the interest of Muslims to stand "shoulder to shoulder with English, French, Polish and Czech soldiers" against fascism despite their colonial empires.

These views rendered Sidqi politically homeless—a socialist internationalist who believed that it was politically and morally unacceptable to align with fascism, even if it temporarily served the state interests of the Soviet Union, and an Arab nationalist who rejected the dictum that the enemy of my enemy is my friend. Operation Barbarossa, the Nazi invasion of the Soviet Union on June 22, 1941, vindicated Sidqi and other anti-fascists who had objected to the Hitler-Stalin pact. By then, Sidqi had abandoned politics for a career in literature and journalism. His memoir stands as a lesson in the historical significance of politically homeless dissident voices—in his case, of those who fell between the emerging poles of twentieth-century politics, denounced as Trotskyists in the Soviet camp and labeled "premature anti-fascists" by American McCarthyites.

THE MEMOIR OF NAJATI SIDQI

INTRODUCTION

Margaret Litvin and Gideon Gordon

Najati Sidqi—print and radio journalist, early Palestinian recruit to the Communist Party, outspoken anti-fascist, literary translator, and short story writer—has been recognized as an important figure in many fields of Arabic culture. For scholars of Arab anti-Nazism, Sidqi stands as "a bold voice raised against the raging waves" of Hitler's appeal to the Palestinians, steadfast in arguing that fascism (whether in Spain or in Germany) contravened both Islamic tradition and socialist principles.[1] Political scientist Musa Budeiri flags Sidqi as "probably the first Palestinian to try and acquaint his readers with the ideas of Ibn Khaldoun, Darwin and Descartes."[2] Novelist Ghassan Kanafani praises him as the earliest materialist chronicler of Arab nationalism.[3] The

1 Mustafa Kabha, "A Bold Voice Raised Above the Raging Waves: Palestinian Intellectual Najati Sidqi and His Battle with Nazi Doctrine at the Time of World War II," in *The Holocaust and the Nakba: A New Grammar of Trauma and History*, ed. Bashir Bashir and Amos Goldberg (Columbia University Press, 2018), 154–72. See also Israel Gershoni, "Why the Muslims Must Fight against Nazi Germany: Muhammad Najātī Sidqī's Plea," *Die Welt Des Islams* 52, no. 3/4 (2012): 471–98; John Broich, "Did the Muslim World Really Fall for Hitler?," *Slate*, March 13, 2017.

2 Musa Budeiri, *The Palestine Communist Party, 1919-1948: Arab & Jew in the Struggle for Internationalism* (London: Ithaca Press, 1979), 70. For Sidqi's presentation of Ibn Khaldun, "the first Arabic philosopher to attempt a materialist interpretation of history," see *Al-Tali'a* 1, January 1, 1937, pp. 6-13, online at *https://archive.alsharekh.org/Articles/266/19169/434411.*

3 Ghassan Kanafani, *Palestine: The 1936–39 Revolt* (London: Tricontinental Society, 1980).

Palestinian Ministry of Culture sponsors an annual short story prize in Sidqi's name.[4] But very few readers have encountered what we believe to be Sidqi's masterpiece: this memoir, completed in the late 1970s.

Born in Jerusalem in 1905, Sidqi died in 1979 in Athens, Greece—his second exile—leaving behind his wife Lotka Lorberbaum Sidqi, their three children in three different countries, a good shelf's worth of short stories and radio scripts, and this memoir. Edited by Palestinian writer Hanna Abu Hanna and published by the Institute for Palestine Studies in 2001, the memoir is a fun and idiosyncratic read. Sidqi was both energetic and unlucky enough to experience many of the early twentieth century's upheavals: the first decade of Stalin's USSR, the Arab-Jewish intercommunal violence of 1929-31 (a national liberation uprising to some, a pogrom to others), the Spanish Civil War of 1936, and the rise of the Nazis. He would later experience the loss of Palestine in 1948, the failure of Arab nationalism, and finally the Lebanese Civil War, in whose shadow the memoir was written. To this dizzyingly eventful life full of historically significant encounters he brought his wide-ranging intellectual curiosity, wry sense of irony, and lively prose style. This English translation, introduced and annotated with a bibliographic essay for undergraduate readers, presents his full memoir in a European language for the first time.

Sidqi's memoir is a story of Communism from the movement's margin. Recruited to the movement in 1923-24 while working as a postal clerk in Jerusalem, he became one of the first Arabs to join the majority-Jewish Palestine Communist Party (PCP), which sent him to study at the Communist University of Toilers of the East (KUTV) in Moscow from 1925 to 1928. He analyzes the party's underground organization in the crucial British Mandate

4 For a recent announcement, see Al-Mayadeen.net, "I'lān natā'ij jā'izat Najāti Ṣidqī lil-qiṣṣa al-qaṣīra," Shabaka al-Mayadeen, January 8, 2023, *https://www.almayadeen.net/arts-culture/إعلان-نتائج-جائزة-نجاتي-صدقي-للقصة-القصيرة*. The Ministry held the competition in 2024 as well.

period, illuminating some of its paradoxes: a liberation movement nonetheless marked with subtle racism, an atheist group bound by ritual and dogma. (As Joel Beinin notes in his foreword, this part of Sidqi's account also includes some puzzling moments of vagueness.) While he is relatively successful at gaining a voice in the PCP itself, joining its Central Committee in 1930, Sidqi soon antagonizes powerful figures in the stiffly hierarchical Comintern and French Communist Party, which do not welcome his support for liberal Arab nationalism in the Levant and anticolonialism in the Maghreb. As Sidqi navigates the dangers of interwar politics, he develops his own political voice, which puts him at odds with the party line.

This memoir covers roughly the years 1923-1940, from Najati Sidqi's recruitment into the party to his separation from it during World War II. Besides describing political intrigue in Jerusalem, Jaffa, Haifa, and Acre—where Sidqi first dodges arrest for clandestine political activity, then vividly encounters British Mandate courts and prisons—the memoir ranges across an astonishing swath of interwar Europe, chronicling Sidqi's adventures in Stalin's Moscow, 1930s Paris, and Republican Madrid. As a student in Moscow he suffers a close brush with Bolshevik doctrine, hastily recanting some Trotsykist-sounding heresies before a jury of his Arab peers. Later he finds himself debating nationalities policy with Comintern leader Georgy Dimitrov and Chinese revolutionary Mao Zedong. In Paris, he evades the police while editing a clandestine Communist newspaper. In the Spanish Civil War, he rubs shoulders with key Republican figures, joining Dolores "La Pasionaria" Ibárruri at supper and trying to persuade the Republicans that Franco's Moroccan conscripts are not savage enemies but fellow victims of fascism.

Sidqi's account of these adventures sparkles with a mixture of earnestness and bemused detachment; the latter has frustrated some readers. Historian Salim Tamari calls Sidqi "the enigmatic Jerusalem Bolshevik": a memoirist stingy with private details, strangely aloof from the momentous events he has witnessed, even guilty of an "inability to come to grips with his personal and intimate relationships."[5] A more generous view, we believe, would be to read Sidqi's memoir in light of the family members he sought to protect and the literary tropes he channeled. Therefore, rather than reproduce Abu Hanna's detailed 2001 introduction, which specialist readers can access in Arabic, the rest of our introduction will sketch in two figures conspicuously missing from Sidqi's account: his wife Lotka Lorberbaum Sidqi (1905-2000) and their daughter Dawlieh Saadi (1930-2018). It will then point out a few of the familiar tropes that animate Sidqi's autobiographical narrative.

A DAUGHTER NAMED INTERNATIONALE

Sidqi was raised in an art-loving household with Ottoman heritage; his father Bakr Sidqi Alai Amini taught Turkish, and his mother Nazira Murad hailed from a prominent Jerusalem merchant family. In 1919, the 14-year-old Sidqi tagged along as his father traveled to help Prince Faisal battle the Wahhabi movement in the Hejaz, perhaps preparing him for a life of political adventure. Najati was close with his older brother Ahmad Sidqi (1903-1965), who would join him at KUTV in the late 1920s but then testify against him in a British court in Palestine in 1931, sending him to prison as a Communist for two years. Their younger sister Fikriyya (1919?-1979) stayed in Palestine, becoming an early feminist journalist and schoolteacher.[6]

5 Salim Tamari, "Najati Sidqi (1905-79): The Enigmatic Jerusalem Bolshevik," *Journal of Palestine Studies* 32:2 (2003): 79–94, 83. See also Tamari, "The Enigmatic Bolshevik from the Holy City," in *Mountain against the Sea: Essays on Palestinian Society and Culture* (Berkeley and Los Angeles: University of California Press, 2009), 167–75.

6 Nadia Harhash, *Nisā' al-Quds: al-Mar'a al-Filasṭīnīyah fī fatrat al-intidāb al-Brīṭānī* [Women of Jerusalem: Palestinian Women in the British Mandate Period] (Ramallah: al-Ri`a, 2018), 71, 90. See also 'A'ida al-Najjar, *Al-Quds wa-l-bint al-shalabiyya*, 2nd ed. (Amman: Dar al-Salwa 2012), 239. Al-Najjar reports that Fikriyya Sidqi's attendance at a Jerusalem YMCA lecture by Lebanese poet Ameen al-Rihani prompted a supportive comment from the stage and a writeup in the newspaper *Filastin*.

Meanwhile Najati's future wife Lotka, born in 1905 like Najati, was growing up in what was then Lwow, Poland. (It was seized by the Soviet Union in 1939 and today is Lviv, in western Ukraine.) Perhaps because Lotka's Jewishness was a sensitive topic, she appears in Najati's memoir only as a shadow. She is never named, described only as "my wife, a Ukrainian from the city of Lvov." She takes action only twice: once on the border crossing between Palestine and Lebanon, nodding silently to help fool a border guard, and once in Jerusalem, helping Najati evade police surveillance. According to her surviving children and grandchildren, Lotka was a secretive woman who never spoke about her life, let alone her Jewish origins or her tumultuous communist past.

Lotka's original name was Batsheva Nena Lorberbaum; her ancestors were rabbis and her parents shopkeepers who had relocated from their small village of Nadworna to the Austro-Hungarian city variously known as Lemberg, Lviv, and Lwow. Other families in Eastern Poland made similar moves, fleeing cholera outbreaks and anti-Jewish pogroms.[7] Sloughing off identities as she outgrew them, the teenaged Batsheva adopted the more European-sounding name Charlotte (which became Lotte, then Lotka), joined a Zionist youth group, and in 1924, aged 19, moved to Palestine alone on the heels of her older brother Zalman (1899-1972). Their parents Yakov and Tsippora Lorberbaum were killed in the Holocaust in 1941; the fate of Lotka's two younger brothers is unclear.[8]

Lotka met Najati Sidqi in Jerusalem in 1929, soon after his return from Moscow's Communist University of the Toilers of the East, and embarked

7 For a memoir by another Polish-born Israeli Jewish communist of similar age, see Leah Trachtman-Palchan, *Between Tel Aviv and Moscow: A Life of Dissent and Exile in Mandate Palestine and the Soviet Union*, trans. Nir Arielli (London: Radcliffe Press, 2015).

8 We rely on family details and Yad Vashem certificates kindly shared by the Dafni family of Tel Aviv and Eilat. A Russian-language family tree handwritten by Dulia (Dawlieh, also called Dawlat) Saadi late in life, apparently with her mother's help, names two younger brothers, Yakhil (b. 1907-8) and Shahin (b. 1909-11), adding that Shahin moved to Palestine and became a rabbi.

with him on an activist romance. They communicated in a mix of Arabic and Russian. In a period when many Communists married citizens of Palestine to evade deportation by the British, this relationship was real. By August 1929, as Arab-Jewish riots convulsed Palestine in what one historian has called "Year Zero of the Arab-Israeli Conflict,"[9] Lotka was already pregnant with an Arab-Jewish baby. Stepping outside the *yishuv* Jewish community, she converted to Islam and began answering to Sitt Khadija. At times she wore a black headscarf, likely a ploy to help her convert Arab quarry workers and women to the communist cause, as the American consul in Jerusalem lamented.[10] The couple married before their daughter was born on March 17, 1930. They named her Dawlieh, meaning *Internationale.*

Arrested by the British in 1930 and again in 1931 for allegedly running an underground Communist printing press, Lotka braved a trial much like Najati's trial described in this memoir. Najati's brother Ahmad testified against her as well. The spectacle fascinated Jerusalem's Hebrew press: "She, who looks like a typical Jewish girl, sat cross-legged before the judge. She smiled sometimes and appeared irritated sometimes . . . These two lovers had the same views, they were enthusiastic disciples of Lenin, the rabbi of Moscow."[11]

However, their defiance would carry a terrible price. While Lotka and Najati were in prison, they sent their infant daughter away for safekeeping by the International Organization for Assistance to Revolutionaries (Russian

9 Hillel Cohen, *Year Zero of the Arab-Israeli Conflict 1929*, trans. Haim Watzman (Waltham, Mass.: Brandeis University Press, 2015).

10 Records of the Department of State Relating to Internal Affairs of Palestine, 1930-1944, Roll 3, American Consulate General—Jerusalem, Review of Communist Activities in Palestine, 1929 to March 31, 1932, Confidential, Jerusalem 13-7-1932, 33 pp.

11 "She Remains Loyal to Marx and Marries a Muslim," *Do'ar Hayom*, 1 December 1931, p. 1, kindly shared and translated by Yair Wallach. Explored in Wallach, "Lutka and Najati: Love and Communism in British Mandate Palestine," Ayin Press (blog), March 15, 2025, *https://ayinpress.org/lutka-and-najati-love-and-communism-in-british-mandate-palestine/.*

acronym MOPR). Dawlieh's last name became not Sidqi but Saadi, her father's revolutionary alias. Raised in Soviet orphanages, she would live in Russia for the rest of her life, despite her and her parents' fierce efforts to reunite. Lotka was particularly affected by the separation from her child. During the height of Stalin's purges (1936-39), while Najati sat in Paris or pursued glory in the Spanish Civil War, she lived for three precarious years with Dawlieh at the Comintern's Lux Hotel in Moscow, trying to secure custody and gainful employment. She failed. Instead Dawlieh was raised at the Interdom International Children's Home in Ivanovo alongside other children of world revolutionaries, surrounded by a warm transnational community but painfully severed from her parents and her language.[12] In a letter to her younger siblings Hind and Said in 2005, Dawlieh/Dulia/Dawlat wrote:

> I am 75 now and I lived all my life without my family, without my motherland, without my native language and culture. This is a great tragedy of my life. My childhood was warped, for I lived without my parents [and] my sister and brother who were alive and with whom I could have joined if not for the terrible communist distortions and cruelty, which sometimes were absolutely senseless and unexplainable.[13]

Written in Russian, the letter had to be translated for her siblings to read.

The Sidqis suffered other losses as well. Expelled from the Communist Party for his trenchant 1940 Islamic-based critique of Nazism, Sidqi lived the rest of his life apart from his Party colleagues, scraping by financially only

12 This poignant predicament is explored in Amal Ramsis's feminist documentary about the Sidqi family, *You Come from Far Away* (2018).

13 English and Arabic translations (not the Russian original) in Najati Sidqi Papers, folder 6, Institute for Palestine Studies, Beirut.

through ceaseless writing: journalism, short stories, and translations. The 1948 Nakba, or Catastrophe (as Palestinians refer to the expulsion of Palestinians that accompanied the founding of the State of Israel), separated both Sidqis from their respective siblings in Palestine. Najati's brother Ahmad and sister Fikriyya stayed in Jerusalem with their mother under Jordanian and then Israeli rule; neither ever married. Both siblings sent warm letters to Najati in Cyprus and then Beirut, commenting on his publications and listening avidly to his radio broadcasts, but they never saw him after 1948. Meanwhile, Lotka's brother Zalman and his family lost track of her; only through Amal Ramsis's 2018 documentary did the Jewish branch of her family became aware of her fate. That branch's name is Dafni (i.e., Daphne), the Hebrew translation of Lorberbaum, which means "laurel tree" in German—a fitting Ovidian metamorphosis for Lotka's much-transplanted family tree.

A THEMATIC READING

Though not consciously intended as a literary work, Sidqi's memoir plays with many elements of the Arabic travel writing tradition. The most obvious is attention to the texture of language: different registers of slang and jargon, translation slippage, and the distance between words and deeds. Sidqi frequently forgets dates and details of events—he places an anecdote about U.S. President Herbert Hoover anachronistically in the mid-1920s, and even bungles Vladimir Lenin's first name—but he recalls many punchlines and witty turns of phrase decades after he uttered them. Describing an argument with his Arab fellow students at KUTV, Sidqi shows them yelling in Egyptian dialect while he responds in mellifluous literary Arabic. Translating the Internationale and other socialist hymns into Arabic, the comrades disagree over word choices and finally opt to sing the Russian. Recalling how he met a Spanish Republican militia leader in Barcelona, Sidqi portrays himself as a polyglot cosmopolitan choosing every winged syllable with care:

I declared with a smile, in French, with the enthusiasm of youth: "I am an Arab volunteer, come to defend liberty in Madrid, Damascus in the Valley of Stones [Guadalajara], Jerusalem in Córdoba, Baghdad in Toledo, Cairo in Cádiz, and Tetouan in Burgos."

In this alliterative and chiastic *tour de force*, the young Arab volunteer envisions nothing short of liberating the Arab world from its imperialist occupiers, starting with the once-great cities of historical Muslim Spain and North Africa. The boundary-melting idealism of his "belief in social justice and international solidarities" continues to inspire leftist scholars today.[14] But Sidqi is equally attuned to the limits of transcultural organizing, transcribing the broken Moroccan Arabic of his own failed call to Franco's conscripts. He also mentions the Spanish Republicans' caricature of the Moroccan fighter who pretends to surrender, shouting in ungrammatical Spanish, "Yo estar rojo" (I being red). We have tried to honor Sidqi's love of language and his curiosity about foreign words throughout our translation.

As Roxanne Euben and others have noted, the medieval Arabic literary genre of *riḥla* (journey narrative) emphasized the pursuit of knowledge.[15] Starting in twelfth-century North Africa and Muslim Spain, scholars would write a *riḥla* as a kind of curriculum vitae enumerating the centers of learning they had visited, the luminaries at whose feet they had learned, and the religious authority they had thus acquired. The typical *riḥla* described a voyage eastward to the

14 Sana Tannoury-Karam, "Not Monolithic: Reflections on the Communist International in the Levant," *Rosa Luxemburg Stiftung* (blog), *https://www.rosalux.de/en/publication/id/40817/not-monolithic*.

15 Roxanne Euben, *Journeys to the Other Shore: Muslim and Western Travelers in Search of Knowledge* (Princeton: Princeton UP, 2006), especially 34-8.

traditional centers of Islamic learning: Baghdad, Damascus, and Jerusalem.[16] During the *nahḍa* or Arab Renaissance of the nineteenth century, students sent abroad to pursue (secular) knowledge took this premodern *riḥla* genre as a model. Their voyages explicitly referred to the early modern tradition —but now headed mostly north and west: to Paris or London, or even St. Petersburg (an 1840s travelogue survives).[17] Twentieth-century *riḥla* narratives continued to visit those centers of learning but added others: Berlin, New York, and notably Moscow. Sidqi's book joins that tradition, highlighting themes of wonders and marvels; encounters with foreign women; and religious and national identity.

Joining the communist movement at its internationalist height, Sidqi evidently enjoyed traveling to distant shores and climes. His long chapter on 1920s Moscow reads like a modern *riḥla*, with details of the locals' clothing, foodways, religious observances, and jokes as well as his coursework at the Communist University of the Toilers of the East (KUTV). His prose is most vivid when reporting on foreign *'ajā'ib wa-gharā'ib* (strange and marvelous sights). However, unlike earlier travel writers who stressed natural wonders such as hitherto unknown landscapes or animals, Sidqi recalls his encounters with technological wonders: live translation headsets at a conference, gigantic planes, the German airship *Graf Zeppelin*. Raised in a progressive home in late-Ottoman Palestine—his family is said to be the first to have brought a

16 On the medieval *riḥla* tradition see Houari Touati, *Islam and Travel in the Middle Ages* (Chicago: University of Chicago Press, 2010).

17 See Rifā'a Rāfi' Ṭahṭāwī, *An Imam in Paris: Account of a Stay in France by an Egyptian Cleric (1826-1831)*, trans. Daniel L. Newman (Saqi, 2004); "An Egyptian Teacher Heads to St. Petersburg: al-Tantawi's *Gift of the Wise in the Account of the Land of Russia* (1840)," translated and introduced by Suha Kudsieh, chapter 4 in Eileen Kane, Masha Kirasirova, and Margaret Litvin, eds., *Russian-Arab Worlds: A Documentary History* (New York: Oxford UP, 2023).

phonograph to Jerusalem, provoking passers-by to listen to the "strange music" from the square outside[18]—he is fascinated by modern machines.

Twentieth-century Arabic *riḥla* narratives often dramatize the cross-cultural encounter through a romantic relationship: one local woman stands in for her whole society, acting as both a tour guide through Europe and a microcosm of it.[19] Travel writing about Russia, too, often refracts cultural difference through a single blue-eyed, rosy-cheeked Russian love interest.[20] Najati Sidqi, perhaps because his own family situation is so complex, avoids this trope. As we have seen, by the time he completed the memoir he and his Polish-born wife Lotka had been together for more than fifty years, living together in at least five countries where neither one of them was a typical representative of his or her respective society, and often communicating in a language, Russian, that was native to neither. Despite their different origins, there is no evidence that they ever exoticized each other.

Instead, the women in Sidqi's memoir signal the diversity of Soviet people and attitudes. This approach challenges both the clichés of Arabic *riḥla* literature and the USSR's official narrative about the Soviet New Man and New

18 Abū Hashhash, Ibrāhīm, "Najātī Sidqī: Al-qāṣṣ, al-mutarjim, al-nāqid wa-l-siyāsī" [Najati Sidqi: Short Story Writer, Translator, Critic, and Politician], in *Mawsū'at abḥāth wa-dirāsāt fī al-adab al-Filasṭīnī al-ḥadīth* [Encycyclopedia of Studies in Modern Palestinian Literature], ed. Yāsīn Kittānī (West Bank: Al-Qasimi Group for Arabic Literature, 2011). Also mentioned in an authorized profile of Sidqi by Jordanian historian Ya'qūb Al-Adwat, published under the pseudonym "Al-Badawi al-Mulatham" (The Masked Bedouin) in *Al-Adīb* magazine, May 1, 1968.

19 Benjamin Smith explains: "A motif employed by many texts is to dispatch an Arab male protagonist to Europe where he meets a female European counterpart. This relationship becomes the prism through which that Arab male learns about the West and its cultural and social mores." Smith, "Writing Amrika: Literary Encounters with America in Arabic Literature" (PhD, Harvard, 2014), 18-19. See also Rasheed El-Enany, *Arab Representations of the Occident: East-West Encounters in Arabic Fiction* (London: Routledge, 2006).

20 See, for instance, the character of Zoya in Egyptian writer Sonallah Ibrahim's 2011 novel *Ice*.

Woman that socialism would create. Rather than an exotic Russian other or monolithic New Society, Sidqi portrays friendships or flirtations with multiple women, each representing a different region and social class: "Shura from Ryazan," widowed by the Russian Civil War; Lyuba, a "fat village girl from near Rzhev" who is pregnant by an unknown partner; Valia, whose bourgeois and Christian Moscow family enjoys telling snide Stalin jokes. Sidqi is ironic about the romantic lives of his fellow Arab students, particularly those who womanize or are "captivated by the idea of free love." By contrast, he writes with compassion of the Soviet women left stranded by Arab lovers, Soviet partners, or their own dreams of freedom. In one section titled "Mingling with the Russians," he recounts:

> Kaba from Kaluga, a wheat-haired girl with a quiet nature, invited me one day to the dormitory where she lived and introduced me to a girl there. That girl was melancholy and sad, and asked me about life in the countries "beyond the border," about people who enjoy their lives, who wear what clothes they like, who read whatever books and magazines they want. A few days later, I learned from Kaba that the girl had hanged herself. This event was a violent shock to me, and I found it strange—as did the girls—that this girl had committed suicide, though there were many others like her in those days.

Other vignettes, ordinary and banal—a teenager invites Sidqi to an outdoor concert to make her boyfriend jealous; an elderly churchgoer is terrified to see Sidqi's African-American comrade and calls him a "demon"—reveal communism's failure to cultivate a New Soviet Person along the lines taught in the KUTV curriculum.

Religion, Karl Marx's "opiate of the masses," is another stubborn presence in Soviet society. Though the USSR and the communist movement are both officially atheist and rationalist, Sidqi's ethnographic eye is drawn to religious practices surviving in the margins of the Soviet space, sometimes in quiet coexistence with communist political education and sometimes in tension. A Muslim KUTV classmate brings his prayer rug to the dormitory, prompting a self-criticism session (the teachers are "lenient" because he is new).[21] A Russian woman attending Christmas Mass insists her ardent communist faith does not contradict her Christianity. On a visit to Soviet Tashkent, Sidqi recounts how an Uzbek official uses a Qur'an-based vodka toast to play on the post-Muslim status he and Sidqi share.[22] Later Sidqi is dismayed to find Franco's Moroccan troops ignoring his anti-imperialist arguments but heeding a Sufi saint who appears to them in dreams. Many people, in short, identify at least as strongly with some version of their religious heritage as with political ideals. Sidqi will apply this lesson when he publishes *Islamic Traditions and Nazi Principles: Are They Compatible?* (1940), the religion-based anti-fascist tract that precipitates his expulsion from the Communist party.[23]

Back home from Moscow, Sidqi attends to the vexed question of ethnicity and belonging. As an Arab Muslim in Palestine during the British Mandate, he navigates a complicated landscape of ethnic boundaries and wears—literally—many hats. A well-chosen disguise can transform his self-presentation from one ethnicity to another, but physical danger or arrest can result from a poorly-chosen alias or the wrong headwear: a tarboosh (fez) in a Jewish neighborhood during a British police sweep, or a Jewish-identified hat (a fedora or, less likely, a yarmulke) on a train during the 1929 intercommunal violence. In one of the only passages mentioning his wife Lotka, the Arab cloak (*milāya*) pulled over her head both explains her silence and veils her Jewish—and hence fugitive Communist—identity.

21 Masha Kirasirova, "The 'East' as a Category of Bolshevik Ideology and Comintern Administration: The Arab Section of the Communist University of the Toilers of the East," *Kritika: Explorations in Russian and Eurasian History* 18:1 (2017): 7–34.

22 For an astute reading of this encounter see Masha Kirasirova, *The Eastern International: Arabs, Central Asians, and Jews in the Soviet Union's Anticolonial Empire* (Oxford: Oxford UP, 2024).

23 Muḥammad Najātī Ṣidqī, *al-Taqālīd al-islāmiyya, wa-l-mabādi' al-nāziyya, hal tattafiqān* (Beirut: n.p., 1940).

According to the Sidqis' two surviving children Said Sidki (b. 1941) and Hind Sidki Zeibak (b. 1945), their father silenced and veiled their mother's presence in his memoir for the same reason he gave her the milaya: "to protect her." Downplaying his family life may have offered emotional protection to him as well. He never mentions Lotka's 1930s stay in Moscow, their failed ten-year custody battle with the Soviet state, or the other personal costs of their cloak-and-dagger revolutionary adventures.

But in the background of Najati Sidqi's rollicking tale, a sensitive reader can hear echoes of these struggles. His detailed description of the Comintern's Lux Hotel, where he personally spent only a few days, suggests his painful awareness of this building and its dark place in his family story. His description of Dolores Ibárruri notes with odd specificity that she sent her daughter to the Interdom in Ivanovo, outside Moscow; she and Sidqi's daughter would have been classmates. His tales from Moscow pay special attention to stories of relationships between Arab men and Soviet women, including an Egyptian student named Hassuna, who marries a Russian pharmacist named Shura and abandons their son Marun in the Soviet Union. (As Dulia Saadi once told an interviewer, a half-Egyptian young man named Marun was her only Arab classmate at the Interdom.) Among the stories he tells of his Arab classmates at KUTV is the dramatic story of 'Abd al-Ghani al-Karmi, who struggles to obtain an exit visa from the USSR and is finally arrested on accusations of espionage for trying to contact the British embassy for help. We hope our readers will experience Sidqi's memoir in its full depth, reading it with an awareness of the shadows that underlie Sidqi's colorful account of his brief and eventful communist career.

This book aims to serve several audiences: scholars of global leftist movements, scholars of Palestinian or Middle Eastern history, and students coming to these topics for the first time. Many of Sidqi's own footnotes and those added by editor Hanna Abu Hanna offer background facts that are easily searchable online today; we have omitted these, keeping only those that are obscure or show Sidqi's mind at work. Rather than annotate every peculiarity in Sidqi's text, we have silently corrected some small lapses, kept bracketed interpolations to a minimum, and provided some annotations in the bibliographic essay. We hope that the bibliographic essay provides students and teachers with more context as well as a jumping-off point for further research projects on Sidqi, which—like this remarkable man himself, and like the Palestinian intellectuals of his era—can branch out in many fascinating directions.

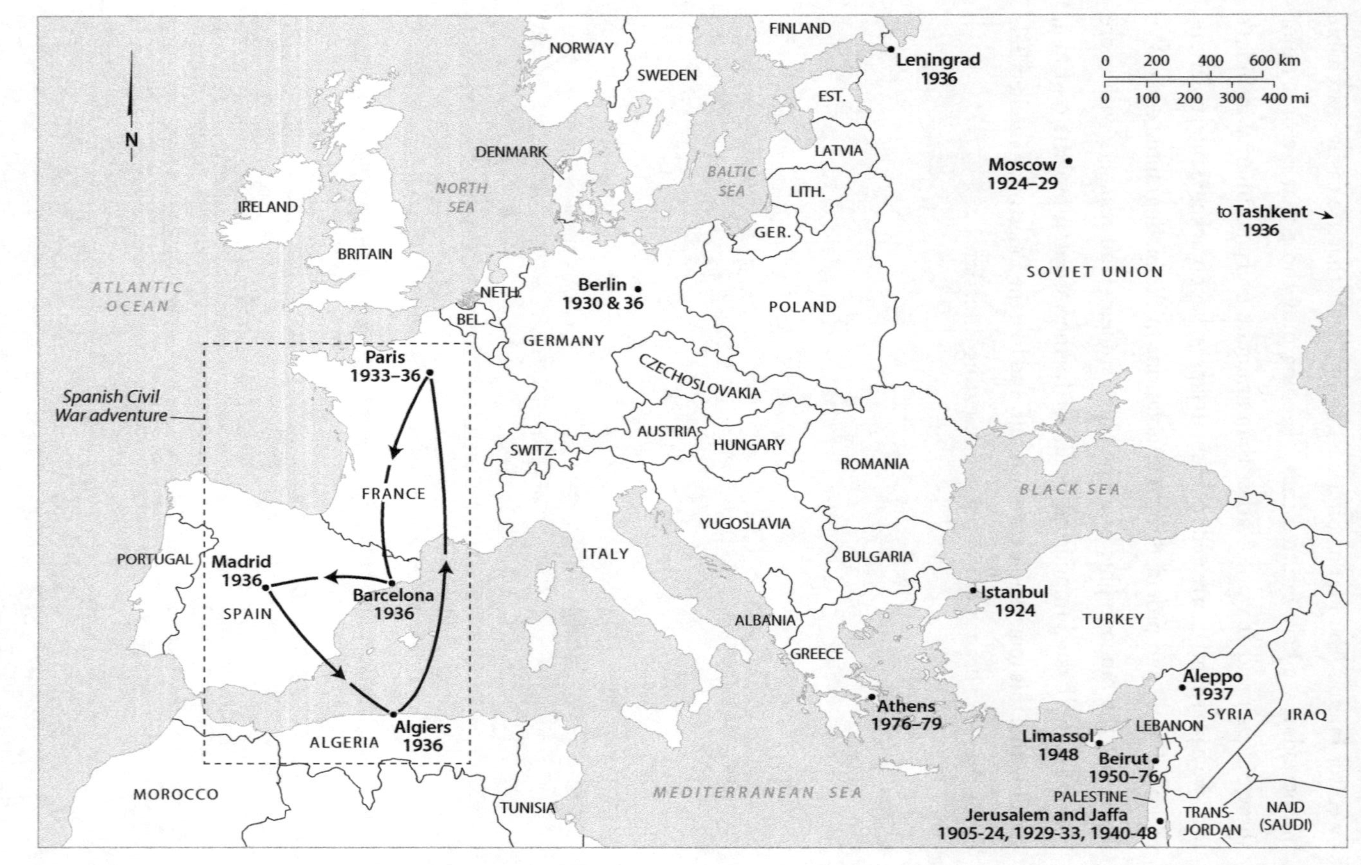
N
0 200 400 600 km
0 100 200 300 400 mi
FINLAND
NORWAY
SWEDEN
Leningrad 1936
EST.
LATVIA
LITH.
GER.
DENMARK
NORTH SEA
BALTIC SEA
Moscow 1924–29
to Tashkent 1936
IRELAND
BRITAIN
ATLANTIC OCEAN
NETH.
BEL.
Berlin 1930 & 36
GERMANY
POLAND
SOVIET UNION
CZECHOSLOVAKIA
AUSTRIA
HUNGARY
SWITZ.
ROMANIA
Paris 1933–36
Spanish Civil War adventure
FRANCE
BLACK SEA
YUGOSLAVIA
ITALY
BULGARIA
PORTUGAL
Madrid 1936
Barcelona 1936
SPAIN
Istanbul 1924
TURKEY
ALBANIA
GREECE
Aleppo 1937
Athens 1976–79
SYRIA
IRAQ
LEBANON
Algiers 1936
ALGERIA
Limassol 1948
Beirut 1950–76
MOROCCO
TUNISIA
MEDITERRANEAN SEA
PALESTINE
Jerusalem and Jaffa 1905-24, 1929-33, 1940-48
TRANS-JORDAN
NAJD (SAUDI)

1
COMMUNISTS IN PALESTINE
(1920–1924)

Jewish immigration to Palestine brought customs, ideas, and social practices alien to the conditions of Arab life in Palestine. In the early 1920s we started hearing of Bolshevism, of Anarchism, of Marx, Lenin, and Trotsky, and of [Theodore] Hertzl. We got to know the workers' movements among the Jewish immigrants, such as the Histadrut (the Federation of Jewish Workers), the Fraktsiya (the leftist opposition within the Histadrut), the Poalei Zion (Workers of Zion) party, and the *kibbutzim*, which were cooperative semi-socialist encampments for Jewish workers newly arrived in the country.

The Jewish workers with leftist inclinations sought to propagandize among the Arabs. The first demonstration they held in the streets of Jaffa was for May Day 1921: they raised red flags in the Manshiyya neighborhood and called out various chants in Hebrew and Arabic, as the Arab inhabitants watched them dumbfounded, unsure what these protestors were talking about or what they wanted. One group of knowledgeable Arabs said, "These Bolsheviks came from Russia influenced by the principles of the Revolution, and they're trying to apply those principles to the Arab milieu." Another group said, "These Red Zionists have called for a revolution against the Arabs. Let's have a revolution against them in return." The Jaffa Uprising of [May] 1921 was the first Arab revolt in Palestine.

The leftist workers' movement was represented among Jewish immigrants by the Poalei Zion party, which called for the establishment of a socialist Jewish state in Palestine instead of a bourgeois State of Israel. This group didn't recognize the Arab community; they considered the Arabs socially backward, the furthest people from adopting socialist theory. The party thought that the only solution to the Arab problem in Palestine was to integrate Arabs with Jews through assimilation and intermarriage. It would not be long before the Arabs dissolved into the socialist Jewish state.

An opposition emerged within the party, the seed of the communist movement in Palestine, calling for the establishment of a socialist state in Palestine in opposition to British colonialism and the Zionist bourgeoisie. Jewish workers would helm this state, as they were more conscious of class struggle. But the Arabs would continue to enjoy their distinct communal existence: there was no need to assimilate them into the Jewish people. Their workers and peasants would work towards the destruction of the effendi class with the help of their comrades among the Jewish workers, who were full of the revolutionary socialist ideas they had brought from Russia and Eastern Europe.

Russia's Bolsheviks at that time tended to support this opposition and agreed with a large part of its program, so they provided it with funding and direction. In 1923, the opposition group applied to join the Communist International (Comintern). Their application was accepted, and they became known as the "Communist Party of Palestine," replacing the name they had given themselves, "The Workers' Party of Palestine." They were given this name because the overwhelming majority of them were Jewish, and based on the understanding that this name would change to "The Palestinian Communist Party" when the number of Arabs in the party matched the Jews or outnumbered them.

At the time, I was an adolescent boy working at the Jerusalem post and telegraph office, which was located in the old Italian consulate, across from the

Barclays Bank today—that is, it stood on the dividing line between the Jewish and Arab neighborhoods outside the city walls. The office had employees from both communities, and I encountered a range of ethnicities and sects there. You would see your countrymen wearing Arab clothing, and Ashkenazis (the Jews from Germany who immigrated to Palestine before World War I for purely religious reasons) dressed in colorful velvet coats and wearing fur caps that looked very much like Tatar caps—they may have borrowed this whole style of dress from the Tatars when they reached the boundaries of Eastern Europe in their march. There were *halutzim*, the immigrant "pioneers," who wore short trousers whether they were men or women; and there were Sephardis, the remaining Arab Jews who had been displaced from Spain after the fall of Arab rule in the late fifteenth century. There were also Georgians, Jews who had been exiled by the Assyrians in the time of King Shalmaneser in 730 BCE, some of whom later returned to Palestine.

Najati Sidqi at the Post and Telegraph Office, Jerusalem, 1923

At this post office a variety of languages could be heard, and you could see costumes representing the different peoples and sects—or strange mixtures of them. You might see a Jewish girl in short trousers but with her head wrapped in an Arab keffiyeh; a Jewish boy wearing a sheepskin jacket; an Englishman wearing an immense qolbaq on his head (intending to arouse fright in the hearts of the population); or a peasant in a woolen abaya shod in heavy British army surplus boots.

We would rub shoulders with Jewish immigrants in this office in the course of work or in order to get to know each other. We would also drop by a small coffee shop, behind where the Barclays is today, owned by a tall, huge Russian Jew who wore white trousers and a black shirt that buttoned at the left shoulder. His head was shaved to keep him cool in the summer, and he had a round beard and mustache trimmed Russian-style. An attractive Polish girl worked at his cafe, with blond hair, a peaches-and-cream complexion, and blue eyes. In this little café, we would get together every evening and meet various visitors from abroad. There was a white-bearded Tsarist who said he had been captain of a Russian warship, but that the Bolsheviks had seized his ship in the port of Odessa. There was a young man with a Russian father and an Arab mother who worked in the municipal services. There was an immigrant painter who would draw portraits for a few piasters, a stylish woman who spoke a lot about her property in Ukraine, and immigrant girls and boys moistening their throats with swigs of soda water.

Conversation in this circle centered around a variety of topics: Jewish immigration, the Arab struggle, the mutiny of [Vladimir] Jabotinsky (the Russian Zionist extremist), the Battle of Tel Hai in northern Palestine during which the Jewish commander Joseph Trumpeldor was killed, the uprising in Jaffa, and the armed clash between Jews and Arabs in Jerusalem after Jabotinsky's march to the Wailing Wall in the Old City. These conversations pulsed with ideological questions, which some immigrants who spoke colloquial Arabic translated for us. We learned that socialism sought to extend its authority through representative bodies, that anarchism didn't recognize any sort of government and looked to manage the people's affairs through trade unions, and that Bolshevism (Arabs hadn't yet learned the term "Communism") had established a socialist government in Russia through a coup and the Red Army.

For us at the time, these events were opaque, distant from our local concerns. The things that mattered to us and which had seized our attention were the "frightening and mysterious future," "the English occupation," and "the Balfour Declaration." We had heard from our fathers that the British and French had come as liberators, that T.E. Lawrence was a friend of the Arabs, that the rebellion of Husayn bin 'Ali was intended to unify the Arabs and establish a state for them. We were attracted to the slogans written on the walls along the street, such as: "Long live independence!", "Down with colonialism!", "Down with the Balfour Declaration!", and "Give us independence or give us death!"

We grew up in this atmosphere. Hordes of colonists and Zionists burst into Palestine, while international ideologies invaded our impressionable minds. We were ready to listen to anything, to accept anything that might lift from us the nightmare of this new occupation that had followed Turkish rule.

At the Post Office Café, I got to know a group of immigrant youth who had come from Russia. They belonged to the Fraktsiya and the Workers' Party of Palestine, and they began to agitate among us, making the following points: First, British imperialism was an enemy of Jews and Arabs alike, and its policies were built on the principle of "divide and rule." Second, Jewish immigrants consisted of two groups, a wealthy bourgeoisie and desperate workers. Zionism was a bourgeois movement that benefited only wealthy Jews, but the interests of Jewish workers lay with international socialism, and they would work to overthrow their masters sooner or later. Third, the Arab effendis were opportunists collaborating with imperialism, and no good could come of them. And fourth, because the Workers' Party was for all inhabitants of Palestine, it was able to reconcile the interests of the working classes of both communities and to solve the Palestine problem in the fullest sense.

These were new and seductive ideas, proposals that called for careful consideration. The immigrants invited us to their club, located behind the German hospital in Jerusalem. There they told us about the arrest of their colleagues in Egypt and the death of one of them, a Lebanese Arab named Anton Maroun, in prison during a hunger strike. They presented us with an Arabic newspaper called *al-Insaniyya* (*Humanity*), published in Beirut by Yusuf Yazbek; on the front page was a drawing of the hunger striker praying to heaven. They also gave us a little pamphlet in Arabic about anarchism penned by Prince Kropotkin.

The meetings continued; sometimes they were held in the club, at other times in the Schneller Forest or among the rocks in the Ratisbonne area. One day in late 1924, when I was nineteen, they asked me, "Would you like to travel to Moscow to study at the university there without having to pay for travel, education, or housing?"

I didn't hesitate a moment before accepting their offer, and they told me to get ready to travel in six months. So I bent my efforts toward studying the basics of the Russian language with the help of an Arabic-speaking Russian youth; I learned Russian letters and spelling from him and memorized a few essential phrases. Meanwhile, the group held a conference for their youth in Haifa and invited me to it; they elected me as a representative of the Youth Central Committee. This proclaimed my official entry into the pro-Bolshevik movement. From then on, I was included in all the secret meetings, and I contributed to spreading the word and distributing pamphlets.

2

ON THE ROAD TO MOSCOW

(1925)

The time came for me to journey to the lands of the north. It was a dangerous adventure for a young Arab man to leave his home, his family, and his job to seek education in a strange place about which he knew nothing, not even a single word of the language. But he was driven by a thirst for learning and education, by the urgent need to fill the knowledge gap torn by World War I in the ranks of the rising Arab youth.

I worked to prepare a false passport, and I asked my father's permission to spend the week with family in Jaffa for the Prophet Reuben festival. I headed to the Jaffa port, where the steamer *Chicherin* was anchored. There, a Party member greeted me and passed me an entry visa for Turkey. Then he led me to the steamship and said, "Board as if you're a traveler going to Istanbul, but when you get aboard, ask for Comrade Orlov, the head of the Communist group on the ship. He's waiting for you and knows about your trip. Safe travels."

Before I left, I gave the party member a letter. I asked him to leave it in my father's mailbox three days after I set out, and he promised me he would. The letter said:

Jaffa, September 16, 1925

Dear Father,

When you receive this letter of mine, I will be looking out at the Mediterranean

Sea, on my way to Moscow to seek an education. Don't be worried or upset. The trip is very comfortable, and I am being treated excellently. I will live in the Russian capital for three years, then I will return to you, having received a great education in the arts and sciences. Don't imagine that I'm going to the North Pole! I will be only a ten days' journey from you. As for the cold there, I took along a thick military jacket just in case.

I ask that you forgive me. I will write to you constantly from Moscow.

Greetings from your obedient son,

Najati

My father later told me that when he received this letter of mine, he frothed and foamed. He went to Government House and shouted, "Bolshevism has stolen my son!" He demanded that the British send a warship after me to bring me back over the sea whatever the cost. But they explained to him that this was impossible and asked him to bear his shock with patience. They made do with recording his complaint.

The small merchant steamer *Chicherin* set off from the port of Jaffa heading west. Standing at its stern, I watched the customs office disappear, then the merchants' warehouses, the sailboats, the Hasan Bey Mosque, the orchards and orange groves spread out along the coastline. I bid farewell to the family in Jerusalem who thought I was enjoying myself at the Prophet Reuben festival west of Jaffa. As soon as evening had drawn its curtain over the old Palestinian port, I was reassured that the moment of danger was behind me. I went looking for the person I wanted, and saw a Russian sailor gathering up ropes. I approached and asked him, "*Tovarishch Orlov*?"

He realized that I was searching for Comrade Orlov, and he smiled, patted me on the shoulder, and indicated that I should follow him. He led me to the lower deck of the steamer and knocked on the door of a chamber. A voice from inside called out, "*Da*?", meaning "Yes?"

The sailor opened the door, revealing a giant Russian man with a shaved head who looked me over, then said, "Ah. Moscow University?"

I nodded to him in the affirmative. He took my hand, led me to the crew quarters and said to me in broken English, "*Hir you slip… Odessa*!" pointing to one of the beds. I took this to mean that I would sleep in a hammock in the quarters of the steamer's crew until I reached Odessa.

The first night was terrifying. The steamer was small, and the rough sea toyed with it as it pleased while my hammock tilted left and right. The steamer's bow rose high on the swells and then plunged towards the depths. You could hear the sailors' voices rising in shouts, sharp breaths, and grunts over the clatter of tea jugs and pots, the slap of wooden clogs on the deck, yelling, singing, the strumming of a balalaika.

During the first day, the second, and the third, I got to know the ship and its passengers, most of whom were Jews returning to Ukraine. I joined in nighttime celebrations full of song and folk dance, and also attended party meetings. Though I didn't understand all the topics discussed, I gathered that they were talking about the eighth anniversary of the socialist October Revolution.

On the fourth and fifth days, we replenished our supplies at the island of Rhodes, then continued through the Greek archipelago. We entered the Aegean Sea, took on supplies at the Dardanelles, and the coastline's beautiful natural scenery appeared on both sides. Then at night we entered the Sea of Marmara. When dawn came on the sixth day, Constantinople appeared before us in all of its glory and grandeur. One who sees this eternal city from afar imagines it choked in factory smokestacks, but in fact those are the marvelously designed minarets of priceless ancient mosques.

Comrade Orlov said to me as we entered port, "Turkish security officials will ask you, 'Aren't you staying in Turkish territory?' Tell them, 'No, I'm going to Odessa' without giving any further explanation or details." And so it was:

The steamer anchored at the docks of Galata, and I was invited to the captain's quarters, where one of the Turkish security officers, smiling broadly, asked me, "On your passport is an entry visa to Turkey, aren't you going to use it?"

I said to him, "I've changed my mind—I'm not going to the Turkish mainland."

He asked, "Why?"

I replied, "Because I want to visit the port of Odessa."

He said, "A boy like you, visiting Odessa?"

I said, "That's my business, not yours."

He asked, "Where's your entry visa for Russia?"

Here the captain jumped in and said, "That's our problem. I as captain of this ship allow this boy to travel to Odessa, and there the Russian authorities will grant him an entry visa for Soviet territory after he pays the fee required by law."

The Turkish officials shrugged and left the ship. Our journey continued through the Bosphorus towards the Black Sea. After we had crossed only a short stretch of the Bosphorus, at about nine o'clock, Comrade Orlov approached me while I was leaning on the deck railing and began to tell me a story in English. He said something like this:

"There were a number of Turkish soldiers in Russia in 1917 who had been taken prisoner during the World War. These soldiers were excited by the Russian Revolution and joined it alongside the Russians. They lived with the Russians until last year, 1924, when the Greco-Turkish War was at its height and Mustafa Kemal was winning victory after victory in Anatolia and achieving worldwide renown. The Soviet government extended financial and military aid to him.

"It was no surprise that these Turkish soldiers, having imbibed the principles of the Bolshevik Revolution, wished to return to their homeland Turkey and participate in the national struggle alongside Mustafa Kemal Pasha. They landed in Anatolia, almost 30 in number, and presented themselves to the warrior Mustafa Kemal. He welcomed them and commanded them to use their military experience to help.

"These Turkish soldiers believed that the Kemalist revolution was a democratic revolution like the Kerensky revolution in Russia (the Revolution of February 1917), and that it would certainly turn into a socialist revolution like the Revolution of October 1917. They worked in that direction, spreading the call among the Turkish peasants, workers, and soldiers, encouraging them to imitate the socialist Russian Revolution and proclaim Soviet rule in Turkish lands.

"When Mustafa Kemal heard the news about these soldiers, he ordered their arrest and issued a harsh sentence against them. Since then, all traces of them have disappeared. It is said that they were bound in chains and cast into the depths of the Bosphorus."

Orlov sighed and said, looking into the waters of the sea, "Who knows... we could be passing over them at this very moment."

We entered the Black Sea, a sea that really does tend to be dark in color. It is surrounded by land, and its depth reaches 7,200 feet. It is a choppy sea with heavy waves; we were tossed about like a feather in a gale.

An incident happened to me as we approached Odessa which can only be explained by my ignorance of the new system and adherence to obsolete customs. On the ship I had gotten to know a young Greek man who managed the food stores aboard. Throughout the journey, he was always hanging out with me and helping me whenever he could. We became close friends. He told me that he didn't get involved in politics, although he sympathized with the Soviets. As we approached the port of Odessa, he said to me, "Could I ask you for a simple favor?"

I said, "Go ahead."

He said, "In Istanbul I bought some leather for shoes and an amber necklace. They're a gift for a friend of mine in Odessa. The port customs office charges a high tariff, which I can't pay, so I wanted to ask you to carry them in your bag and pretend that they're yours."

I said, "Okay, I can say the leather's mine, but what do I say about the necklace?"

He said, "Say you're carrying it as a gift for a girl you know from Palestine."

I was confused. This Greek youth had helped me with my work aboard the steamer and was now asking me for a simple favor. The obligations of friendship, of bread and salt, required me to fulfill his request. So I put the necklace in my coat pocket and left the shoe leather atop my clothes.

When they opened the bag at the customs office the officials spotted the shoe leather but did not search the coat and so did not stumble upon the necklace. They asked me why I was carrying shoe leather with me, seeing as I was coming as a student.

I said, "I brought it with me to make myself shoes."

They consulted with one another and it seemed they weren't convinced by my story, but they suspected that one of the sailors had taken advantage of me and left me alone.

In Odessa I stayed at the "Bulgar House," which was the home of some revolutionaries who had fled Bulgaria after the failure of the 1924 workers' revolution in Sofia. After a few days, the Greek sailor came to me and received the necklace and the shoe leather with thanks. I couldn't have known that there were eyes watching us. Three days later, one of the Bulgarians said to me, "The Greek sailor who took advantage of your ignorance has been arrested. Importing a piece of leather or a necklace in your country or mine doesn't raise any suspicion; nobody would pay any attention. But here it's considered an 'instrument of bourgeois commercial speculation.' So watch out!"

I stayed in Odessa for four days, awaiting instructions from Moscow. While I was in Odessa, I attended a public performance. The weather was cold, and I wore the military coat I had brought with me from Jerusalem. The coat had two shoulder straps on which to attach badges and pins, and the people in the theater stared at me in confusion. When I asked why people were staring at me, I was told, "You're a boy wearing an officer's coat! The Revolution removed the shoulder straps from the coats and jackets of officers and soldiers, while the Tsarist forces were decorated with them; this had distinguished the 'Whites' from the 'Reds.' So you appearing in a coat with those straps piqued people's curiosity and interest." Later that evening, I returned to the Bulgar House, borrowed some scissors, and cut off the straps entirely.

Permission came for me to travel to Moscow. I received a pass document and got on a train to the Soviet capital. This trip took thirty-six hours; we passed through Kharkov and Kursk, Oryol and Tula, before reaching Moscow. The travelers on the train were peasants, soldiers, workers, and middle-class youth. My attention was drawn to a Russian peasant with long hair parted in the middle who wore a tunic called a *tolstovka*, based on the shirt worn by the great Russian author Leo Tolstoy. This shirt was embroidered colorfully on the front, the collar, the sleeves, and the hem. The shirt hung down over his trousers and was tied together with knots of braided cotton. The ends of these knots made up the right side of the shirt. The tunic's front opened on the left side of the collar. In the summer, this peasant would wear cotton-padded pants and straw shoes and wrap his legs in cotton garters, while in the winter, he would wear thick felt boots called *valenki*.

Russian peasant women tend to wear colorful clothes and wrap their heads in scarves that vary in color based on their age and particular circumstances. Peasant women typically wear men's shoes.

As for Russian soldiers, or to be more precise, Red Army soldiers, they wore unique uniforms at that time. These consisted of a long tight-waisted coat that almost reached their heels. Every button on the front of the coat passed through a horizontal red strip ten centimeters long. The soldiers' hats were of a style based on those worn by Russian fighters in the past; they were conical and had earflaps that could be lowered in times of extreme cold. Placed in the exact center was a red star.

The Russian workers I saw wore black leather coats and thick leather boots, and they wore *casquette* hats also made of black leather.

State employees usually wore green uniforms with gold buttons. Their hats had shiny leather brims and green flaps.

As for middle-class girls, all of them highly educated and refined, they grew out their hair and braided it about their heads, and wore long modest openwork dresses and shoes that rose above the ankle and were knotted tightly. Some among them spoke French or German, but they spoke not a word of English.

The train passengers sipped tea frequently, and at every stop on the railroad there was a big tank of *kipetok*—that is, hot water. The passengers took the boiling water they needed from the tank and put a bit of tea in it. They nibbled a bit of sugar with every sip of their beloved hot beverage.

Almost everyone smoked strong-smelling and dark-colored *makhorka* tobacco, which the peasants would grow and dry, then break into small pieces and wrap in thick or thin leaves, or they would place the tobacco in a small, rough wooden pipe.

These were my companions on the road from Odessa to Moscow: the hubbub in the train, the continual clatter of the wheels, and the locomotive's whistle, which echoed through the wide forests to either side. At every stop, the locomotive thundered and stormed and puffed steam to either side. Then I would hear the shouts of the vendors, calling out "*yablochki!*"—little apples—and "*kvass!*"—a drink made from starchy local rye—and "*pirozhnoe!*"—cake.

There would be a newspaper vendor calling out "*Pravda*!," "*Izvestiya*!," "*Trud*!" and "*Vechernaya Moskva*!" Then the bell would ring to announce the coming departure and the whistle of the locomotive would follow it. Lanterns would be raised as well if it was nighttime.

On the way, I mostly saw dense forest, fertile fields, and green hills. Russian villages appeared on both sides of the tracks, with wooden log houses one or two stories high in a uniquely Russian style. Some were constructed with great artistic taste such that they resembled fairy-tale cottages.

As we passed through the major cities, I beheld beautiful buildings, predominantly of nineteenth-century design, with decorated exteriors. Many of them had porticoes with white pillars, resembling Greek and Roman architecture.

At last we reached Moscow, the capital on which the world's attention had been fixed since the World War. The train stopped at *Kurskiy Vokzal*, Kursk Station. Then I rode in a small one-horse carriage driven by an *izvodshchik*, a driver. The driver is usually a bushy-bearded man wearing a tight-waisted coat and a fur hat. The carriage proceeded through streets laid with black stones, passing walls and old Russian buildings until we traversed the square with the great—in Russian, *Bolshoi*—theater, then turned right onto Tverskaya Street (which today is called Gorky Street). We stopped before the door of the hotel for foreigners, called the Lux.

The Lux is a large and old hotel that was well-known in Moscow before the revolution. It consists of three floors of many rooms, each of which contains one or two beds and a telephone set. There's one bathroom on each wing for men and another for women, a barber for the whole building, an ironing room, and a center for phone calls. A person called the *zaveduyushchii* oversees the hotel administration. This administration assigns rooms to those who arrive at the hotel, whether for long-term or short-term stays, and sees to their comfort, laundry, and bathing. Most Comintern officials, whether single or married, live in the Hotel Lux, as it is the headquarters of the Communist International. So does every foreigner who comes as a student or is dispatched to Moscow on an official visit.

I stayed in this hotel for three days, during which I went through the process of enrolling at the Communist University for Toilers of the East, or KUTV. I then moved to a dormitory, called an *obshchezhitie*, located on Tverskoy Boulevard, which is known as Pushkin Boulevard today.

The enrollment process at KUTV's Foreign East section usually went through the Comintern. There a short man named Kitaigorodsky greeted me; he worked in the section specifically dedicated to Palestine. He told me that he had a brother in Jerusalem who ran a shop on Jaffa Street. I remembered this name; I knew his brother's shop. It sold household goods and was on the northern side of the municipal park.

Kitaigorodsky conducted the necessary interview with the help of an interpreter, who asked me about my "social situation," that is, which social class I came from, and I told him I was a simple employee at the post and telegraph office, my family was middle class, and my father had been an officer in the army of the Arab Revolt. The interpreter passed on what I'd said, prompting a loud guffaw. I asked the interpreter, who had mistranslated because of his ignorance of Arabic, what was going on. He said, "The comrade found it strange that you'd said you were an officer when you were still an adolescent boy, and I told him jokingly that maybe you had been an officer in your mother's belly!"

I explained the mistake to the interpreter, telling him and Kitaigorodsky that they should obviously understand that I meant my father, not myself. Then the interviewer stopped the discussion of this matter and advised me never to mention that my father had been an officer, as Russia remained in a state of civil war and the people wanted to take vengeance on the officer class. He crossed out the word "officer" in the box for "father's occupation" and replaced it with "office employee."

3
THE STALINIST KUTV UNIVERSITY
(1925–1929)

The university for eastern peoples in Moscow in those days was called KUTV, an acronym for *Kommunisticheskii Universitet Trudiashchikhsia Vostoka*, or the Communist University for Toilers of the East. The word "toilers" was used to indicate that it accepted every wage worker, anyone who came from a working-class family, or anyone who considered themselves part of the working class. This definition included the manual laborer, the office employee, the factory worker, the peasant, the teacher, and every tradesman.

This university was founded in Moscow in 1921 to accept Soviet students from the peoples of Uzbekistan, Turkmenistan, the Caucasus, Armenia, Tajikistan, Georgia, and Mongolia. It was also to accept students from the capitalist world—from China, Japan, Indonesia, India, Indochina, Turkey, Iran, Afghanistan, and the Arab countries.

KUTV had one curriculum for eastern Soviet students and another for eastern students from countries held in the grip of, or struggling against, foreign rule. Domestic students learned the history of Russia, from when the Rus' were tribes living on the banks of the Dnieper River until they became the wide-ranging Tsarist empire, then the Soviet state; they analyzed the history of all its peoples according to socialist principles. The university trained students in this section to take on party administration and public authority in their homelands. Most of the men who administered the eastern Soviet republics in those days had graduated from KUTV.

The second section of the university, Foreign East, for students coming from abroad, focused on the history of colonization and European conquest, from the march of the Crusaders to that of the merchants and explorers, to when Europe began to launch imperial conquests for the benefit of manufacturers and financiers. The university sought to train students in this section for party leadership and public authority in their countries; many of the East's leftist politicians graduated from this section. Among those who studied there or visited were Rüştü Aras, the former Turkish foreign minister; Ms. Vijaya Lakshmi Pandit, sister of Jawaharlal Nehru; Nazim Hikmet, the well-known Turkish poet; the son of Chiang-Kai Shek; and others. I recall on this note that Ms. Nehru was a beautiful young woman, tall, with dark hair, a sharp nose, and sparkling black eyes; she was very perceptive and quick-witted. Shortly after her arrival she invited me to get a drink of the Caucasus' famous wine with her. She did not stay with us for long, as not many luxuries were available at the university, and she had grown up in a rich family surrounded by wealth and comfort.

The university buildings were spread throughout the city center. The dormitory was on Tverskoy Boulevard; the classrooms were in a building located on the eastern side of Tverskaya Square; the dining hall was beside a church on the eastern side of the square; the gym was where the offices of the *Izvestiya* newspaper are located today. A statue of Pushkin stood at the western end of Tverskoy Boulevard; it was later transferred to the eastern end and the street was renamed Pushkin Boulevard.

KUTV was organized as a single college where the only topics taught were those related to politics, economics, and society; it was exclusively a university of political science. Its graduates led parties, unions, or governments, and some showed the potential to become heads of state, parliamentary representatives, or ministers, either in the eastern Soviet republics or in countries freed from foreign rule.

The three-year curriculum covered the following topics:

1. POLITICAL ECONOMY

This course dealt with the topics of labor, capital, and surplus value. The bourgeois economic theories (of [Adam] Smith, [David] Ricardo, and the like) claim that capital does not grow at the expense of labor, but rather because of consumer choices, according to the law of supply and demand. The Marxist theory says that "surplus value" is the money the capitalist accumulates directly from the pains of the workers. Supply and demand influence the growth of profits or losses, but have no relation to the core of the surplus value which accrues to the capitalist. Karl Marx had explained his theory and his analysis of the capitalist system in his famous book *Das Kapital.*

2. MARXIST-LENINIST PHILOSOPHY

Marxism analyzes the law of societal development based on the natural historical process of class struggle: between masters and slaves; feudal landlords and the oppressed peasantry; usurers and merchants; nobles and bourgeoisie; capitalists and laborers. The revolutionary class destroys the ruling class and establishes a new society, which in turn creates new social circumstances.

Marx's theory says that modes of production are constantly developing, and that newer modes of production collide with the old modes of production, destroying them to clear the way for the new. He identifies revolutionary changes in the mode of production, such as the Industrial Revolution. This collision between modes of production is reflected in social relations, leading to a conflict between the owners of the old means of production and the new; this is known as a social revolution. Authors, poets, and artists pave the way for the revolutionaries by exposing the ugliness of the old ways and celebrating the new; this is known as an intellectual revolution.

Leninist analysis in turn says that western capitalism cannot survive without control over the markets of economically backward countries to which it can sell its goods; imperialism turns populations of colonized countries into nothing but consumers, then by one means or another gets its hands on their natural resources to supply the factories of the West. The working hands of the East are thus turned into labor harnessed to do nothing but export raw materials in exchange for western products.

Lenin said that imperialism, in contrast to colonialism, does not require direct military occupation; rather it is enough for it to wield control through capitalists, known as financial capital, mediated by the exploitative institutions known as cartels and monopolies.

Lenin focused on the useful effects of the nationalist movements in the colonies in bringing about socialist revolution in the West. Excluding western capital from control of production and finances in the East, following the success of revolutionary nationalist movements, would break the strength of western capitalism and lead to the establishment of a socialist system in its place.

This was Lenin's theory regarding the East, which Karl Marx had not mentioned in any way. It was a fundamental point of disagreement between democratic socialism (the Second International) led by the German Karl Kautsky, and the dissenting Communist group (the Third International) led by the Russian Vladimir Lenin: the first was limited to the socialist movement in industrialized countries alone, and especially in the western world, and relied for its realization on representative bodies. The second also included the working class in the West, but linked it to the national liberation movements in the East. The Leninist movement had global relevance: it dealt with all deprived and impoverished people wherever they were, regardless of their countries' levels of social, economic, or intellectual development. It called upon them to "leap over the capitalist stage into socialism." To realize its goals this movement relied on revolutionary activity by all available means.

3. IMPERIALISM AND THE NATIONAL ISSUE

This course dealt with the means, known as "settler-colonization," by which merchant capital infiltrated the East, beginning with the Dutch and Spanish conquests and followed by those of Britain and France starting in the fifteenth century.[1] This became the infiltration of "industrial and financial capital" in the twentieth century, known as imperialism. The course also discussed the situations of the people of the East: their history; their kings; their leaders; their parties; their factions; their customs; their creeds; their conflicts; their religions; the relations of ruling nations to the peoples they rule; and finally the implementation of the principle of self-determination, and the right of underdeveloped peoples to choose whether to be linked to the ruling nation or separated from it. In party and university circles, Stalin was considered the foundational authority on this topic, as he had written detailed studies of it, including his book *The National Question*. All his writings included dry technical definitions; in many cases Stalin wanted those formulations to be used verbatim as a kind of scientific constitution.

Stalin did not follow any coherent philosophy or theory. The term *Stalinism* means simply "the policies Stalin followed"; it went no further than the speeches, lectures, and guidance that the previous dictator, Lenin, had presented at party conferences and other occasions. Stalinism mostly revolved around

1 Sidqi quotes what seems to be a hybrid French-Arabic term for "settler colonialism": "kūlūnīzāsiūn–al-istīṭān" (Arabic text, p. 32). The second word is Arabic for "to settle." It is possible that these are two words in different languages for the same thing; however, Arabic has a separate word, *al-isti'amār*, that means "colonization" or "colonialism." The contemporary Arabic expression for "settler colonialism" is *al-isti'amār al-istīṭānī*. —Trans.

Stalin's constant revisions to the history of the Soviet Communist Party, his constant debates with Trotskyite and Bukharinite opposition, his outlines of the successive Five-Year Plans, his *kolkhoz* and *sovkhoz* collectivized farms, his opinions on the nationalities question in the colonies, and his campaigns against the remnants of Russian bourgeois society—and alongside this came the executions of most of the notable figures in the Bolshevik party and a bloodbath for many leaders of the Soviet Army, and for many more Communists, both Russian and foreign. This terror reached its climax in 1937.

Stalin had a negative view of the nationalist movement in the East. He did not see a positive historical role for the nationalist bourgeoisie and did not note how it was oppressed by colonialism, which struck heavy blows against it and passed unjust laws that limited its economic growth. He always referred to it as an "opportunistic" movement that worked with colonialism. His views inflicted serious harm on Arab Communists and subjected them to suspicion and hostility.

4. DIALECTICAL MATERIALISM

Dialectical materialism is a basis for intellectual analysis, which Marx, Lenin, and their followers consider a basic touchstone for avoiding deviations and for reaching correct and reliable results in both theory and practice. This theory goes: If logic means that yes = yes, and no = no, then the dialectic means that yes = no and no = yes. Nothing is completely negative, and nothing is completely positive; everything has an antithesis; in every system, what opposes it comes from within it; in every situation one thinks is entirely bad, there is something that contradicts it and works to eliminate it; in every situation there is a thesis, an antithesis, and a synthesis. When an infant goes out into the world, it carries the seed of death in its swaddling-cloth. The tree grows and flourishes, but it already contains the elements that will rot it from within once it has given root to new growth. The social structure of the nation produces a class that holds the reins of power, but each ruling regime also produces the people who will undermine its foundations and destroy it.

The study of dialectic or "the logic of contradiction" is based on the work of the German philosopher Georg Hegel (1770–1831), to which Karl Marx was devoted, and which Marx used for his socio-economic philosophy; he applied it to the course of human development, calling it "dialectical materialism" or "historical materialism."

But Marx disagreed with Hegel about the substance of his analysis. While Hegel considered human thought the origin of the real world, Marx believed that human thinking was a product of the physical world and, inescapably, a reflection of it. Hegel said that the state was an ideal, born of imagination and the reality of reason, while Marx said that the state was a force imposed on human society—an oppressive force. In this dispute between two philosophies, it is said that Marx set Hegel on his feet, before turning him on his head.

KUTV devoted special emphasis to this topic because—as I said—of its substantive criteria for understanding reality, and its reliable technique for avoiding error and avoiding the tendency to stray onto the wrong path.

On this topic, I recall that one day I visited a prison near Moscow, and the prison director led me to a room crowded with suspects, fugitives, thieves, and *khuligany*, that is, riff-raff. Then the director led me on a zig-zagging route to the prison yard and said, "Here the prisoners entertain themselves by presenting dramatic and musical performances; we want to support them in becoming educated in the sciences and arts, so that they can become upstanding citizens."

I asked him, "Do you teach them dialectical materialism?"

He got flustered and said, "No, no, only the material bit!"

5. THE HISTORY OF WORLD REVOLUTIONARY MOVEMENTS

This course covered the great French Revolution (1791), with its various stages and prominent figures, which served as the paradigmatic revolution of the bourgeoisie (the financiers, merchants, and industrialists) against feudal and royal power. We also discussed:

- The English Revolution (1649) led by Cromwell, who beheaded King Charles I then united England. He occupied Ireland and wiped out Irish landowners, taking over their land and turning it into pasturage for sheep to benefit English industry by providing wool as a raw material.
- The American Revolution (1776) led by Washington. This revolution unleashed American capital, which had been oppressed and mistreated by British colonialism. The American Civil War (1861) under Lincoln's leadership freed the slaves to become wage laborers destined for the nascent American industrial and agricultural establishments.
- The Russian Revolution of 1905 responded to the terrible losses which Russians suffered in the war against Japan. This revolution failed, leading to a regressive backlash and terrorism.
- The Chinese Revolution (1911), led by Sun-Yat Sen against the feudal monarchy and foreign imperialism. It is considered the earliest of the nationalist movements of the East, large or small.
- The Arab Revolution [Arab Revolt] (1915), which rose against the feudal Turkish occupation (Ottoman Sultanate) and the Committee for Union and Progress's pan-Turkish nationalism. It led to the rise of emirates, statelets, sheikhdoms, and nationalist governments deceived by the French and British mandates.
- The Egyptian Revolution (1919), which challenged the British occupation and demanded the liberation of Egyptians from slavery on cotton plantations.
- The Turkish Revolution (1924) under Mustafa Kemal. It destroyed both Ottoman rule and the Caliphate together, setting the Turks on a westward path.

The study of all these revolutions and upheavals was conducted through a Marxist-Leninist theoretical lens, based on investigating the details of material reality.

6. HISTORY OF TRADE UNION MOVEMENTS

This subject covered how unions were established in England, France, and the United States, the nature of their organization and their laws, and the manner of their contribution to public life. Then, it covered the spread of unionist ideas in the East; what leads to strength or weakness in the Arab trade union movements (especially looking at the case of the Egyptian movement); the Profintern, the revolutionary international federation of unions, and its stance on the "federation of yellow unions," that is, the International Federation of Trade Unions, which is subordinated to financial institutions, just like the All-Trade Union in England, the *Confédération Générale du Travail* in France, and the American Federation of Labor in the United States.

These were the main courses in the curriculum of the Eastern University in Moscow, which were accompanied by courses in Russian language and literature, the tactics and strategy of political struggle, underground organizing, and military science—a theoretical course in Moscow in the winter, and a practical course at the Udel'naya encampment near the capital in the summer.

STUDENTS FROM EGYPT

Coming to KUTV in 1925, I met the Egyptian students who had arrived in 1924 to study in the Soviet capital. They came in the wake of the reactionary developments in Egypt that followed the assassination of Sir Lee Stack Pasha, which included the execution of numerous Egyptian youths. I knew these students by the following party names: 'Aziz, Hamdi, Fahmi, Hassunah, 'Umar, and Zanberg. 'Aziz, skinny with wide eyes and a nervous temperament, had worked at the railroad in Cairo and had come to Moscow to pursue Marxist studies. He always swore that he would only return to Egypt to raise the red flag atop the Great Pyramid. Hamdi, a first-year medical student, was short and stocky with a slight limp and claimed that he was "the brains of the Egyptian revolutionary movement." Fahmi had studied engineering at Alexandria University. Skinny with a calm temperament, he liked to draw and avoided arguments about complex ideological questions. Hassunah, tall and slightly slouched, with small bright eyes, had been a dentist's assistant in Alexandria. He argued often and dreamed of becoming an important minister. 'Umar, short and stocky, had come to Russia before the socialist revolution with a foreign circus troupe: his specialty was fire eating and glass chewing. He would strike a match and extinguish it in his big mouth, or swallow a glass and crush it to smithereens. Finally, there was Zanberg, of Polish Jewish origin. He was short and fair with blue eyes. His parents had immigrated to Egypt during World War I, and he had become naturalized there. He joined the Socialist movement of Husni al-'Arabi in 1923 and was subsequently arrested and exiled to Russia. These were the first Arab students to arrive in the Soviet Union in the year of Lenin's death, all Egyptians. I was the first Arab to arrive from the Asian parts of the Arab world. As it was customary to use pseudonyms, the Egyptian students decided to call me "Mustafa Kamel." The Russians, however, or at least the students from the eastern Soviet Union, thought my new name was "Mustafa Kemal" and looked askance at me until Nazim Hikmet intervened and explained.

The student dormitory housed most of the foreign students from outside the Soviet Union. Each national group had its own activities. The most active was the Turkish group, which was headed by the poet Nazim Hikmet. He was a young man of twenty-five when I met him, tall with blond hair, blue eyes, and a ruddy complexion. Constantly moving and full of energy, he used to wear golf pants and a jacket almost fully buttoned up and would stand among the Turkish students reciting revolutionary poems he had composed. The students would then move on to a comic performance ridiculing the Turkish sultans. Someone would ride around on a broomstick, saluting the people to his left and right, while his classmates would recite the sultan's anthem in a derisive way.

I was new at the university then. I was standing at the top of the staircase, watching the whole show and laughing. Nazim Hikmet came up to me and began asking me questions to get to know me. When he asked my name, I told him that my university name was Mustafa Kamel. A shudder passed through him and he said, "What?! Mustafa Kemal? Who gave you this name, who?" I told him that it was Mustafa Kamel, the Egyptian nationalist leader, not Mustafa Kemal [Ataturk]. He still did not like the name, as he said it confused freedom with despotism, and suggested that it be changed to Mustafa Sa'adi to honor the Persian poet. This was how Nazim Hikmet and I became friends. He often invited me to visit the Turkish students and even insisted that I join their group and attend their meetings, since both our peoples had been living under the same despotic rule until the recent past.

Time passed, and I continued my university education. I used to meet Nazim Hikmet at the university club, in the lecture hall, or at the university's summer dacha in the village of Udel'naya outside Moscow. But suddenly the Turkish poet disappeared. I found out later that he had returned to Turkey and was in prison for publicly declaring his hostility to the Turkish leader and calling for his removal and replacement by a socialist republic across Turkey. Turkey at the time was not socially or historically ready to accept this leap in thinking. Indeed, even replacing the fez with a Western hat had caused Mustafa Kemal lots of problems and led to numerous plots against him, to say nothing of accepting a Bolshevik ideology in place of Islam. Besides, Turkey had just emerged victorious from the Turkish-Greek war and was full of admiration for the leader it saw as a great savior. And so Nazim Hikmet remained a poet living with his dreams and pains, until, after fifteen years in prison, he was able to escape with the help of one of his guards. He then lived between Moscow, Havana, and Prague until his death.

THE WALL NEWSPAPER

One custom followed by students at the university, as at other Soviet institutes and organizations, was to produce wall newspapers. Students from each national group would edit a newspaper in their own language and choose a name for it.

Each editorial board would expertly decorate and arrange its newspaper. It was about two meters wide and a meter high; its title was written in beautiful bold lettering, and it was decorated with caricatures and pictures. As for the texts, they were articles with brief, colorful headlines, interspersed with jokes and anecdotes, sharp critiques, and letters. The purpose of the letters was, in general, to offer guidance and to correct behavioral and political deviations by discussing or criticizing a colleague on some matter. The article would be read by the members of that department or section, who would debate it in the pages of the newspaper or in the halls of the university. No one would dare to insult his colleague, because the court of their peers and the Party would hold him accountable.

Initially, the Arab group did not have a wall newspaper for lack of members. However, early in 1926, a number of students flocked to us from Morocco, Tunisia, and Algeria; a number of students from Syria and Palestine followed. With this influx of Arab students, there was an urgent need for an Arabic wall newspaper, which was titled *al-Hurriyya* (*Freedom*). Hamdi was its editor-in-chief and Fahmi its illustrator, while Hassunah and I were its editors—this was the beginning of my journalistic career.

The first issue of the newspaper was published, and in it, Fahmi drew a large, colorful drawing of a wide field, a red sun rising from the east, and men wearing hats, fezzes, and turbans, all in a state of terror. There were cattle fleeing, horses neighing and kicking, and domestic birds flapping their wings in panic, wailing.

We said to Fahmi, "Explain this, by God!"

He said, "The field is Arabia, the sun is the flame of freedom and the hats, fezzes, and turbans represent colonialism and Arab reactionaries. As soon as they saw the sun shining, their limbs trembled and they fled in such a state of terror that the cattle and birds went crazy and started chasing after them!"

Once, 'Aziz sent an article to the wall newspaper, but the editorial office did not approve it. He came to me inquiring about his article and our reason for not publishing it, so I said to him, thoughtlessly, "This writing is *galiata*!" He boiled with rage and shouted so all the world could hear. The comrades asked me to apologize to him, so I explained that I did not know the word "*galiata*" in Egyptian had a different meaning. And that was it.[2]

THE CONSEQUENCES OF THE CIVIL WAR

In those times, Russia was in a deep economic crisis. It was still trying to recover from the effects of the revolution and the civil war, and signs of poverty and hunger were visible everywhere. At times, we would stand in a long queue for breakfast, each holding a piece of dark bread and a glass of tea while a Russian girl would pass down the line, putting two spoons of sugar in each glass and spreading a little butter on the bread. However, the university administration was providing us with the best available food compared to other universities. Normally, breakfast consisted of bread and butter, tea, and caviar—caviar was part of the everyday diet then due to its abundance. The midday meal was *borshch* (a soup of cabbage leaves, beets, small meat slices, and cream), followed by white or black *kasha* (a kind of cereal resembling burghul that is cooked over a low flame) served with a sauce, a piece of rather tough meat, and a cup of *kisil* (apple puree). Supper was a glass of buttermilk with a single spoonful of sugar,

2 Sidqi appears to have tried to address 'Aziz in Egyptian Arabic here. However, he misunderstood how intensely negative *galiata*'s connotation in Egyptian is. See Further Reading essay. —Trans.

a Russian salad of chunks of boiled potatoes and boiled eggs with chopped onions and parsley, and a glass of tea—or glasses of tea, provided the student was sparing in his use of sugar.

We wore military-style clothing: a jacket with four pockets buttoned all the way up to the neck, a coarse pair of trousers, a thick pair of shoes, a heavy coat stuffed and lined with cotton, and a hat of cat fur or rabbitskin with flaps over the ears and laces tied under the chin for the cold. In the summer, we got either a khaki military uniform or a pair of Russian pants and a shirt similar to what I described from the train journey.

Regarding the weather in Russia: winter begins in September, when clouds begin to gather in the sky, then from amid the clouds, it starts to rain. The weather gradually gets gloomy, and some light snow falls in October and November. The temperature falls from 0° to sometimes -30° or colder. I remember that when Lenin died on January 21, 1924, the cold reached -35°, and when people began to cry for this great loss, it was so cold that their tears turned to ice on their cheeks, mustaches, and beards!

The people dealt with the severe cold by wearing warm thick clothes and constantly stomping on the ground when they were forced to stand in one spot. Sometimes, you would see a person approaching you with a handful of snow in his hand, and he would vigorously rub the snow on your nose, saying, "Your nose turned white without you realizing it," which meant you were starting to get frostbite. The only treatment for this was snow, according to the proverb that says, "Cure it with its own cause."

One of the most wonderful sights in winter was seeing water particles in the atmosphere, in an extreme degree of frost, transformed into crystalline geometric models. You could look at your sleeve, for example, and see water droplets transforming into small round, cubic, rectangular, oblong, rhomboid, and hexagonal shapes, all of them perforated in an amazing artistic way. You would take it between your fingers, wishing it would stay this way forever, but soon it would thaw and return to its original essence: a drop of water.

Snow would continue to fall until March, when spring would arrive, bringing rain and mud, and then would come the summer season with its extreme heat, sometimes up to 30°. People would wear white clothing, and many men would shave their heads. Often, during summer, the clouds would suddenly gather in the sky and heavy rain would fall, as if pouring from an open tap.

The stores of the capital were empty. In their windows were only empty cartons and empty boxes next to naked mannequins. People stood in front of government shops and stores in a long queue known as a *khvost.* Woe, absolute woe, betide anyone who attempted to usurp the place of another citizen. Whoever tried would be met with a wave of condemnation and yells of "*Ochered'*!"—meaning "Queue!"—and would retreat to his place, humiliated and harried. Everyone, however, was allowed to leave his place in line to run other errands, provided those standing in front and behind him attested that he had been between them.

During the civil war and in the first year of Soviet rule, the state introduced an emergency economic system known as war communism. Under this system, the authorities seized all foodstuffs and distributed them to people using ration cards. When inflation had made the Russian ruble worthless, since it was no longer pegged to gold or any other commodity, the modern Soviet authorities decided to completely abolish tsarist cash. They replaced it temporarily with colored cards given to soldiers, employees, workers, and others, which served as vouchers for purchases. They could also go to public cafeterias and get meals in exchange for certain vouchers, the value of which varied by color.

War communism did not last long, as the Soviet regime quickly established its foundations, issued a new currency, and returned to conducting financial operations. They canceled the voucher system. The ruble, equivalent to one hundred kopecks, became the basic unit of exchange, guaranteed by the state bank with gold bullion. In addition Lenin enacted the NEP (Novaya Ekonomicheskaya Politika, or New Economic Policy) plan, which allowed small Russian capitalists to recover and work alongside the socialist system of work and production.[3] It also allowed foreign industrialists to establish factories in Russia in exchange for limited and specific profits; the state would contribute money and supervise, and the workers were authorized to strike if the foreign industrialists breached their commitments.

The NEP was introduced because the new socialist economy could not meet the needs of a population that numbered 170 million at the time (they have reached almost twice that number today). The population was also forced to coexist peacefully with small-scale capitalists, who would produce goods and receive limited profits.

As a result of the civil war and the accompanying famine, which woke the conscience of the world, groups of homeless children known as *bezprizorniki* spread all over the country. Their plight worried the country's leaders more than the enemies of the revolution did.

THE HOMELESS CHILDREN

One morning, I left my dormitory with Hamdi. When we approached a huge water tank that was used to melt tar, ten children burst out with tar-blackened hands and faces. Frightened, I asked my friend, "What's this I'm seeing?" He laughed and replied, "These are homeless children with no place to sleep except the tank, which lets them spend the night in a warm place until morning."

The Soviet authorities of the time spent a great deal of time and effort to help these homeless children. They set up shelters to house them and gave

3 Sidqi gives the Russian transliteration of NEP as well as the translation. —Trans.

them training in various skills. But the children often rebelled against these constraints on their freedom and destroyed the shelters, even killing the directors, and fled to the forests or to villages or suburbs.

That year, I remember watching a movie about homeless children, the hero of which was a young man named Mustafa. This Turkestani youth lives in a Russian town and is rendered homeless by the civil war. With his fellow homeless friends, he commits burglary and robs people. One day he is arrested and put in a shelter; there, his character changes and his behavior improves, and he becomes a skilled carpenter. Some time later, the homeless shelter residents revolt, attack its director, and climb into the treetops like hundreds of birds. Mustafa, who understands what it is like to be a homeless child, intervenes, controls them, and returns them to the shelter so that they can continue on their educational journey and one day become useful for the country.

The problem of homeless children was the state's main concern. At first the state was unable to find and count them, as they numbered hundreds of thousands, spread through every part of the vast Russian land. Some had lost their fathers, brothers, or relatives in the war against Kaiserist Germany, while others had been separated from their families during the civil war between Whites and Reds that had raged all over the country. These children ranged from five to ten years of age, deprived of the blessing of education by incessant battles and perpetual displacement from one place to another, clumping together in dreadful little gatherings. They wore the coarsest clothing, with hats of the skins of all types of animals, and wrapped their little legs in leather, woolen rags, or anything else they could find.

These children had a famous song that went,

"I'm dying, I'm dying
And insects are in the soil,
In vain, people try
To find my grave."

TRAGEDY OF A POET

In those days, people were moved by the story of a young Russian poet named Sergei Yesenin. This Russian village poet was not very interested in writing about social issues; rather, his poetry was limited to depicting the village, rivers, treachery, love, pubs, the moons and stars, his home, and his mother. In 1922, this pure Russian poet met an American dancer named Isadora Duncan, who had come to Russia during the days of the revolution and had begun performing for workers and soldiers. One of her most famous dances was the "Red Flag" dance: moves taken from ballet, performed while carrying a large red silk kerchief in one hand, and a group of flags of capitalist countries in the other. She set up a battle between the red kerchief and the other flags, which all fell to the ground one by one. Then, she finished her dance by wrapping herself in the big red kerchief, to the fans' applause and cheers.

Yesenin saw her performing this artful dance. He admired her, got introduced to her, fell in love with her, and married her. This happened in 1922, when he was twenty-seven years old and she was forty-four. The dancer saw in this young Russian poet the ideals of masculinity, semi-civilization, and forest instinct.

The poet and the dancer separated; she traveled to France, Yesenin joined her afterwards, but then returned to his country in agony. He met his demise on December 28, 1925, committing suicide in an authentic Russian bog near Leningrad, though he had said in a verse of his poetry,

> In the crooked streets of Moscow
> God has fated me to die!

As for Isadora, she grieved greatly for the poet; to make matters worse, her two children from a previous marriage drowned. She died in Nice in 1927. The long scarf she wore around her neck got caught in a car wheel and strangled her.

Yesenin's suicide was the news of the hour; institutes and clubs were instructed to hold discussions about the poet and his poetry—he had composed about a thousand poems in ten years. A meeting was held in the university club, filled with students and guests, young Muscovite men and women. Orators started talking about the poet who committed suicide. Some of them slandered and attacked him, while others praised him for his poetry and intelligence. The audience was divided in two: his supporters and his opponents. Some began screaming, and the girls got overexcited. The campaign against Yesenin led to a ban on the circulation of his poetry, which remained in place for a long time.

The charge leveled against the poet-suicide was that he did not participate in the Revolution but continued to live in his own narrow circle of flirtations, love, the soil, and the pub, which brought despair into his soul and drove him to commit suicide in an absolutely Russian way as no one had ever done before, which was, as I said, by diving into a quagmire such that the body decomposed and became sludge.

I was among those who attended this meeting, following the discussion through an interpreter. A Russian student I knew approached me and said with a smile, "What do you think of Yesenin? Was he a glorious poet? Should his poetry be read by young people?" I told the girl that I was new to the Russian milieu, and I knew little of the Russian language and its literature; therefore, I could not express an opinion on this poet or anyone else. However, the uproar that arose around him in early 1926 motivated me to get acquainted with his poetry. I admired his aesthetic talent, and I liked his short poems about the Russian East, which he visited at the end of his life, including "Farewell, Baku, I Will Not See You Again," "Persian Considerations," "You Said That Sa'adi the Poet," "Firdausi's Blue Homeland," "Shaganet, Dear Shaganet," and others.

When news of Yesenin's suicide reached Maxim Gorky, he said, "Sergei Yesenin was more of an organ than a human being! Nature produced him only for poetry—describing sad fields, expressing love and tenderness for all living things in the world." So Yesenin's problem, then, was that he was more of an organ than a human being, meaning that he was less sensitive to social tragedies. But what can we say about Vladimir Mayakovsky (1893–1930), the poet of Russia's socialist revolution, who also committed suicide for the same reason, even though he was "more of a human than an organ"?

THE ARAB SECTION

By the beginning of 1926, more Arab students arrived at KUTV, with some of the older students becoming translators and teachers. The Egyptian called Hamdi was very keen on translating Marxist writings from English into Arabic and received a good fee based on the number of English words to be translated. Often he would take me on as his assistant. He would have me sit at the desk while he paced back and forth, swaying a bit on account of his limp, dictating to me in Arabic the parts he understood from Karl Marx's writings on surplus value or Frederick Engels's *The Origin of the Family, Private Property, and the State.* When he encountered a complex idea, or a complicated word with several possible meanings, he would become very agitated and try to enlist the help of 'Aziz, Fahmi, Hassunah, and Zanberg. This would result in a mishmash of opinions and produce disagreements, until 'Umar would intervene with his opinion on the matter, aided by what knowledge he had of Marxist writings. As soon as they agreed on the meaning, Hamdi would turn back to me to dictate, but often by that point he found that I had gotten tired of it and left.

The various groups at the university were competing to translate the Internationale into their own national languages, and we got very excited about translating it into Arabic as well. But then our Russian language teacher, Vladimir Androvich, told us not to bother, for it had already been translated by the late Professor Mikhail 'Attaya. "Who is this professor 'Attaya?" we inquired. He told us that he was the colleague of Dr. Bandali al-Jawzi and Mrs. Kulthum 'Awdah and a friend of Professor Ignatii Krachkovsky. The Tsarist

Russian Imperial Orthodox Palestine Society in Nazareth had sent him and others to pre-revolutionary Russia to teach Arabic at the College of Oriental Languages. He died in the Russian capital in 1924, leaving behind valuable textbooks in Arabic and Russian. He had also translated the Internationale. Our teacher gave us a copy of it, which I did not preserve for security reasons, but I remember the first line of the anthem, which goes:

Arise, ye markéd with damnation,
Ye mistreated and ye poor,
Your mind and marrow bid you hasten
To enlist in a dangerous war!
We'll demolish this whole world of evil,
From the foundations on up!
And build a new world for the people,
That's never been seen before! (*'Attaya dropped the rhyme to fit the tune*).

Come and join the struggle . . . Come and join the struggle . . .
Come and join the struggle . . .
The human race will rise!

We differed on whether to accept this translation as it was, since we found it a bit more "philological" than necessary, in that it was a literal translation of the Russian text. We formed a committee to edit it and give it a simplified populist flavor, but the committee didn't reach a conclusion and the project was eventually abandoned. We all preferred to sing it in the foreign languages we had mastered.

Then it occurred to 'Aziz to compose a song for the Arab students, so we worked on it collaboratively. After many meetings, lots of back and forth, adding and deleting and editing, we came up with a song in Egyptian dialect. I remember the starting bit of it:

The world is what it is! Life is what it is!
Hey, Uncle Hamza! We're the students,
We don't care if we sleep in the citadel or the governorate
Not one of us is afraid
of your force. We stand, despite our fear!
We're used to plain bread
We sleep without a blanket
We are the students: Long live the struggle!
(Then the chorus): *Bonjour, ya khalayiq*!
You crooked one, you thief,
While the bourgeois employs workers for dirhams,
And gets rich off of them,
This worker is an animal!
We are the youth,
The people of discernment
We are the students,
Long live the struggle!

This song didn't last long. It quickly got muddled and we grew tired of singing it. Instead, we memorized Russian revolutionary songs, and sang them on all occasions.

By the beginning of 1927, the Arab group had grown even more. It now consisted of ten Egyptians, fifteen Palestinian Arabs, five Palestinian Jews, seven Syrians, ten Lebanese, three Algerians, and two Moroccans. Most of them took pseudonyms, such as Subotin, Saul, Namitov, Ahmedov, Maykhan, Muhammadov, Khaltorin, Ibrahimov, and so on.

Some of them are still alive, and some of them have died, like Maykhan ('Abd al-Ghani al-Karmi), Ibrahimov ('Ali 'Abd al-Khaliq, who was killed in the Spanish Civil War), and 'Aziz the Egyptian, who died in the Citadel Prison in Cairo. And there are students whom I never heard from again after World War II; some of them may have died, but some may still be alive, spending their old age reminiscing about the days of their rebellious youth and bad luck. I shall write about some of my classmates' stories where appropriate in these memoirs.

The Arab group had a political committee that supervised the Arab students' general and private affairs, directed them ideologically and politically, and monitored their conduct. It also had an arts committee, which presented Arabic song and dance at club parties and university events. As at other Soviet institutions and colleges, the political committee organized a yearly event called Reckoning Day, where the students exposed their peers' deficiencies and celebrated their strong points. For example, someone would stand up and say, "'Aziz is a good guy who cares for his comrades, but he is selfish. His behavior seems to follow the example of petit-bourgeois children. Picture this—he stands before the mirror for half an hour arranging his hair, sprays himself with cologne, and wastes a lot of time flirting with girls. This behavior must influence him ideologically, because his adventures, learned from bourgeois society, take him away from his political duties." This would be the text of the accusation, which would then be followed by students' comments, refutations, condemnations, and exonerations, until nerves were tense, minds agitated, and spirits disturbed. Reckoning Day ended with each student receiving a *kharakteristika*—a classification of his ethics and character—including his good and bad attributes, praising him if he deserved praise or rebuking him if he deserved rebuke, with appropriate warnings and scoldings.

There were also "self-criticism" sessions in which the students had to engage all year. In these meetings, which were organized by section or university class, students would stand up and criticize themselves, or they could defend themselves against criticism presented to them, provided that they showed openness and a readiness to admit their mistakes, as well as complete acceptance of the ethical and moral principles called for by the new society.

An example of this was when one of the Palestinian students did not neglect to bring his prayer rug with him from Jaffa. He was caught "in flagrante delicto" and was referred to a court of self-criticism. He argued forcefully and defended himself on the grounds that Islam is the religion of socialism. He said that prayer is to the spirit what exercise is to the body, posing no contradiction to the goal of breaking the chains of exploitation and ridding society of capitalism and colonialism. People were very lenient with him because he was a new student. One of the professors was assigned to explain to him the history of the development of religions, beginning with man's instinctive fear of the elements, moving on to paganism and idolatry, and then to the monotheistic notion of a god who created the heavens, earth, mankind, and all living things.

The practice of self-criticism and the annual Reckoning Day were the ethical examinations through which students were to be directed to the right path, virtuous morals, and the highest ideals.

On the topic of self-criticism, I want to mention an incident that happened to me and nearly caused me many problems. Moscow in 1926–27 was thinking constantly about Trotsky and Trotskyism, first thing in the morning and last thing before bed. Indeed, the country became divided between two camps: Stalinists and Trotskyists.

Stalin maintained that it was possible to establish a complete socialist system inside the Soviet republics without linking it to the establishment of socialism in the rest of the world, and that the country would be able to overcome its economic problems through universal electrification, strengthening of heavy industry, and destroying the *kulak* class—the small agricultural landowners whom the revolution had tolerated during the NEP period.

Trotsky and Zinoviev, on the other hand, insisted that it was impossible to establish a socialist society in the Soviet Union alone. They argued that Moscow must think not only of itself but pursue "permanent revolution," i.e., it should not invest its financial and scientific resources only within its own borders but should put them at the service of world revolution until socialism was realized worldwide. Trotsky also thought that the Soviet Union should not get carried away with socialist industrialization but should grant contracts to foreign capitalist companies. Similarly, it should not depend on socialist agricultural cooperatives but instead have agricultural work performed by "educated tenants."

The result of all this was that Trotsky was expelled from the party in 1927 and exiled from the Soviet Union. He lived in Turkey, then France, and then Mexico, where he was killed by one of his followers. It is said that his assassin was a Stalinist agent. His colleagues and aides were purged from the party, exiled, or executed.

But back to my story: the Arab group in those days used to hold meetings at which Zanberg would present Trotskyist ideas and then refute them. We would agree with everything he said, adding side remarks to prove that we were up to date with what was happening in the country. One day, I decided to study the topic and speak up at the meeting. A Palestinian Jewish woman named Chaya confronted me and began provoking me. I remember saying, "It is well known that the country is suffering from agricultural shortages and needs to win the farmers' trust and support to increase production and strengthen cooperation between the urban proletariat and the rural peasantry. Thus, would you not think that turning against the small landowners at the present time will cause the country numerous problems, potentially leading to famine?"

Instead of an answer to my question there was an eruption of anger. Zanberg jumped up and said, "We should thank Chaya for pulling you out into the open!"

Hamdi sprang up too, and said, "God, what's all this? Where've you been hiding all this?" Then 'Umar rose, shaking, and said, "No, no! This is dangerous stuff! This stuff could drive you nuts. We're not gonna let this pass!"

This was how I got in trouble and struggled to fend off the accusation of Trotskyism. I defended myself, but in vain. 'Aziz suggested convening an extraordinary session to examine my case. We all walked out to the street, the other comrades muttering darkly. Hassunah approached me and said, "So, Mr. Mustafa, you want to cause drama wherever you go. Did you have to flap your gums? Couldn't you just have waited until you left? Go back to your country, then say whatever you want! Listen, you should apologize at the next session; just say you made a mistake, and that's it."

When the extraordinary session convened, I stood up and said, "Comrades, I expressed an opinion at the last session that was closer to Trotskyism than to Stalinism. I wish to reassure you that I do not share the views of the Trotskyists. It was a slip of the tongue, or rather a confusion in my understanding of the meaning of *kolkhoz* and *goskhoz* farms and an insufficient appreciation of the necessity to eliminate the *kulaks* as a social class. I acknowledge my mistakes and apologize." As soon as I finished, everyone visibly relaxed, and the students came up and congratulated me on my return to the Stalinist fold. Thus fell the curtain on this "opposition," which had lasted less than twenty-four hours.

One day the arts committee of the Arab section of KUTV received an invitation to attend a Red Army Day celebration hosted by the workers from a factory in the town of Orekhovo Zuyevo. So 'Aziz, 'Umar, and I headed to that town, where we were welcomed warmly. In a gymnasium, speakers competed, while performers presented all sorts of traditional songs and dances and played musical instruments. Then they asked us to say a word at the festivities and to present some Arab arts. It was up to 'Aziz to speak, as he was the oldest and the most advanced at the university.

He looked at me and said, "Whaddo I do, Mr. Mustafa?"

I said, "Improvise a few words in Arabic."

He said, "Okay, but whaddo I say?"

I said, "Say anything that suits the occasion, and I'll translate."

So we got up on stage amid applause and cheers, and then 'Aziz began to give his speech, starting with the following poem:

"If my strong arms can't guard my king,
My name's not Saladin!
Though my king cares not for me,
I'm there through thick and thin!" (Etc.)

Then he gave a speech that contained some improvised praise and greetings. The time came for translation, and I had to save the day. I began by telling the public that my comrade had begun his speech with a poem about how the army is the nation's protector, and about how when the Red Army had defeated General Kolchak in the Urals and Siberia, General Denikin on the Central Front, and General Wrangel in the South, it was a victory for freedom everywhere, and that no doubt the Arabs too would taste the fruits of this victory sooner or later.

'Aziz left the stage, panting with exertion. I followed him to our seats and asked, "What was that speech?"

He said, "What matters is, in your translation you said all the stuff I didn't think of. *Merci* so much."

Then 'Umar got up on stage and gave a speech in Russian about cocaine, which the colonizer uses to numb the mind and soul. He recited the poem "A Sniff of Cocaine" by Sheikh Sayed Darwish, using his hands and eyes for emphasis:

"A sniff of cocaine
Leaves me insane,
burns at my nose,
Makes me morose,
Rolling my sight
To the left and the right . . ."

And so on.

They applauded him heartily, and we returned to Moscow.

HASSUNAH AND SHURA

Something happened to Hassunah which produced much tumult at the university. He fell for a Russian girl named Shura who worked as a pharmacist there. He spoke to her and professed his love for her and his desire to marry her. She reciprocated his love and desire, and they were married; she bore him a son named Marun.

It became clear that Hassunah was not serious about this marriage and neglected his Russian wife. He started avoiding her, so she followed everywhere he went and watched him until she discovered that he was partial to another woman. She was not strong enough to bear this shock, after having fallen in love with this Egyptian youth with his wavy black hair. She trudged back to her pharmacy, mixed up a draught by hand, and drank it. She rested her head on the table and never rose again.

Shura left no note explaining why she had ended her life in the prime of youth, but the students who knew about her relationship with Hassunah realized the secret behind her suicide and blamed Hassunah. He suffered greatly from her loss but never admitted that she had ended her life because of him. He would say at the time, "What, am I 'Umar ibn Abi Rabi'a, or some sorta Rudy Valentino?" Despite this arrogant response, deep in his heart he knew he was guilty.

The story of Shura and Hassunah continued to be the main topic of discussion in the KUTV Arab section until it gave way to the story of the new Egyptian student, Fathi. The gist of it was that he married a Russian woman and she bore him a daughter, but that very day he changed his mind and repudiated her with the "triple divorce." Then we intervened in the matter and passed a judgment on the two protagonists that the oath of divorce was null and void. The marriage had been made under civil law, and recording it as a Muslim marriage would require returning to Egypt and going to shari'a court. Since the marriage had not been recognized under Islamic law, neither was the Islamic oath of divorce.

On the topic of love and marriage, I note that when the Arab students came to Moscow at the outset of Soviet rule, they were captivated by the idea of "free love." This idea grew from the Russian Revolution, which in its first year freed people from many chains and led them to reject many customs. The revolt against the priesthood was violent, and more violent still was the revolt against traditional social norms. A nudist movement arose among women, and young people joined a movement for "free love." They engaged in both practices constantly, until the Soviet authorities cracked down on both movements, subjecting them to surveillance and persecution. The Soviets insisted that the new regime did not want to eliminate the family, but rather to establish a new form of family appropriate to the new circumstances. Despite these policies, middle-aged people continued to follow Church dictates in many private matters, albeit secretly, while the revolutionary generation lived according to its own lights, interpreting things however they pleased.

The news of this sexual aspect of the revolution spread abroad, and people called it "Russian debauchery." They exaggerated it, imagining all of Russia to be falling into moral degradation. Marriage contracts at that time ran through the office known as "ZAGS," the Russian acronym for the Registry of Acts of Civil Status. This process in the early years after the revolution was very simple. The bridal couple would go to the aforementioned office, often wearing flowers and beautiful clothing, and sit in front of the official in the presence of a few witnesses. The couple's names, professions, and place of residence would be recorded; the official would bless their marriage and wish them a happy life.

Over time, as Soviet family life stabilized, the ZAGS office tightened the requirements for a marriage contract, including verifying that those seeking marriage were not bound by a previous marriage contract, ensuring their financial and physical health, committing them to take joint responsibility for the family, and requiring strong reasons for divorce. Restrictions like these were not in effect in the early days of the revolution, so it was said that Russia believed in "free love," which meant freedom of sexual relationships. This news reached us in a distorted form, and Arabs imagined that sexual anarchy prevailed in the country. But the ZAGS office today does not differ one bit from civil marriage registration offices in any other part of the world, and its contracts contain requirements drawn from church and shari'a contracts. They are distinguished only by the latter having religious status and responsibility to clerics, and the former having civil status and responsibility to fellow citizens. Also, those getting married are required to go to the Tomb of the Unknown Soldier and place a bouquet of flowers on it, and they must visit Lenin's tomb in wedding clothes. These traditions were incorporated so people would forever remember the victims of war and the founder of the socialist state.

THE SUBBOTNIK

One day we were told that KUTV students were included in a list of *subbotniki*, and that we needed to go out and work. At the time, we could not distinguish between the word *subbotnik* and the word *sputnik*.[4] The former means working on Saturdays, and the latter means "escort" or "travel companion," and would later come to mean a satellite that orbits the globe.

The civil war and the revolution had greatly reduced the workforce, so most public utilities were short of workers, and the towns and social service offices lacked people to maintain vital services. As a result, Lenin was seeking a way to support the country, and thus the *subbotnik* plan was invented. This meant conscripting youth, especially students, to perform a full day of unpaid work on Saturdays to support the public utilities as directed by their institute, school, or organization.

Subbotnik labor was used for the following tasks: gathering firewood from the forest; harvesting fruit and vegetables; transporting merchandise; carrying furniture and luggage; cleaning public parks; cleaning public graveyards;

4 Arabic uses the same letter for the *b* and *p* sounds. —Trans.

helping deliver construction materials for public buildings; and bringing foodstuffs to the institutions, nurseries, orphanages, shelters, and prisons. In general: for any unskilled collective labor. In this unique way, the country would conscript hundreds of thousands of young people to perform labor and public services on Saturdays, paying them nothing but a midday meal. By this method, Lenin was able to save the state millions of rubles, ensure the cleanliness and order of the cities, and provide food and fuel to the people.

The Arab section went out with the other sections to work on Saturday. Our job was to clean the graveyard on the northern side of the capital. The graveyard was ancient; it may have been the Golovinsky cemetery, where there are many gravestones, statues, and tombs. Some bore dates going back to the sixteenth century. The Russians write things on their gravestones like: "so-and-so, servant of her God"; their gravestones also have plenty of passages of prose or poetry honoring the virtues of the deceased.

While I was involved in cleaning a grave with some of the other Arab students, an old Russian woman approached us, brandishing a stick, and said, "Clean it well! What's with this playing around?"

I said to her, "What's it to you?"

She said, "That's the grave of my grandmother, Vera Alexeyevna Goncharova."

I said, "It's no concern of ours whose grave it is, we'll do a good job regardless."

She said, shaking the stick, "You're lazy, you don't deserve to be paid!"

Then she left, frothing and fuming. We laughed, and kept working all day until the graveyard looked like a park in wintertime.

On the topic of Russian graves, most of those who died in those days were burned in crematoria. The family was given a bit of their ashes in a vial, and what remained was thrown in a big pit.

The crematorium was something like a fancy house, well-designed, with a wide, scented hall full of flowers. At the front of the hall was a high platform, in the open space of the hall there were seats, and in the center of the hall, there was an oblong platform on which the coffin was placed. After people eulogized the deceased, recalling his achievements and virtues, someone pushed an electric switch, and the platform descended, carrying the coffin with it. Below, stove-keepers received the corpse, put it in a steel coffin that would not melt, then pushed it into a high-temperature electric oven. After a short while, the dead body and all the microbes in it turned to pure ash. The platform returned to the upper floor, carrying the urn for commemoration by the family or for placement on the wall of the dead, where a small tile was inscribed with the name of the deceased and the dates of birth, death, and burning.

4
MINGLING WITH THE RUSSIANS
(1925–1929)

MINGLING WITH THE RUSSIANS

There was a school for Russian nurses located near KUTV's club on Tverskoy Square, and many of the nursing students enjoyed coming to the club to meet the students, who had come from Easts both Near and Far, to get to know them and ask them about the ways of life and customs in their countries.

Among those whom I got to know at the club was Shura, blonde and blue-eyed, who lived with her elder brother and had lost her husband in the civil war. It was thanks to this Shura that I learned to pronounce Russian correctly.

Then there was Zina, from the city of Ryazan, with carob-colored hair and dark eyes, active and lively. She forced me to chat in Russian, and when I stumbled on a word, she poked me with a pin. Once, she pressed her lit cigarette to the back of my hand—I let fly a fluent string of Russian curses.

Kaba from Kaluga, a wheat-haired girl with a quiet nature, invited me one day to the dormitory where she lived and introduced me to a girl there. That girl was melancholy and sad, and asked me about life in the countries "beyond the border," about people who enjoy their lives, who wear what clothes they like, who read whatever books and magazines they want. A few days later, I learned from Kaba that the girl had hanged herself. This event was a violent shock to me, and I found it strange—as did the girls—that this girl had committed suicide, though there were many others like her in those days.

Ksenia was from Tula, which was famous for producing knife blades and samovars. She was from a middle-class family, cultured, slim and fair-skinned, with blue eyes. She wore smooth gold earrings decorated with precious stones. This girl did not complain in difficult circumstances, and her attention was bent towards marriage. From her I learned about the poetry of Pushkin and Lermontov.

Vera was a high schooler, fifteen years old, a sweet, playful, sturdily built and long-haired girl who lived on the northwest side of Moscow, whom I knew through the University club; she invited me to her house and introduced me to her parents. This girl was betrothed to a Russian boy, but he annoyed her and made her jealous. She saw in me a young man who could make her fiancé jealous in return. One day she brought me to a public park where there was what is called in Russian an *estradnyi kontsert*, that is, an open-air concert, and seated me not far from where her fiancé was sitting. She turned around from time to time to attract his attention. I realized then that I ought to distance myself from them both, so I did.

There was Lyuba, a fat village girl from near Rzhev; I got to know her at a New Year's party. She was drunk that night, and very cheerful; she promised that she would take me to her village so I could see Russian village life, but I didn't trust her and made my escape from her. The next day, a friend of hers told me: You did well to run away from Lyuba. She's pregnant by someone who dumped her, so she wanted to stick you with the responsibility.

Valia, a girl who had completed high school and spoke a little English, lived on Sadovaya Street in Moscow, on the eastern side of the canal. I met her through the club. She was always by my side, with a smiling face and good heart. Through Valia I got to know her middle-class Russian family, a class known in Russian as *meshchiani*. In her family, the lady of the house was wealthy. The father used to be a high-ranking bureaucrat in the Tsarist regime, and the brother was a candidate for military school, while the three beautiful and well-educated sisters lived on memories alone. Their maternal uncle was a priest, who disguised himself in normal clothes, while their paternal aunt was an orphanage director.

I can't say that this family had any affection for the new Soviet regime. The petty-bourgeois class remained nervous about the new regime, as it had lost the economic base on which it had stood under Tsarist rule. In this class were merchants, brokers, landlords, owners of small businesses and banks, and small-scale shopkeepers who sold groceries, meat, clothes, or cosmetics. There were also civil servants and officials in great numbers, and others who had lived in the shelter of the imperial court and who had built their independence on the promises of courtiers.

Valia's family was from this class, and they constantly grumbled about the new situation, expressing their discontent indirectly, including with pointed jokes. Valia said one evening, "One Russian is unimportant. Two Russians are unimportant. But three Russians together are a revolution against that Georgian, Stalin!"

Her sister said, "Let me tell you a quick story. Chamberlain, Hoover, and Stalin all get together, and each is determined to prove that he's more stubborn than the others, more able to withstand adversity than the others. They agree that each will enter a goat pen and live there, and the winner will be the one who lives in the goat pen longer than anyone else. So Chamberlain goes in, and after just a few moments he's leaving the pen and shouting curses. Hoover opens the door and walks in, takes three steps, then turns on his heels and rushes out, covering his nose. Then Stalin goes in, spreads out a mat on the floor of the pen, and falls into a deep sleep."

The aunt said, "Stalin was walking down a narrow country path when a cow blocked his way. His men tried to get the cow to move, but they couldn't. Then Stalin walked up to the cow and whispered a few words in her ear, and the cow nodded her head and moved out of the road. So his men asked, 'What did you say to get her to move?' Stalin smiled and told them, 'I promised she'd get to go to one of the cooperative farms!'"

Everyone was engulfed in laughter after every joke they told. They reassured me that they didn't intend to speak against the regime, just to criticize the ruler jokingly and to have some fun.

The uncle, who was a priest, came to a party one night. He looked normal, like an ordinary person. He had a fur hat, a thick coat, and knee-length boots. There was absolutely nothing suspicious about him. When he entered the house and took off the coat, priestly robes appeared, and he had a cross pressed against his chest.

I asked for an explanation: "What's the reason for all this subterfuge?"

He said, "I was avoiding hostility and harassment."

I said, "Why would there be hostility and harassment toward you, a man of God?"

He said, "These are the consequences of the Revolution. It's not unknown to you that the Russian Orthodox Church was always a powerful supporter of the Tsarist government. So when the Revolution came, a number of priests joined counter-revolutionary forces. They encouraged people to fight the Reds, injuring the Church's honor; they allowed cannons and Maxim guns to be placed in bell towers to fire on the revolutionaries from above. From this emerged hatred for men of religion. They were pursued, and mocking songs were written about them, and they were made to wander about in the streets, at great risk to them."

I asked him, smiling, "Did you also allow them to deploy machine guns in your church?"

He said, "God forbid! I'm a religious man and no more; I don't get involved in politics at all. All I strive for is to serve the church and the people."

The priest began to recite his prayers in his pleasant voice, and Valia accompanied him on the piano. Then they passed around aged wine, followed by tea and sweets. As they became drunk, they struck up Russian folk songs. I remember among them was the song the tune of which Mohammed 'Abd-al-Wahab "borrowed" for his song "*Oh Lovely World*." The Russian lyrics are similar to those in Arabic, in which the narrator is a girl flirting with her boy, saying:

You come and go uselessly, Kolya,
You uselessly wear out your feet,
You'll never succeed at anything,
Go home, you fool, in defeat.

These Russian dinner parties frequently occurred at Valia's house, or in the homes of her friends, or in the rural cabins where we were hosted for Christmas and New Year's. They invited us to homes surrounded by woods, snow, and fierce cold, with fireplaces blazing, tea and sweets, dance, the music of the guitar and the balalaika, and exchanges of kisses.

Valia invited me over on Christmas Eve 1927 to visit the Isayevsky Church by the Moscow River on the southern side of the Kremlin. Accompanying me was an African-American student, Jones, a stout man, wide-nosed, with heavy lips and watery eyes.

The church was redolent with the smell of frankincense. The priest stood for the service, while people circumambulated the church, moving from icon to icon. I noted at first sight that most of the visitors to the church were elderly, or peasant men and women who had come to Moscow to sell fruit and vegetables, though there were a few young people among the worshippers.

As we were wandering inside the church, an old Russian woman carrying a candle in her hands passed the African-American, Jones. When the light of the candle fell on his face, she drew back and made the sign of the cross before her face, shouting, "*Chert, chert*!" This means, "Demon, demon!" We had a hearty laugh at this odd occurrence. Some of the other worshippers told us they had never seen a black person before in their entire lives. And so the old woman was startled to see a black person, in a church on Christmas Eve of all places.

When we left the church we met a Russian woman in her thirties. We spoke about religion and the new regime, and she said straightforwardly, "I am a supporter of the new regime, but I'm also a believer; religion in my opinion does not contradict the new government."

So Valia said to her, "But the revolutionaries put up a big sign at the southern entrance to Red Square saying, 'Religion is the opiate of the masses'!"

She replied, shaking her head, "I don't endorse that view, but every side is free to think whatever they want."

We returned to the University, and Jones was holding his face in his hands and laughing, saying, "*Chert*, *chert*! Oh, if they could hear her in Harlem..."

A TOUR OF THE KREMLIN

On the first day of the new year we took a comprehensive tour around the famous Kremlin palace. The Kremlin is practically a small walled city unto itself, with gates and towers, and its architecture includes elements going back nine centuries.

The Kremlin was the original center of the town of Moscow, established by Prince Yuri Dolguriki in 1106, and subsequent Russian princes expanded the castle and surrounded it with wooden walls made of tree trunks, then with walls of white stone. They built twenty towers there, the most famous of which is the "Secret Tower," built by the Italian architect Anton Fryazin, which was connected to a secret tunnel which ran under the Moscow river. After that, there was the Borovitskaya Tower, built by the same man in 1491. In the same year, the Russians built Spassky Tower, the most beautiful of the round towers.

The Kremlin's main entrance is on Red Square, with a big clock on top of it—the Big Ben of Moscow. It used to play the Tsarist anthem, then it played the state anthem, and now it plays the Soviet anthem.

There are a group of ornate cathedrals, like the Uspensky Cathedral, built by the Italian architect Aristotele Fioravanti in 1475–1479, and the Blagoveshchensky Cathedral, built in 1484–1489. The latter contains beautifully-crafted icons, considered among the greatest works of Russian artists such as [Theophanes the] Greek, [Andrei] Rublev, [Prokhor of] Gorodets, Feodosii, and others. The Arkhangelsky Cathedral was constructed by Russian architects who were inspired by the Italian architect Alfizano in 1505–1509; Russian tsars and princes were later buried there.

In the center of the Kremlin's courtyard is a bell tower begun by Tsar Ivan the Great in 1505–1508 and completed during the reign of Boris Godonov. The tower is 81 meters high, and the largest bell in it weighs 70 tons. In the year 1735, Russian artist Ivan Motorin cast an immense bell weighing two hundred tons, which was called the Tsar-Bell. He hung it on the bell tower, but the fire of 1737 caused part of it to crack off and fall. The part which broke off weighed 11 tons.

In the year 1586, the Russian Andrei Chokhov cast an enormous cannon which he called the Tsar-Cannon. It weighed 40 tons and was 5.34 meters long, with a caliber of 890 millimeters, decorated with beautiful Russian engravings. There was an arsenal constructed in 1702 under the oversight of the architect Christopher Konrad, and in its hall are displayed a number of cannons which the Russians captured from Napoleon during his retreat in 1812.

In front of the arsenal is a beautiful building, the construction of which was overseen by the Russian architect Kazakov in 1776–1788. During the era of the Tsars, it was the headquarters of the Senate, then Lenin took it as his office and headquarters in 1917–1922, and today it is the headquarters of the council of ministers.

On the southern hill of the Kremlin, the Grand Kremlin palace was constructed in 1838–1849, incorporating older palaces which are still standing. These are the Palace of Panels from the fifteenth century, the Golden Hall of the Tsars from the sixteenth century, and the Rest Hall of the Tsars from the seventeenth century. The Grand Palace was taken over in the Soviet period as a place to hold party conferences and meetings of the high councils of the Soviet Union and the Russian Soviet Republic. Meetings of officials in the industry, agriculture, science, and culture departments were also held there, as were all political and diplomatic meetings.

Near this palace was the Hall of Arms, built by Peter the Great in 1720 and completed in its present form in 1801. Today, expensive and historic works of art and valuable antique weapons are stored there, including some unique things placed there by prominent princes: Tsarist treasures, antique weapons, shields, sheets of gold and silver, beautiful clothing, and other treasures of cultural and historical value.

RED SQUARE

Many people think that the Revolution gave the name "Red Square" to the square in front of the Kremlin. But it is in fact an old name going back many centuries. The Tsars used to hold public festivals here, including coronations, receptions, and holidays. They also enjoyed watching public boxing matches held here, known as *kulachniy boy*. The contestants would shout out to the Tsar and his entourage, then they would meet in combat. Each wore a glove on his right hand, padded on the inside and iron on the outside. They circled around and shouted at each other until one was able to land a blow in the chest of the other contestant, then to throw him to the ground dead before the Tsar, the bodyguards, the onlookers, and the people.

The Russian Tsars used to chop off the heads of enemies and criminals on Red Square, and the platform for the executions still stands today. On that very platform in 1681, the Tsars beheaded the legendary peasant rebel Stenka Razin.

While in Red Square, we thought we ought to stop at the most beautiful house of worship in Russia, the Cathedral of St. Basil the Blessed, also called the Pokrovsky Cathedral. It was built in the reign of Tsar Ivan IV, called "the Terrible," son of Ivan III ("the Great"). This tsar ordered two of the most skilled architects in Russia to construct a church, seminary, or cathedral in Red Square which would be truly great and majestic. Its design and adornment were to make it an everlasting work of art. The architects devoted care to bringing Russian folklore to life in their design and built the Pokrovsky Cathedral, which astonishes and captures the hearts of everyone who enters it. Ivan the Terrible was among its greatest admirers, and he favored the architects with positions close to him at court.

One day the English ambassador to the Russian court visited the cathedral and was enchanted by its beauty and artistry. When he returned to London, he told the story of the cathedral to the Queen, and she wanted to build something like it in London. She wrote a letter to Ivan the Terrible, asking him to lend her the two architects so they could immortalize Russian architecture in the English capital.

When Ivan received the letter, he called the two architects and asked them, "Are you able to build a more beautiful holy place than the one you have built?"

They responded to him in unison: "Of course, master. We're ready to construct a more beautiful and majestic church."

And that night, Ivan the Terrible ordered that the eyes of the two architects be gouged out. Elizabeth awaited a response for a long time to no avail, until her ambassador returned from Russia and informed her of the tragedy which had befallen these two men, who had built a cathedral in Moscow's Red Square unlike even those imagined in legends and stories.

In Red Square today, near the walls of the Kremlin, there is the mausoleum of Lenin, made of black marble, based on the Babylonian-Persian architectural tradition. The founder of the state was entombed there in a tightly sealed glass coffin, wearing a military uniform, with his right hand formed into a fist and placed on his chest, and his left hand placed straight at his side. His mausoleum today is considered a global destination, and is guarded constantly by soldiers who stand reverently around it in complete silence and prevent visitors from conversing or wandering about. They urge visitors to go directly inside and to leave by the other door of the mausoleum.

Along one wall of the mausoleum, the one adjacent to the wall of the Kremlin, are the graves of Party leaders and state and international Communist leaders, including the American writer John Reed, the author of the book *Ten Days that Shook the World*.

On that topic, Stalin after his death was entombed in a glass coffin alongside Lenin's, but Khrushchev's reformist movement stripped him of this honor, transferred him from the mausoleum, and reinterred him elsewhere. A simple gravestone sufficed for him: "Stalin, 1879–1953."

Official parades were held in Red Square on major occasions. The Armed Forces paraded there, with their combat vehicles and, later, with intercontinental ballistic missiles. They were followed by teams of workers, students, and athletes. These groups performed artistic displays and waved flags of every type and color, while leaders of the Party and state stood atop Lenin's Mausoleum, continually waving at the crowds and exchanging greetings with everyone they saw.

In the days when I studied there, these celebrations began with the arrival of Marshal Semyon Budyonny. He was a big deal, having commanded the Red cavalry during the Civil War, and he arrived riding his lean steed, resting his saber on his shoulder, and loudly announcing the opening of the parade. Then the crowds of paraders would pour in, carefully organized in ranks of four, intermittently calling out slogans.

This custom was also later practiced by Marshal Klementy Voroshilov, who rode a white horse and wore military finery.

TO THE HEALTH RETREAT IN CRIMEA

I came down with an illness in the summer of 1928 and reported it to the university clinic. After the doctor ran some required tests, he informed me that

I had been exposed to intense cold and had come down with an inflammation in my airways called *bronkhit*, and that I had to be sent to a health retreat in the Crimean Peninsula to rest and recover. He issued his medical report, and accompanied it with a direction to prepare a *putevka*, a travel permit to go to the south of the Soviet Union.

The University doctor was a cheerful old man who never missed an opportunity for a joke. After he found out that I was an Arab, he said, "You've jumped from the desert to socialism in a single leap!"[5]

I said, "I come from a country that has made immense achievements in the medical field you practice. Have you heard of Jabir ibn Hiyyan, or Abu Bakr Mohammed al-Razi, or Abu Nasr Mohammad al-Farabi, or the great Abu 'Ali ibn Sina, or other learned Arab doctors and chemists?"

He said, "That's a different matter. What's important is, the desert and socialism do not meet, since socialism is the fruit of the stage of industry, not the stage of poverty."

I said, "Then how did the Uzbeks, Caucasians, Mongols, Kyrgyz, and Tatar peoples become your fellow-travelers?"

He clapped me on the shoulder and said, "You've answered your own question." He gave me the medical report and the recommendation for a *putevka* to the Crimean Peninsula and directed me to a resort in the town of Simeiz, where the climate would restore me to good health.

On June 20, 1928, I took my seat on a train from Moscow to the Crimean Peninsula (which extends 200 kilometers north-south and 325 kilometers west-east), until we reached the Perekop Isthmus, which links the peninsula to the mainland. Then we switched to a big tourist car and headed towards the southern point of the peninsula, where wonderful views overlooking the

5 A play on the common Leninist slogan that colonized areas should jump "from feudalism to socialism in a single leap," without the intervening capitalist stage expected by traditional Marxism. – Trans.

Black Sea were revealed to us. Then we took a route through the center of the peninsula until we reached the city of Simferopol and went from there to Yalta. Many health resorts spread along the shores of the southern tip of Crimea to either side of Yalta.

I went to the Simashko resort in Simeiz. The climate there was wonderful, rich with greenery and fruit. Thousands of patients and vacationers were attracted to the amazing coasts. Overlooking this town is "Cat Mountain," Mount Koshka, which looks like a cat lying down, and to its right is a string of mountains, 1200 meters high and covered in pine trees and vineyards that stretch up the slopes. There are very beautifully organized parks all over these mountains.

The nature of this town affected the great Russian writer Leo Tolstoy, who visited it in 1885 and wrote to his wife: "I am very comfortable here . . . isolation, beauty, and splendor!"

The residents at the health resorts in Simeiz spend their time according to the treatment regimens assigned to them, and according to their doctors' instructions if they came for treatment and recovery. The mornings and evenings are filled with walks to nearby healthful places, including climbing the Ai-Petri peak, 1233 meters high.

In the town of Alubka is the palace that housed General Vorontsov, the governor-general of the peninsula in the Tsarist era. The palace is considered among the most beautiful palaces in the whole world. It took 18 years to build it, from 1828 to 1846. Great Russian artists have stayed there, including [Ivan] Aivazovsky; Maxim Gorky, who is known for his book "Wonders of Crimea"; and the Poet of the Revolution Vladimir Mayakovsky, known for his poem "Crimea."

In the Alorka park stand three immense trees. One is a Lebanese cedar, another is a Mexican pine, and the third is an Italian pine.

Yalta itself is surrounded by cypress trees, acacias, laurels, and magnolias. There are 130 health resorts in this area, and every year about 300,000 people are drawn there. The great Russian storyteller Anton Chekhov settled there in 1898 and built a house overlooking the Black Sea, where he composed many of his literary works. The house was later turned into a museum about his Crimean influences. It has become a destination for every visitor and vacationer who comes to Crimea.

In the square in Yalta, the Soviet government set up an obelisk on which was engraved in gold letters: "These splendid vacation houses and hotels were once the preserve of emperors and great princes, but now the workers and peasants will benefit from them as centers for healing and relaxation."

The name "Yalta" became famous at the end of World War II, when Roosevelt, Churchill, and Stalin met there from February 4 to 12, 1945, to draw up plans for the future of the war and peace, and wrote the Yalta Formula, the basis for the United Nations Security Council.

The town of Gorzov is another beautiful resort. The great Russian poet Alexander Pushkin visited it in the spring of 1821 and stayed there as a guest of the family of General Raevsky, a hero of the national war against Napoleon in 1812. There he wrote his two long poems *The Caucasian Prisoner* and *The Fountain of Bakhchisarai.*

The town of Feodosia is famous for its fifteen kilometers of golden beaches, which Tolstoy described as follows: "By her beautiful blue and foaming sea, a man can live on the beach for a thousand years and never tire of it." Greek merchants knew Feodosia in the sixth century BCE and established a colony there by this name. Then the Tatars lived there and gave it the name Kaffa, after which it was sold to the merchants of Genoa, who made it a base for trading goods and slaves. Then the Turks lived there in the fifteenth century, making it their base in the peninsula, working hand in hand with the Tatar people there. The Russians captured it in the seventeenth century and restored its original name, Feodosia, which means "Gift of God" in Greek.

The Aivazovsky museum is in this town. It features 2,290 artworks by Russian and global artists, including 389 works of the Russian artist Aivazovsky, and a four-thousand-volume library.

On the western coast of Crimea is the town of Yevpatoria, considered the best resort for children, or for any who suffer from osteomyelitis or ailments of the joints, blood vessels, or nervous system.

Among the advantages of this town are its constant sun, clean air, the sea breezes that moderate the climate, and the shallow waters of its coast, which warm quickly in the sun and in which children can swim safely. It has no dangerous currents, nor freshwater streams, which would otherwise reduce the water's healthy salinity, nor are there factories and industries there, so the air remains clean and free of pollution.

This health resort had become famous in 1882 and later in the early twentieth century as a favorite place for gatherings of nobles and their retinues.

We briefly visited a number of other places on the Crimean Peninsula. Among them were the capital Simferopol, whose Tatar name is Akmesjit, and Sevastopol, called Akhyar by the Tatars. Sevastopol is Crimea's primary port and the main Soviet naval base on the Black Sea. It was annexed by Russia in 1783. It played a key role in the Crimean War (of a Turko-Anglo-French coalition against Russia in 1854–1856), and in the Second World War, in which the Nazis occupied the Crimean Peninsula in the spring of 1942; the Russians resisted this occupation and overcame it.

Crimea was an autonomous Tatar republic before the war. But the Tatar inhabitants fell under the influence of Nazi propaganda during the Second World War and declared the independence of Crimea from the Soviet Union. Stalin, the Party, and the state canceled the autonomous status of the Crimean Republic in 1946, returning it to the Russian Soviet Republic.

I returned from Crimea to Moscow, having recovered from my bronchitis, my eyes and spirit having enjoyed the nature of those beautiful surroundings, and having learned much about its history and art. I returned to studying at the university in due course.

NEHRU AND BUKHARIN

We were told early in 1929 that Gandhi's second-in-command as leader of the Indian National Congress, Sri [Jawaharlal] Nehru, would soon visit Moscow. They told us to go greet him at the railway station, and we wore our fancy clothes, representing a mix of Eastern peoples.

With us standing around the train, the band played the national anthem, and Bukharin stepped forward wearing his black leather coat, representing the Soviet Government and the party (he was at the time a member of the Politburo in the party's central committee). He extended his hand to shake hands with Nehru, but the Indian leader replied with a half-smile and turned down the handshake. Bukharin, shaken by this insult, slowly withdrew his hand and placed it in his pocket.

Nobody at the time understood Nehru's reason for insulting Bukharin in this way, which remained a closely held secret. But I thought Nehru did what he did for the following reasons: First, he was greeted in a "comradely" way, and he didn't want to seem like a "political follower." Secondly, his reception had not followed official protocol, which required the presence of civilians from the foreign ministry. Thirdly, Stalin had not come in person to greet Nehru, despite Nehru's status as the second-ranking leader of the Indian people.

Nehru took a car with a few of the Indian students to the Metropol Hotel, while Bukharin called us over to take a commemorative photo with him. Though the photos were distributed to us, we later had to tear them up, as his opposition to Stalin's policies caused issues to emerge. We will come to those issues in a later section.

THE BRONZE-SKINNED SPEAKER

In 1929, units of the British fleet blockaded Alexandria under orders from the second Ramsay MacDonald government, in the time of Egypt's Mustafa Nahhas Pasha government. Soviet circles were enraged by this imperialist action, and people went off at the behest of state and Party authorities to hold meetings and demonstrations against "the barbarity of the Labor Party," as agents of colonialism and capitalism. It was self-evident that the students at KUTV would hold loud demonstrations in Tverskoy Square. The students wanted to make sure that an Arab was brought forward to speak to them, and they chose me to speak. They put me up at the podium and I got up to call excitedly for the fall of imperialism, cheering on the Egyptian people and the Egyptian Wafd party.

The next day, the newspaper *Izvestiya* published a story describing the demonstration and said, "Suddenly, an Arab youth got up on the stage, bronze-skinned, with dark hair and eyes, and inspired the demonstrators' enthusiasm with strongly phrased Arabic expressions. He protested against the MacDonald government for its artillery bombardment of Alexandria."[6]

6 Sidqi's footnote: "Earlier, as a young man, Ramsey MacDonald had done a big favor for Lenin. After the failure of the 1905 revolution, with the Russian security forces pursuing them, the Russian Social Democratic Labor Party decided to hold its fifth congress in a European country. So they gathered in London in 1907, but were in serious need of financial support. Ramsay MacDonald as head of the Socialist Party of Britain undertook to support his Russian guests. He convinced a group that followed Christian Socialism, based in the Brotherhood Church in Whitechapel in East London, to clear the space so that the Russians could hold their conference in that church for three days only. But the Russian, Polish, and other delegates, 336 of them in total, remained in the church for three weeks. The English begged them to leave the church, as they were unable to perform prayers for all of that time. Only Maxim Gorky, who was also in attendance, could save the day: he raised some money for his colleagues from English comrades, and they also agreed to borrow a total of three thousand pounds sterling from an Englishman who owned a soap factory in London. Thus they were able to manage their affairs. It is known that Lenin repaid the factory owner this amount after the revolution, with his thanks."

THE GRAF ZEPPELIN

One day in 1929, the German blimp *Graf Zeppelin* passed over Moscow during its trip around the world. People gathered in the squares and streets, staring up at this flying giant, waving their hands, caps, and handkerchiefs. The next day, a picture appeared in *Pravda* of a Russian looking at the blimp with resignation and saying in Russian: "*Khorosha Masha, da ne nasha*," which means "Masha is lovely, but she's not for us." The newspaper responded to this with an expression of reassurance, saying in Russian, "*Masha da budet nasha*," which means "Masha will be ours!" They meant that the Russians too could manufacture a blimp of their own.

THE GIANT PLANE

The Russians didn't build a blimp, but in 1929, they began to construct a giant eight-engine plane with two floors, a luxurious reception hall, and comfortable seats. In 1931 this plane was completed and named *Maxim Gorky*, in recognition of the writer's forty years of literary life. It rose into the Moscow sky carrying a select group of official personages as well as a band playing marches and dance melodies.

As this aerial display was passing, people below gazed up at it cheerfully. Then, a young pilot circled the behemoth in his small plane, doing aerobatic stunts above it. He lost his balance and struck it, destroying the plane along with himself.

It was a great national tragedy. The newspapers vented their spleen on the young pilot, describing him in abominable terms, such as "the child pilot," "the murderous aerobat," and "flying trash."

The Russians never tried to manufacture a plane like that again.

THE METRO AND THE METROPOLITAN

A topic of conversation at that time was the building of an underground train in Moscow. The people were thrilled about the metro project and sang its praises. *Izvestiya* encouraged this excitement by publishing two photos, one of which was of a statue of the top Orthodox bishop, called the "Metropolitan" in Russian. The caption said: "The country has moved from one era to another."

The project developed, and the first line of the Metropolitan subway opened atop the rubble of the Metropolit's statue on May 15, 1935. Today Moscow's metro stations are considered modern tourist attractions, as every station is constructed of marble and multicolored granite and decorated with oil paintings and mosaics, all in an artistic framework presenting the stages of Russian and Soviet history.

MATCHBOXES

That year people lacked liquid cash, causing many difficulties on transit systems like the tram and the bus. If you paid the ticket collector in rubles and exceeded the price of the fare, he would make change with a matchbox. Then, you were entitled to board the tram and pay with three unopened and unused matchboxes!

This farce did not go on for long.

A RIVER BATH

Among the amusing events from this time was the publication of the satirical magazine *Smekhach* (*The Jester*). One issue contained a cartoon criticizing the state of public baths. It showed a man in the winter using a hammer to break a hole in the ice on the river to take a swim. His friend Grisha walks by, and the guy in the river asks him, "Grisha, where are you going?"

Grisha replies, "I'm going to the public bath."

The first man says, "No need to walk all the way to the bathhouse! Come get in the water here, it's warmer!"

STALIN AND UZBEK POETRY

No leader in history enjoyed the level of veneration that Iosif Dzhugashvili Stalin did, to the point of worship. And no person received as many wearisome compliments and expressions of praise as Stalin.

At the university I met an Uzbek student who showed me a poem written by an Uzbek poet from Ferghana in praise of Stalin, entitled *Happiness*. I memorized it and translated it. It goes:

When the sun sparkles on the shore
When the sun blazes, smiles and shines
My eyes laugh with delight
And I find joy in the sunlight

My country is happy in May
My land of Ferghana in May
Its gardens full with a floral display
Their scents rise thickly in May

The pomegranate branches dance
Filling my lungs with sweet fragrance
The country delights in its pure spring
When garden branches bow in greeting

I make my way through the cotton fields
I reach and touch their blooming yields
I call out loud to the fields where I stand:
"All of this cotton belongs to my land!"

Blessings to you, my happy land
May you find joy, my ancient land
My blessings to the peoples' Union!

Praise to you, oh leader we love,
You, Stalin, are the poor man's balm
O Stalin, words cannot express your praise
You, Stalin, are the people's protector

Stalin, you are the foeman's fear
You bring water to the wasteland
New happiness to the wasteland
A spring of freedom to the wasteland
Burned tyrant's yokes with your blazing brand!

You are our sun, O knight of joy,
You spread your joy far and wide
Stalin, you send forth light and joy
To Soviet lands, you are a world of joy

You are our beloved Father Stalin,
Maker of the constitution, Stalin,
A thousand greetings to you, Stalin
From hearts brimming with grateful joy, O Stalin!

GOODBYE, MOSCOW!

The Arab group threw a goodbye party at the graduation of the first class of Arab students. At this party there were speeches by the Tunisian student 'Ali al-Hamami (he was from the left wing of the Tunisian Destour party); the

Algerian student Mohammed Bousfir from the town of Sidi Bel-Abbes; the Egyptian student 'Aziz mentioned above; and the Egyptian Jewish student Zanberg, who later became a teacher at the university for his mastery of Marxist theory. They all spoke about the five years they had spent at the university and all the amusing and amazing things those years had contained, and they offered advice and instructions to the new cohort of students sent from Syria, Palestine, and Egypt.

One day in February 1929, I submitted my university thesis on the subject of "The Arab Nationalist Movement from the Unionist Coup to the Period of the National Bloc," and it was accepted. I have attached it to the end of this book.[7]

7 The "Unionist Coup" is now called the Young Turk Revolution. We have not translated Sidqi's senior thesis. For the Arabic, see pp. 189-228 in *Mudhakirat Najati Sidqi*. —Trans.

5

RETURNING TO THE HOMELAND

(1929–1930)

I caught a steamer from the Odessa port to Istanbul. In my pocket was my real passport, which bore no Soviet entry or exit stamps. I had to arrange matters in Istanbul to prove that I had been there during the years I had spent in Moscow, 1925 to 1929. This mission was quite daunting, as I knew no one in the Turkish capital. One day, as I was walking near the Galata Bridge, I met a young Greek man who had studied in Moscow. He smiled at me and gestured that I should follow him, then led me to a café in the Taqsim neighborhood. There I told him that I was returning home and needed to prove that I had lived in Istanbul for the duration of my absence. To do so, I had to receive an official exit stamp from Turkey. He told me that doing this would take time, and he proposed that I leave the Jerusalem Hotel, where I was staying, and move to the house of another Greek comrade who had studied in Moscow.

I took up residence in the home of the Greek comrade, saving the money I would have spent on a hotel and restaurants, and his kind family surrounded me with attention. After about two weeks, my host told me that he had arranged matters with a broker, and that I had to follow the broker to a Turkish security office to receive a long-term residence permit for Istanbul and an exit visa.

I went with the broker to complete this mission. On the way, he said to me in Russian, "*Vy rabotchii narod?*"—that is, "Are you from the working people?" This was all the Russian he knew. And I said to him, "*Da, da, rabotchii narod,*" that is, "Yes, I'm from the working people." And when we neared the Turkish security offices, he recommended that I reply to every question the employee there asked with "*Evet, efendim*": "Yes, sir."

And so it was. The broker and I strolled to the office of a big Turkish official, a tall, bulky, pale-skinned man, who looked from me to the photo affixed to my passport. He asked me a few pro forma questions; I replied to each question with "*Evet, efendim.*" He smiled and stamped the passport and affixed a travel permit. I left his office almost flying with joy. Honestly, if not for my Greek comrade, I would have run into insurmountable obstacles.

The next day, I bought a third-class ticket on a French steamship bound for Jaffa. We arrived after a week at sea, and the steamer anchored offshore, as the city did not have a port where steamships could dock. The sailors put on loose pants and boarded longboats to take the passengers to the dock, myself among them. No sooner had I set foot on the customs dock than I spotted the English chief of police, one Mister Rex. I knew him, though he did not know me. Because my passport had no trace of where I had actually lived abroad and where I was returning home from, the passport office approved my passport for official entry. So I set off for a friend's house to contact the Party's local committee. After a few days there, I was on my way to Jerusalem to meet with the central committee of the Palestinian Communist Party.

THE PARTY'S JEWISH LEADERSHIP

Leadership of the Palestinian Communist Party was in the hands of a number of Jewish Communists, most of whom had come from Russia, Poland, or other European countries. Here they are:

1. **The party's general secretary** had a few names, which has confused everyone who has written about the Palestinian Communist Party, leading them to believe that these were the names of a number of different Jewish Communist

leaders. His names were: Eliyahu Tepper, Der Alter—Yiddish for "The Choice,"[8] Abu Siam, Haydar, and Shami.

Tepper was born in Vilna in 1869. He was influenced by Socialist ideas in his youth, then joined the Poalei Zion (Workers of Zion) party, which was founded in the Vilna area in the early 20th century; he became one of its leaders. As this party combined Marxism and Zionism, Eliyahu Tepper moved to Palestine around 1922. But soon afterwards he left Poalei Zion, influenced by the Arab reality in Palestine, and joined the international Communist movement.

He worked on founding the Communist Party for Palestine—the name reflects the fact that it was not local—and tried to join the global group of Communist parties, the Comintern. First, the Comintern required him to open spaces for Arab elements to integrate into the movement. The Comintern then allowed him to call the party the Palestinian Communist Party, as it had become local. In his time, he set out to implement the "Arabization" of the Party, which required assigning some sensitive positions to Arab Communists.

Among his other activities, he went to Lebanon in 1924 and met with Yusuf Yazbek, Fu'ad al-Shamali, and others, to try to inject revolutionary socialist ideas coming from Haifa into the romantic Lebanese socialist movement, which was centered in Zahle around the Wandering Journalist newspaper. But the French Mandate authorities arrested him and deported him from Lebanon.

In 1932, Eliyahu Tepper was called to Moscow to be investigated for "Zionist deviations" and was thrown into the Lubyanka, a prison specifically for political criminals. After a while, he was released. He disappeared from the political scene when he was almost in his seventies.

8 Der Alter actually means "the Old Man." Tepper was substantially older than most other members of his party. —Trans.

2. Joseph Berger-Barzilai was a journalist of Austrian origin, Tepper's trusted assistant who took his place when he was absent. Within the party he handled foreign relations and official communications, and he printed discussions and articles about Arab-Jewish issues in the newspaper *International Press Correspondence* (Inprecor), published in Berlin. He also reported on the party's administrative, political, and financial decisions to the Comintern organization in Moscow.

Among other activities, he traveled ahead of Eliyahu Tepper, or Abu Siam, on his visit to Lebanon in 1924, smoothing the way for his leader in organizing the first cells of the Communist movement in Lebanon and Syria. He also taught the members of these cells the song "L'Internationale" in French and encouraged Yusuf Yazbek to translate it into Arabic.

In 1932, Joseph Barzilai was called to Moscow for an investigation into the Palestinian Communist Party. As soon as he reached the Soviet capital, he was arrested on the accusation that during his visits to Berlin he had met members of the German Nazi party. It was rumored at that time that he had been tried and sentenced to execution by firing squad, but he returned and appeared in Israel having reached his eighties. By that age he was wholly immersed in the study of the Mishna (a book of Jewish law) and the Jerusalem Talmud.

3. Nakhman Litvinsky, originally from Russia, came to Palestine with the first immigrants. He married a woman named Anyuta, the daughter of a bathhouse owner in Haifa. She was Russian by birth as well, and very smart and capable.

Nakhman and his wife joined the Party and primarily worked in the central committee; he spoke Arabic fluently and was proficient in Russian, French, Yiddish (Jewish German), and Hebrew. The Party sent him to Lebanon in the early thirties, but he was arrested and expelled to Alexandria with his wife. The two returned to Beirut in 1933 and stayed in the Danai' neighborhood. They then traveled to France and lived in Paris, where Nakhman worked with the League

Against Imperialism and published a book in French on "the Eastern Question" in which he analyzed the history of colonialism in the East. All traces of him and his wife disappeared during World War II.

4. David Lichtinsky came to Palestine in the early 1920s, and the Party sent him to Egypt on August 31, 1930, to help renew Communist activities there after the destruction of the first Egyptian cell in 1924. That cell had been led by [Joseph] Rosenthal and Anton Maroun; the first was exiled abroad with other foreigners, and the second went on a hunger strike in prison until he died.

Lichtinsky lived in Cairo disguised as a Talmud student, but he was discovered and deported from Egypt on October 11, 1930, along with Paul Dietrich, Mila Normberg, and Sarah Poznansky. After returning to Palestine he joined the Party's Central Committee; he managed the Party's affairs in the Tel Aviv-Jaffa area.

5. Meir Kuperman was assigned to manage the Party's affairs in the Haifa area. He was an educated man, but high-strung; he spoke colloquial Arabic and joined the Central Committee in 1929.

6. Yankel Berman was the head of the Party's committee in Tel Aviv at one point; he then headed the committee in Haifa, and eventually was promoted to the Central Committee. He took part in most meetings and conferences of the party, then traveled to Poland shortly before World War II. We later learned that he had played a significant role during the war.

7. Sarah Poznansky was a capable woman with a wide-ranging education whom the Party sent to Egypt with Lichtinsky. She worked as a nurse in a children's hospital in the Jewish quarter in Cairo under the name "Mademoiselle Ehrlich" until she was caught and deported to Palestine on October 11, 1930.

8. David Avigdor, nicknamed "the Mufti," was a short and laconic man. He was a close advisor of the Central Committee and ran the underground press in Jerusalem in both Arabic and Hebrew. He was responsible for printing pamphlets and publications and overseeing their distribution to different areas.

9. Hayim Davidovich was elected as a member of the Communist youth central committee for the 1924 Haifa conference, then became a member of the local Party committee in Jerusalem. He was arrested multiple times, then traveled to the Soviet Union in 1938 and fought in the Battle of Moscow against the Nazi invasion. He died in battle.

10. "Moshe Mizrahi," or "Musa al-Sharqi,"[9] was Palestinian by birth, and was selected as a member of the Communist youth central committee at the 1924 Haifa conference, then was a member of the local committee in Jerusalem. He was arrested repeatedly, but the British authorities were unable to deport him, because he was Palestinian. In 1932 he traveled to Moscow to try to get Eliyahu Tepper released from prison, after which we heard no more of him.

11. "Stepan" was a tall young man, light-skinned, Russian-looking, who was the line of communication between the Central Committee and the heads of local committees. He was assigned to pick up the mail dropped at certain addresses and to send it out; Tepper had great trust in him.

THE ARAB LEADERSHIP

1. Mahmoud al-Mughrabi was called "Mughrabi" because he was of Algerian origin, and so he was also often known as Mahmoud the Algerian. He worked in

9 The names mean "Moshe the Easterner" in Hebrew and Arabic respectively. —Trans.

construction in the Manshiya neighborhood of Jaffa and owned a small house in that area where he lived with his brother Taher, but he eventually had to sell the house as he was in dire financial straits.

He joined the party in 1928, then traveled to Moscow to study at KUTV for post-secondary education. He didn't complete his studies but instead went directly to Lebanon in the spring of 1930, where he was known in Party circles as "Abu Dawud." The French authorities arrested him at the end of that year and deported him to Palestine, where he joined the Central Committee.

In December 1930, he was arrested with me and sentenced to two years in prison. After he served this sentence the police were still after him, so the party furnished him with travel to Moscow a second time; there he was known as "Comrade Salim." He remained there, involved in Comintern activities, until 1937, when he was sent to Paris to support the activities of the French Communist Party (based on his being Algerian). There, he was surprised by the Nazi invasion and rushed into hiding in the Algerian workers' neighborhoods until the war ended in 1945.

In 1947, he was transferred to Prague to work in the Arab center there along with a number of Arab Communists who had taken shelter in the Czech capital. He later settled in North Africa, where he resides to this day.

2. Ridwan al-Hilu was a construction worker in Manshiya, Jaffa, who joined the Party in 1935 and traveled to Moscow for study in 1937. As he was traveling by train from Odessa to the Soviet capital, one of the Russian peasants with him in the third-class carriage wanted to light a cigarette. Ridwan offered to help. He opened his bag before the eyes of the peasants, who were dazzled by the products he had brought from bourgeois countries. He took out an elegant lighter and lit the Russian peasant's cigarette, then closed the bag and returned it to the shelf above his head. The travelers fell into a deep sleep, the air heavy with the smells of vodka, seledka, and makhorka—those being drink, herring, and peasant tobacco. In the morning, Ridwan had lost his bag and couldn't find it. The peasant disembarked at a village station, cradling a bag full of "capitalist luxuries." As for Ridwan, he ran and shouted in Arabic, "Where's the bag?" as the peasants laughed at him, saying "Nichego, tovarishch": "Don't worry about it, Comrade." He arrived in Moscow complaining loudly and asking how theft could happen in a socialist country.

Ridwan returned to Palestine in 1939 via Beirut and joined the Party's central committee. He was appointed to the leadership of the federation of workers in Jaffa, in addition to his party work. After the disaster of 1948, he went to Jericho, where he has worked on a successful farm until this day.

3. Hasan Malak was a Lebanese man from Tripoli, whom the Palestinian party "borrowed" after its Arab leaders were arrested. He joined the Central Committee in 1931 but was then arrested and sent to the Acre prison, where he served six months on the charge of having entered Palestine secretly, and on suspicion of membership in an illegal organization; he was then returned to Lebanon. Today he is a businessman.

4. Ahmad Khalaf was a farm worker from the village of Beitunia in Palestine, who joined the Party in 1927. He was sent to Moscow to be educated, returning to Palestine in 1930. He was arrested in 1931, and after his release he headed to Moscow a second time to complete his education. Contact with him was lost during the years of the Second World War, but it is believed that he settled there.

5. 'Ali 'Abd al-Khaliq was a farmer whom the Party sent to Moscow with his colleague Khalaf. He did not stay there long, returning to Palestine in 1930, where he worked in construction until he was arrested. He was allowed to leave prison in 1932 and travel to Spain, where he fought and was slain in the Civil War.

6. Taher al-Mughrabi was the brother of Mahmoud al-Mughrabi. He was a construction worker. He went to Moscow in 1932 and was still there during World War II, when we lost contact with him.

7. 'Abd al-Ghani al-Karmi was the son of the scholar and poet Sheikh Sa'id al-Karmi; his brothers included the poet 'Abd al-Karim al-Karmi (known as Abu Salma) and Hassan al-Karmi, an editor and interpreter of ancient Arabic poetry who worked at the London Today radio station. 'Abd al-Ghani joined the Party in 1929, while working as a journalist, and was immediately sent to Moscow for a year to broaden his knowledge of Marxism. They gave him the pseudonym "**Maykhan**" to conceal his real identity.

Educated in France, 'Abd al-Ghani did not enjoy the lifestyle in student housing; he became irritated by it, and he tried to return to his country after a short stay in Moscow. But the officials did not understand the reason for this attempt, thinking poorly of him and believing that he had turned traitor (they neglected to ask him). He spoke that day with a French Communist Party representative in the Comintern named "Barbé," and asked him to help facilitate his exit; Barbé promised to help. But the days went on with 'Abd al-Ghani still not able to leave the country.

In a moment of nervous tension, he sat down at his desk in his room at the Hotel Lux and resorted to drafting a letter to the British ambassador in Moscow. In the letter, he asked the ambassador to grant him a passport, describing himself as being from a country under the British Mandate and asking for help in leaving the Soviet Union. 'Abd al-Ghani left the letter in his room and went to the bathroom, and at that moment, his Egyptian colleague Fathi visited. Fathi spotted the name of the letter's addressee and understood its meaning immediately. He pretended he knew nothing of his colleague's plan, then informed the University. The matter concerned them, and they spoke to the OGPU, that is, the secret police, who promptly raided 'Abd al-Ghani's room. They found the letter, arrested him, and sent him to the Lubyanka.

In the investigation, 'Abd al-Ghani defended himself by saying that he had asked to leave many times to no avail, and that he had felt psychological distress from his living condition, nothing more. The Secretary of the Communist Party of Lebanon and Syria, the respected Fu'ad al-Shamali, was visiting Moscow at the time, and he learned that 'Abd al-Ghani had been arrested. He made a great effort with the Comintern officials to secure 'Abd al-Ghani's release and send him out of the country. His efforts were crowned with success, and 'Abd al-Ghani returned to Palestine in the summer of 1930.

In winter of 1930, a conference of Arab workers was held in Haifa; I attended and gave a speech, and there I met 'Abd al-Ghani al-Karmi in his capacity as a reporter for a Jaffan newspaper.

'Abd al-Ghani remained in Palestine for a few years, then moved to London after World War II and worked there as the head of editing at the *London World* magazine, an attractive, informative, and well-edited magazine. It stopped publication in 1963 after twelve years.

'Abd al-Ghani returned to Palestine in the mid-sixties, then moved to Amman, where he lived until his death.

8. Najib Franjieh was of Lebanese extraction. His father and uncle immigrated from Zgharta to Palestine during the First World War. He was born and grew up in the 'Ajami neighborhood of Jaffa, then became a journalist and translator from English. He edited a Jaffa newspaper and joined the Party in 1934. After some time, he was dispatched to Moscow to study along with his wife. He returned to Palestine in 1932 to work at the newspapers *Palestine, al-Difa'* (*The Defense*), and *al-Iqdaam* (*Boldness*).

In the year of the Catastrophe, 1948, he returned to Lebanon with his family (after the deaths of his uncle, father, and mother) and lived in the Sin al-Fil neighborhood in Beirut, where he worked at the *al-Hadaf* (The Goal) newspaper and produced the Arab Encyclopedia published by the Rihani publishing house. Then he emigrated from Lebanon.

There were a number of other Palestinian students who studied political science in Moscow at different times: some returned to their country, some stayed in the Soviet Union, some were dispersed around the world in both Arab and foreign countries, and some died.

THE PROFINTERN CONFERENCE

(1931)

In the summer of 1931, the Central Committee called a surprise meeting in which we decided to send a delegation to the upcoming Conference of the Profintern (Red International of Labor Unions) in Moscow. A precondition for this was holding a public local meeting of unions whose policy or plans the Party directed or influenced, to hear the concerns of Palestinian unions. These were:

1. The relationship between the Histadrut (the federation of Jewish labor unions) and Arab workers.
2. Wage discrimination between Jewish workers and Arab workers.
3. The Arab Palestinian unions and their role in the national movement.
4. Whether to establish independent revolutionary unions, or merge them into a single national federation of trade unions centered in Haifa.

We looked into these four points in a secret three-day meeting held in the Baqaʿa area of Jerusalem, at which we decided to dispatch a delegation of two representatives to the Profintern, one Jew and one Arab; the attendees chose me to represent the Arabs. I traveled to Beirut, then took a boat to Marseilles, then to Paris, then Berlin, where I had to contact the German branch of the Communist Party. In Jerusalem I had been given the address of a shoe factory in the northern part of the German capital, so I set out for there and asked after a certain person. An elderly bespectacled man greeted me, and I told him the codeword. He nodded and said, "Profintern?"

I replied, "Yes."

He said, "You will go to such-and-such a hotel in the East End area, where you'll stay until your sea travel to Leningrad can be arranged." My comrades and I stayed in Berlin for a week. While I was there, I saw Nazi Party marches and the counter-marches organized by the "Red Front" (*Rote Front*), in which tens of thousands of young men and women took part, wearing military uniforms and raising the red flag, singing "*Rote Wedding, Mir Marschiert.*" This meant, "Oh Wedding neighborhood"—that was a workers' neighborhood—"we are marching!"

People stopped on the sidewalk to watch, hands on hearts. It was as if they felt that the ground of Germany was beginning to shake beneath their feet; that these two sides would certainly collide, and that this collision would change the face of Germany, for better or for worse. Between the two forces stood the German police, who said very politely that there was no need for onlookers to stop on the sidewalk, that they should either go on their way or join the demonstrations!

The sickle and hammer and the "crooked cross"[10] challenged one another on the streets in skirmishes in which some fell dead or wounded. Hatred gathered, and bitter grudges built up. Preparations were in full swing for Germany to enter a world shrouded in ignorance and terror.

The Germans, every one, were saying: *Sixteen years have passed and we are still under the yoke of the Treaty of Versailles, which has drained the blood from us, seized our colonies from us, closed global markets in the face of our commerce, loaded us*

10 *Hakenkreuz*, the technical term for the Nazi swastika. —Trans.

with debt, and humiliated us. The time has come for this to end and for us to re-enter the free world.

The stance of the left regarding this reality was that the only salvation for Germany was to form a popular front including the Communists, Socialists, and Social Democrats to resolve the governing crisis.

The stance of the right, that is, the Nazi Party, was that the only salvation for Germany was to utterly destroy German democracy and to instill the country with the spirit of the police and army, to draft every German to march feverishly to east and west to the rising pounding of war drums accompanied by chants of "Heil Hitler."

The German right had wanted to bestow a philosophical stamp on its movement, and for this purpose it used the book *Mein Kampf* (*My Struggle*) by an ex-painter and ex-corporal in the old German army, Adolf Hitler. On this note, I prepared a study about him, entitled *Islamic Traditions and Nazi Principles*, published by Dar al-Kashaf in Beirut in 1940. It was translated into English in London in 1941.[11]

I left Berlin by train and traveled to the port of Stettin located on the Baltic Sea, then embarked from there on a Soviet steamer to Leningrad. The Soviets provided me with a special travel document bearing the entry visa, instead of stamping the visa on my passport. It was an enjoyable trip, during which I saw the "white nights" (of the summer solstice), nights which are indistinguishable from daytime. The light is continuous: only the silence of the streets and the chill in the air indicate that night has fallen.

We reached the Gulf of Finland, and the steamer then crossed through a canal until we approached the port of Leningrad. Our attention was drawn to the Petropavlovskaya Krepost'—Peter and Paul Fortress—and the palace

11 See this memoir's closing chapter for more on that work. —Trans.

of Peter the Great. Then the steamer reached its mooring in the port, and we disembarked for the customs office, where a careful inspection was conducted, especially on the Europeans. One of the customs inspectors spotted a valuable pair of earrings in the ears of an English woman and wanted to inspect them, so he turned them over in his fingers, tugging on the earlobe in which they were fixed. The woman grew angry and rebuked him, so he refrained from a hands-on appraisal and instead examined the earring visually, recording its appearance and type on a form. He told her through an interpreter: You'll have to present the earrings and this form when you leave the country.

During a quick tour through Leningrad, we got to know the landmarks of this beautiful city, which Peter the Great had wanted to be his "window to the West." We saw the ancient fortress into which the tsars used to throw their enemies and the Peterhof Palace with its famous fountains, by which Peter the Great had hoped to compete with the French palace at Versailles and the tsars' winter palace. We also saw the Hermitage Museum, which contains oil paintings by famous European artists; the museum of Pushkin, prince of Russian poetry; the famous obelisk in Saint Peter's Square; and the splendid boardwalk along the Neva River. After this tour, we took a train to Moscow and stayed at the Lux Hotel, designated specially for foreign party delegations.

The Profintern conference opened in the House of the Federation of Trade Unions, which was once a club for aristocrats. The conference's work continued for about two weeks. It addressed the problems of union organization around the world, "at the stage when capitalism is undergoing its deepest crises as unemployment spreads among the workers; when agriculture is withering; when the revolutionary struggle is crystallizing among the working class and the peoples struggling against colonization; and when the Nazi movement rises to power in Germany, the Italian Fascists are moving to expand their empire in Africa, and Japanese militarism is expanding in the Far East."

The conference took a number of decisions on formulating the approach for labor unions around the world during this historic era. I'll highlight the one it took related to Palestine: "That the labor unions should be organized into a general federation, which should then join the Profintern, and that the federation should demand equality between Jewish and Arab labor in wages and working hours."

The proceedings of the conference, for the first time in the history of Russian conferences, were translated automatically. Every representative had a headset placed on his ears and an electric panel indicating the available languages of translation, so that all the representative had to do was to plug the headphones into the slot for the language he wanted, and he then listened to the translation live.

During the course of the conference, I expressed a complaint to the Russian who was responsible for the delegates' comfort, as he was behaving bureaucratically and neglectfully. I asked, "Do you want me to mention this behavior of yours in my report on the activities of the conference?" He got angry and passed my comments to the high committee of the Profintern conference, whose members included [Nikolai] Shvernik, the president of the Soviet Federation of Labor Unions, and Walter Ulbricht, who later became leader of the German Communist Party and the president of the German Democratic Republic. The two called me before them to look into my complaint. Ulbricht took umbrage and demanded that I withdraw my complaint and the things I had said, and I did so. But Shvernik merely remarked: "Arab blood runs hot!"

After the conference ended, I was provided with specific recommendations regarding both the unions and the party. I returned on the Moscow–Paris–Marseilles route. I then sailed to Alexandria and took a train back to Palestine. As I was sitting in the compartment waiting for the train to set off for Gaza, an English policeman approached and asked me to meet him in the head office. I thought to myself: *I've been caught.* In the office, I found an Egyptian officer and an English officer. They asked for my passport, which was fake; the original picture of the owner had been replaced with my photo. The following exchange occurred:

The officer asked, "Are you the owner of this passport?"

I said, "Of course."

"What's your trade?"

"I'm a carpenter."

"You don't look like a carpenter."

"I own a furniture store in Jaffa."

"Where?"

"On 'Ajami Street."

"Have you ever reported the loss of this passport of yours?"

"Yes, I reported its loss a month and a half ago, but I checked again and found it, and I traveled with it to Germany and France."

"Why did you travel to these countries?"

"To learn about the latest furniture styles."

"Where are you headed now?"

"Jaffa, of course."

The English and Egyptian officers inspected the passport carefully but found nothing about it to arouse their suspicions. The Egyptian officer raised his voice, trying to threaten me, but the English officer calmed him down and whispered a few words in his ear. He returned my passport to me, and said, "You're all set, go on your way." I intuited that the English officer had told the Egyptian, "Let him go. We'll call the Jaffa police on the phone. They can meet him at the station, and we'll leave the examination and investigation to them."

The train set off for Lydda, which we reached at dawn. There I left the train, burned my passport, and hitched a ride on a truck carrying oranges to Jerusalem.

I later found out that at that time, the police in Jaffa were lying in wait at the station; they surrounded it and raided it, searching fruitlessly for the suspicious traveler. They realized that I had slipped through their fingers.

7
THE PARTY'S MAIN ISSUES
(1929–1931)

Five leading issues arose in the time I spent as a party official, from 1929 until my arrest in 1931. The issues were: Arabization; the uprising of 1929; Jewish immigration; the rural land issue; and our stance with respect to the Arab national movement.

1. ARABIZATION

The directive to "Arabize" the party came directly from the Comintern. This meant that the Party had to give more opportunities for Arab members affiliated with it to enter sensitive positions, from the local committees to the Central Committee. This didn't mean that the membership had to become majority-Arab and minority-Jewish, but we were meant to tilt the leadership more towards the Arab side. What drove this decision was that the party's Jewish members and supporters comprised about ten thousand people, while Arabs numbered fewer than one thousand.

Arabization was not easy or effortless. The Jewish communists were very cautious about it, as they were convinced that the Jewish communist was more ideologically and organizationally prepared than the Arab communist, and that the Arab member would collapse if ever exposed to pressure and persecution, causing problems for others.

The Jewish leadership were the ones who put forward this argument. They stalled Arabization, supporting it in theory but impeding it in practice. Meanwhile, messages from the Comintern urged us to courageously implement Arabization. They highlighted how the movement in Palestine was chaotic and confused relative to the rest of the Arab world, and that as a consequence, "the wheat was being separated from the chaff."

The Jewish party leadership wavered about implementing the Arabization policy and could not find the courage to open the doors to Arab leadership. It decided to send the largest possible number of Arab members (and even Arabs who were just sympathetic to the party) to Moscow to be educated. Then when they returned to Palestine, they could take up sensitive positions in the party once the Comintern knew them, had gauged their capabilities, and assigned their role within the party. Agreeing to the leadership's proposal, the party took to sending student missions of every class and profession. These included ironworkers, woodworkers, students, peasants, office workers, journalists, and street vendors.

The party had a fixed leadership, composed of known people like Tepper, Barzilai, Berman, and Lichtinsky, who managed to keep themselves well out of prison, and a shifting leadership in the local committees, composed of people who entered sensitive positions only when spots opened up there, although the nature of their work and their constant contact with the public (running unions, organizing strikes, and leading protests) exposed them to arrest. This therefore produced a "leadership crisis." A matter that exacerbated this serious crisis was that many Jewish communists who carried Soviet passports or Russian birth certificates got deported to the Soviet Union by the British authorities. Some Jewish Communists had every hope that they would meet this fate—until they stumbled into it. They were crammed into prison for three to six months, then were shipped from Jaffa to Odessa on the next Soviet ship.

Despite all this, the party actively worked on the issue of Arabization. In 1931, the Comintern dispatched a representative named Mueller to investigate the progress of Arabization. I joked to him, "In Moscow, the acronym for the Communist Party was V.K.P., the Communist Party for the Nations of the Soviet Union, and they added a B to it, to stand for Bolshevik."

He replied, "Yeah . . . so?"

I said, "We abbreviate the name of the Palestinian Communist Party as P.K.P. So what do you think about adding an A to the end, for Arabized?" He shook his head, laughing, and said, "That could also stand for 'antisemite' . . ."

On that note, Mueller almost fell into the hands of the police in the suburb of Nahr al-Uja near Jaffa. We had held a meeting with him in a safe house, and after the meeting about eight of us set off together in the direction of Jaffa. We were halfway there when we ran into a Jewish cart driver who knew that some of us were Jewish communists. He said, "Don't go on along this route; there's a police squad stationed ahead. No doubt they would love to do you mischief!" We thanked him, split up, and went in different directions, thus evading the trap planned for us. But we were burning to know: who had told the police about our secret meeting? Was the informant among us? Suspicion fell on an Arab journalist from Jerusalem, D. Sh., who had hosted the meeting. Considering the evidence, we decided not to rely on him for party activities anymore.

Anyway, Arabization was a central concern of the party at all levels and during all its conferences. In the end the Jewish communists conceded central leadership to the Arab comrades, while they remained in their leadership positions in Jewish areas. The creation of a sort of "federal" structure within the single party allowed us to implement the concept of Arabization and kept peace with the part of the party apparatus that the Jewish leadership administered.

2. THE UPRISING OF 1929

The uprising of August 23, 1929, shook the Party quite violently, and left the Jewish communists completely at a loss. There were some who defended their countrymen, and others who clung to neutrality and preferred to distance themselves from it. However, this situation created a problem in the party between the Jewish comrades and the Arab comrades. We held a contentious meeting in which we discussed the uprising and its consequences. The main dispute was over how to define the nature of this uprising: was it a nationalist revolt, or a sectarian massacre?

Here a division emerged in the party. Among the Jewish communists, some said that it was a massacre, but others supported the central committee in saying that it was a national uprising caused by unjust British rule, the seizure of lands, and the impoverishment of the fellahin.

After a heated back-and-forth, it was decided that it was a nationalist uprising that had no connection to outbreaks of incidents of sectarian violence like the murder of the Sheikh of the Jaffa mosque and his family, the massacre of students in a Talmud school in Khalil [Hebron], or other anomalous incidents uncharacteristic of uprisings. Some of the Jewish members complied with this decision; others were enraged by it and withdrew from the party, or were expelled by the party until they changed their stance.

At the time, I was overseeing the Party's activities in Haifa in close coordination with the Federation of Trade Unions, which was managed by a Lebanese man, a railroad employee from Qlailah. He had also opened a school to fight illiteracy in Qlailah, with the help of another young Lebanese man, who was from Fathallah.

In Haifa, I communicated secretly with the Sheikh of the mosque, 'Izz al-Din al-Qassam, a towering man who lived on the slopes of the mountain, east of the bridge over the Rushmiya wadi. He told me about his struggle against the French in Syria in 1920, his flight to Haifa since then, his fight with the English in Palestine, and how the authorities were pursuing him. I found out in 1935, while I was in Paris, that al-Qassam had been martyred with four of his comrades near Jenin.

While I was stationed in Haifa during the uprising, I came down with dysentery from eating polluted food at a restaurant in the fish market. I was taken to the government hospital, where I stayed ten days until I had recovered. I had barely left the hospital when I was asked to make my way to Jerusalem to join the Central Committee. So I put on a [Jewish-style] hat as a disguise and took a seat in a half-empty train.[12] When the train stopped at Lydda, I looked out the window and saw two Arab youths approaching my seat. In each one's hand was a knife; they were waiting to attack me once the train was in motion. So I laughed and said, "I'm an Arab, like you." They both put their knives back in their pockets and said, "Take that thing off your head and go away."

The train arrived at the Jerusalem station at nine in the evening. The station was shrouded in darkness, and the streets were empty. Here and there, I heard the whistle of bullets. I hired the only carriage in the square to take me to the home of my coworker from the post office, from before I went to Moscow in 1925. This was Qustandi Rofa, who lived in the Greek colony near the railway station. I knocked on the door; he opened the latch with great caution. He saw me in the dim light after my long absence. But he welcomed me and hosted me for three days until I could rendezvous with my comrades in Jerusalem.

The Central Committee had assigned Joseph Barzilai to rent a house in his name in Beit Safafa, an Arab-majority neighborhood, from an Arab farmer. I moved there and lived there. While in Jerusalem, I contributed to a report to the Comintern about the 1929 uprising and the party's stance on it.

12 The Arabic word used here is قبعة, qub'ah, which means "hat." It is cognate with the Hebrew word *kippah*, or yarmulke, but historians of 1920s-30s Palestine say it is unlikely Sidqi wore a yarmulke on the train. Instead, the word qub'ah here likely refers to a European-style brimmed hat such as a fedora, which would have marked Sidqi as Jewish because a Muslim man would have worn a fez. It is also possible that Sidqi actually wore a yarmulke in public or remembered himself doing so, but pre-1948 photographs and dictionaries generally show the yarmulke to be strictly indoor headwear.

An odd event occurred at the time. The landlord had advised Barzilai to leave the house, so that he and whoever he hosted would not be endangered. The landlord helped Barzilai pack up the furniture, then, pistol in hand, he escorted Barzilai in the moving truck to safety in the Jewish neighborhood of Talpiot, on the eastern side of the al-Fawqa neighborhood. Then the landlord bid Barzilai farewell, saying, "I have fulfilled my duty to you; go on your way. If I run into you again, I'll kill you!"

So the 1929 uprising placed the Party actively on the side of Arab rights, and opened the door to a new push from Arab activists and officials. It also highlighted the Communists as an organized and active party, present and influential in both the Arab and Jewish camps.

In the process, the party's headquarters was transferred to a house deep in a pine forest owned by Jamil al-Shakir al-Husseini, on the western side of al-Fawqa. Joseph Barzilai paid the rent, as usual, using his cover as a journalist.

3. JEWISH IMMIGRATION

The Party was preoccupied by the issue of Jewish immigration and was led to debate it and publish pieces about it more than once. Which stance were we to take on it? There were a few different positions which the comrades took at the time, and they were:

First—that the door should be closed to immigration, since the country's economic situation could not support more newcomers. Among the immigrants were some who competed with the Jewish labor force itself in the fields of manufacturing and agriculture, in addition to their negative effect on the Arab community, which intensified public hostility towards Jews.

Second—that it was impossible to stop all immigration so long as it was a pillar of the Zionist movement, and that it was better to try to prevent illegal immigration and to stick to a stance of limiting Jewish immigration, a policy which the Arabs themselves demanded. This would unite the party with the

Arab national movement, so that cooperation between the two groups could take place on a point of serious political importance.

Third—that we should seek a halt to Jewish "bourgeois immigration" while supporting Jewish "working-class immigration," as workers were the sinews of the socialist movement. Their presence would produce a conscious proletarian movement, which would help to create social change in Palestine.

Those of the latter opinion converged with the theory of the Poalei Zion party, which called for the greatest number possible of Jewish workers in Palestine, considering them the educated and conscious vanguard of socialism. In the Poalei Zion platform, the Arabs would be integrated into Jewish socialist society through social mixing and marriage.

Ultimately, the position the Party adopted was that immigration should be halted in principle, and that immigration should be restricted and limited to a certain number annually so long as it was impossible to prevent it in practice. The party benefited from this stance, which pleased the Arabs and mollified the Jews.

4. THE LAND QUESTION

The agricultural situation in Palestine was not feudal, i.e., one in which the large feudal landowners ruled vast expanses of land while fellahin worked the land like slaves, as was the situation in Russia, Egypt, and Iraq. Rather, Palestinian agriculture consisted of: a relatively limited area of land, distributed among a few large landowners (farms and orchards, including orange groves); "common" land which villagers worked with crude cooperative methods; state land, of which some was useful for farming and some was fallow; and finally, many small plots of lands dispersed among small farmers. The latter category made up most of the agricultural land.

As the Jews were making preparations to establish their state with the help of the Mandatory Power, and as this state required ownership of the land, their leaders established two funds to implement plans for the colonization of Palestine. The first of these was "The National Fund" (Keren Kayemeth), the purpose of which was to collect funds from Jewish capital: donations in "shekels" (an ancient Hebrew unit of currency), levies, investments, and so on. The second was "The Establishment Fund" (Keren HaYesod; the United Jewish Appeal), the mission of which was purchasing land and utilizing it in every possible way. It prevented the resale or transfer of land: the land became the national property of the Jewish people, and only Jewish labor could work there.

The Establishment Fund was active in purchasing land through skilled Jewish and Arab agents. The process of land "purchase" often took on tragic dimensions, as all the departments of the Mandatory government were mobilized to support it, from the agricultural courts to the criminal courts. The result was that the central prison in Jerusalem was overflowing, as were the 'Atlit quarry near Haifa and the Acre fortress, with immense numbers of peasant "rebels." The sentences issued to these people ranged from ten years to life imprisonment to execution.

The Party had taken a unified stance on this land issue, calling for opposition to the Mandate's policy, which was designed to impoverish Arab farmers, coerce them into selling their land, then drive them from that land, and against the "businessmen" and landowners—the wealthy farmers and the effendis—who were selling their land to Jewish institutions. The Party wanted to force them to take responsibility for these sales.

In this position on agricultural policy, the Party worked closely with the Arab national movement, serving our ideological and social struggle.

5. THE ARAB NATIONAL MOVEMENT

The Party took a stance distinct from that of the Arab National Movement, as the nationalists were divided: some were activists struggling against Zionist colonialism, but others were opportunists, collaborating with the occupiers.

The activists were divided into two groups. The first was the Executive Committee, elected by the seventh Palestinian conference in 1928. It was a bourgeois activist group and worked within a framework of Arabism and Islamic solidarity. The second was the leftist nationalist movement, which represented the middle class; it was a petit-bourgeois group that worked in a framework of Arabism combined with internationalism.

The Party cooperated with the Executive Committee, supporting its campaigns against the Mandate and Zionism, and collaborated closely with the leftist activists both individually and collectively, even if we did not fully merge with them in a fixed organization at that time. As for other Arab parties in Palestine at the time, the Party considered them to be either lacking a popular base or opportunistic and paid them little attention.

HAMDI AL-HUSSEINI

This national leader was an object of increasing attention from the Party, as he was known to be a Palestinian leader who worked closely with supporters of global proletarian liberation, as well as an opponent of Nazism and Fascism.

Hamdi "Abu Faysal" was descended from the well-known Hashim family in Gaza, which held many leadership positions, as well as positions in the press, the judiciary, and local administrations. One of its pillars was the martyred Sheikh Mehiy al-Din al-Husseini, whom the Turks executed in Gaza during World War I.

Hamdi was born in Gaza in 1898, and applied himself from a young age to the Palestinian national issue. The Turkish authorities detained him in 1917 and exiled him to Konya in Anatolia, but he returned to Gaza after the war to carry on his national struggle against the new rulers. In 1930, when I got to know him, he saw that the Communist Party was a force that supported his struggle in the national movement, and the Party saw in his democratic movement a sound means to link up with the core groups within Palestinian nationalism.

In 1931, Hamdi established the League to Combat Imperialism, the first nationalist group to espouse reformist social and theoretical ideas that the other nationalist fronts had not adopted at that time. That year, Hamdi called for the establishment of a Conference for Resistance to Imperialism, to be held in Paris, then traveled to Moscow, where he met Stalin in the Kremlin.[13] The Soviet leader wanted to test Hamdi's "sensibilities," so he said to him when he came to sit down, "The King of Afghanistan, Amanullah Khan, sat there before you—on that very seat!" Hamdi replied at once, "If the King of Afghanistan sat there, that's no honor at all to me." So Stalin grasped Hamdi's leftist leanings, and he went on to talk to him about the problems of the East and imperialism. His comments focused on "bribery," saying that it was the most dangerous phenomenon in the nationalist movements. By bribery, he meant the techniques to which the imperialist resorts to buy the consciences of notables and leaders and to win them over to his interests.

Hamdi returned from Moscow to contribute to the establishment of the Arab Palestinian Independence Party (al-Istiqlal) in 1932. Also in that year, 'Ajaj Noueihed published the journal *al-'Arab* (*The Arabs*) in Jerusalem, which was a mouthpiece for the Istiqlal Party. Hamdi published nationalist articles in it under the pen name "An Arab Researcher." He also encouraged me to publish articles in this newspaper; I wrote an article called "Class Conflict in the Zionist and Anti-Zionist Parties."

When the Catastrophe of 1948 occurred, Hamdi was staying in Gaza under the Egyptian military administration, then moved with his family to Cairo, where he stayed for a long time. He returned to Gaza after the 1967 War, and remains there still under Israeli rule. He got a chance to summer in Lebanon

13 Editor Hanna Abu Hanna's note: Hind, Najati Sidqi's daughter, said that her father was the interpreter in this meeting between Hamdi and Stalin.

in the company of his daughter in 1973. Hamdi al-Husseini stuck to a firm and clear nationalist line. He did not negotiate, did not make a truce, was never corrupted, and did not accept any government position, whether under the Mandate, Egyptian military administration, or Israeli rule.

As he said to me when he was summering in Lebanon, "We will continue to fight for Palestinian independence, whatever the cost and whatever the results."

Something noteworthy in this respect is that Prince Shakib Arslan also held a conference for resistance to imperialism, and also visited Moscow, but Stalin refused to meet him, as Arslan called for Islamic unity. Stalin rejected this position just as Stalin had rejected the call for Arab unity.

Stalin's argument regarding Islamic unity was that there was no link among the Islamic peoples aside from a religious link: they comprised a wide range of nations differing in their social situations and their national issues. What was it that could link on nationalist grounds the Muslim of the Caucasus, the Afghan Muslim, the Indian, the Turk, the Arab, the African—all of them living in different historical conditions and each suffering different problems and issues from those of other Muslims?

Likewise, Stalin did not believe in Arab unity as a goal, even though he accepted it as a weapon with which to strike imperialism. His reasoning was that Arab unity was ultimately a force hostile to communism, and even to international socialism, and that in general it played a regressive role both at that specific stage of its social development and in its political foundations.

There was an assumption behind Stalin's refusal to meet Prince Shakib Arslan: he worried that this meeting would be used to propagandize against him and his regime. There was no principle, doctrine, or social theory shared between the Soviet leader, who thought himself well-versed in the issues of the East and easterners, and the Islamic advocate and "Prince of Eloquence," Prince Shakib Arslan.

The hostility between Arabs and Jews intensified after the 1929 uprising. Nobody was safe from the bitterness between the two sides, whether you were an Arab living in a Jewish neighborhood or a Jew living in an Arab neighborhood. In this context, Arab eyes were drawn, always with doubt and suspicion, to that mysterious house standing in a pine grove in the Baqa'a area. We decided to abandon it as soon as possible. So Joseph Barzilai was assigned to rent another house for the Central Committee near Maminallah in Jerusalem, an area divided between Jewish and Muslim neighborhoods outside the city walls.

As for myself, I rented a private apartment on Maminallah Street, in a house not far from the Central Committee's, to live there with my wife, a Ukrainian from the city of Lvov. In this house we had a daughter named Dawlat, also called Dawlieh or Dulia. Today, she is an architect in Moscow. In this apartment, I oversaw the editing of the Party's official organ, *Forward!*, as well as pamphlets and publications, and hosted Hamdi al-Husseini there, where we made plans together.

At one point, I traveled to Haifa on a mission. Meanwhile, my father came to visit my apartment to see his granddaughter. He was followed by a Jewish policeman, a despicable man named Rabinovich, who saw him enter my house. He rushed to tell the police, and they ransacked my apartment, but didn't find me there or anything to charge me with. They left, but assigned Rabinovich to guard the place, stationing him in the courtyard within the building with a window overlooking the street.

I returned from Haifa that evening and was very cautious. I didn't enter the building, instead knocking at the windowpane facing the street. I saw my wife, and she signaled that I should flee, so I sought refuge in the nearby base of the Central Committee.

It was decided after this that the Central Committee should distance itself from my house, and it moved to a house owned by the leftist nationalist lawyer

Yahya Hamuda in the village of Lifta on the Jaffa road, adjacent to the Jewish town of Machane Yehuda.

In that period, I redoubled my activities and participated in the celebration of the Feast of Nabi Musa in Jerusalem, which commemorates the conqueror of Jerusalem, Salah al-Din al-'Ayyubi or Saladin. It is a permanent reminder of the Islamic conquest, much like the Feast of Nabi Reuben in Jaffa. Sympathizers lifted me on their shoulders as I wore a keffiyeh and 'agal on my head, and I covered my eyes with dark sunglasses; they raised me between the flags of the religious orders amid drumming and the ringing of gongs, the singing of folk songs, the playing of mizmars, and the dancing of village dabkes. I called out whatever came to mind, and the comrades raised the red flag, crying out, "Long live the struggle for independence!" The people roared assent and rushed about; the ideas got jumbled, and the clamor intensified for the Arab Bolsheviks!

This incident provoked the Mandatory authorities, so they waged an intense campaign to catch me. Their informants were all around me, engulfed in fantastical confusion: one said he spotted me hiding in women's clothing, covering my face with a black headscarf; another that he saw me in the Christian quarter of Jerusalem, disguised in the long robe of a priest; a third had no doubt at all that I was the beggar wearing rags lying down at the Olive Gate before the Holy Compound.

It was these reports that led the CID unit, that being the Criminal Investigation Department, to continue their pursuit of me day and night. They lacked an up-to-date photo of me, so they grabbed a young Arab man who knew me and brought him to an artist, then demanded that he give the artist a full description of my face, which he did. They then printed out the sketch and distributed it to the police. Within a few days, they had arrested a schoolteacher, a real estate broker, and a wandering fabric salesman! Then they had to let them all go.

8
ON THE WAY TO PRISON
(1931–1933)

THE TRAP

The Central Committee held a meeting in November 1931, in its new headquarters in the village of Lifta, which Mahmoud, Barzilai, and I attended. We discussed internal party issues, and we raised the idea of renting two columns in an Arabic Jerusalem newspaper. We decided by consensus to entrust the editing process to an elementary school teacher from the Barghouthi family who was very fond of the party, but first Mahmoud and I would meet him to sound him out.

The next day, at around seven o'clock in the evening, Mahmoud and I, accompanied by a Jewish intermediary, went to the meeting place with Barghouthi. Our destination was a room located on the second floor of a building in which Jewish families lived, halfway between Lifta and Machane Yehuda. When we arrived at the destination, the intermediary left us for a while and returned with Barghouthi. The room had a single window that looked out onto an empty lot behind the house. As a precaution, we had decided not to wear our tarbushes so that no one would notice that there were Arabs in the room. However, we were incredulous to see Barghouthi putting his tarbush on his head, so we took it off of him. He then put it back on his head again and stood up. We attributed this behavior to an ignorance of clandestine practices, so we nervously made him sit down and threw the tarbush aside. Less than half an hour later, we heard whispering at the door of the room, which was locked from the inside, then someone knocked violently and a voice shouted, "Open the door in the name of the law!"

We ran to the window and looked at the back door of the house, hoping to jump out, but we saw the English police blocking the entrance. We could do nothing but surrender.

As soon as we opened the door, Mr. Rex, the director of the Jerusalem Police, shone a bright flashlight in our faces. He was accompanied by a senior Jewish intelligence officer, Adon Shlomo, and another detective. They took us to the Jerusalem Central Prison at eight o'clock in the evening. Mahmoud, the Jewish intermediary, and I were all put in jail. Barghouthi, on the other hand, was promptly released.

We were received in the prison office by a Syrian man who was known as Wireless Muhammad. In the days of King Faisal's rule in Syria, he had worked as an officer in the telegraph department. He then moved to Jerusalem and worked in the electrical station of the Post and Telegraph Department. Then, he became an officer in the Jerusalem Central Prison. His task there was to search the new arrivals and record their names, ages, nationalities, and places of birth. Then he had to introduce them to prison etiquette. Among his directions to prison newcomers was: "Soon, the director of the central prison, Mr. Steele, will come. He will ask you questions, so always answer him with two words: 'Yes, sir…' Huh, don't forget… 'Yes, sir'!"

After Wireless Muhammad searched our pockets, between our teeth, and inside our underwear, he said, "I will now search a part of the body that may contain smuggled items! This is what the prison regulations require!"

When he had done this, he turned to Mr. Rex and said to him, "Everything's in order, sir." Rex asked us pro forma questions like "Where do you live?" and "What is your job?" He then signed an administrative arrest warrant for us, pending investigation on charges that would merit bringing us to the District Court.

On the day after our arrest, the lawyer 'Umar al-Saleh al-Barghouthi, the informer's uncle, came to the prison and asked to meet me.[14] He tried to convince me that his nephew had no part in our arrest, and that he was not arrested with us only due to the lack of evidence against him.

During the preliminary interrogation at the prison, I told the director of the English police that I was staying in a room in Manshiyya, Jaffa. This room contained no furniture except for a bed, a table, and a chair; we used the place as an emergency bolthole. He asked us to specify the street and the building for his own reasons, but the security services took advantage of this statement: after a period of detention, they decided to transfer us to Jaffa because we had identified it as our place of residence. There, we were put in the prison in Saraya Square. After a week in detention, we were asked to show the security forces to the room where we were staying. So we showed them the room, knowing that it contained nothing that could incriminate us legally, and that this would spare us the pressure to reveal our real place of residence. Several Jaffan policemen began to search the room while Rex distracted us with chit-chat, until one of them yelled, "I found it! I found leaflets under the bed!"

These planted leaflets were the only "tangible" accusation; a pretext to issue an arrest order and consequently a referral to the court. However, this charge

14 Sidqi's note: 'Umar al-Saleh al-Barghouthi was a well-known lawyer. He was born in Jerusalem in 1894. I got to know him when he was in his forties. He was a man of literature and poetry, and a historian who co-authored *The History of Palestine* with Khalil Totah, Director of the Teachers' House (Dar al-Mu'allimīn) in Jerusalem. He used to receive many people involved in politics and literature in his office, located in front of the municipal park on Jaffa Street. 'Umar al-Barghouthi, by virtue of his profession, was a close friend of the heads of the General Security of the British, Arabs and Jews. Nevertheless, as soon as the disaster of 1948 struck, he closed his office and left his house, which contained a valuable library and expensive furniture. The Jews seized its contents, as he went with the refugees to Egypt, and was crammed into Ward No. 5 of the Qantara detention center. He used to spend most of his time sitting on a chair, even sleeping on it, hoping to return to his homeland. After a long wait and great sorrow over leaving his home, he returned to Amman, where he held positions in the Jordanian state. He died in Jerusalem on June 2, 1965, during the period of the unification of the two banks [of the Jordan River].

in itself was not sufficient to get the court to issue a harsh judgment against us. Those accused of possessing and distributing secret leaflets were sentenced to three to six months in prison. The leadership of the Palestinian security services did not like to treat leaders like ordinary party members. So, they had to wait to bring us to court until they pinned us with enough charges to condemn us to a prison sentence of about two years.

We spent about a month in the Jaffa prison awaiting trial. During that time, I got to know a young Jaffan named Youssef al-ʻIshsh, who was accused of a misdemeanor. Every time he saw me in the prison yard, he asked my opinion on the new Soviet Five-Year Plan!

An educated young man named Jabra Nicola ended up becoming our cellmate in prison. I had met him through the journalist Najib Franjieh and had accepted his invitation to visit his modest house in the Manshiyya neighborhood. I realized from talking with him that he had studied English, was good at drawing, and worked in literature and journalism. His mother brought us coffee, groaning. Najib leaned over and whispered in my ear, "She has cancer and she does not know it!" Jabra had been arrested because the police suspected him of political activity; he was imprisoned for a few days and then released.

Also in prison, I met a young man who was a neighborhood tough guy in Jaffa—his name was ʻAli al-Jaraihi. He was tall, stocky, pale-skinned, blue-eyed. This young man used to mess with the prison officials, and so the officers, old and young, liked to challenge him. For example, an English policeman used to provoke him, saying to him in English, "C'mon, fight!" ʻAli would then put up his two strong fists, ready to fight.

ʻAli asked to stay in our cell, because we defied the authority of the Mandate and faced dangers courageously. We knew him to be a bold young man. He always liked to tell us about a mythical being named ʻAwj bin ʻAnaq. ʻAwj was a giant who performed miraculous feats, like squeezing the clouds with his hand to quench his thirst, and roasting whales in the eye of the sun to feed on their meat and oil. The supernatural seemed to have captured 'Ali's imagination. He felt in his heart that he too was a mighty being whom nobody could obstruct or refuse.

One morning, an English policeman entered our room, and we did not stand up for him like the rest of the prisoners, so he got angry and told me to get up and follow him. So I said to him in English, "Do you want to kill me like you killed the Egyptian prisoner?!" The policeman said, trembling, "I didn't kill him. I didn't kill him. He did it. He committed suicide," and hastily left the room.

This incident left a deep impression on 'Ali al-Jaraihi's soul; his admiration for us increased, and he drew closer to us. Later, I learned that he had contracted an incurable disease in prison and been transferred to the government hospital, where he passed away in the prime of his youth—may God have mercy on his soul.

THE TRIAL

We spent a long time in detention: five months in Jerusalem Central Prison, and one month in Jaffa Prison. This prolonged detention was intentional; the security services were hoping one of us might turn and testify against his comrade, tightening the charges against the other. They hoped to build a very strong case, so that the verdict would result in a sentence three times longer than our period of detention, or more! They also hoped to find a witness from our families. They pressured my late older brother Ahmad with both promises and threats, and got him to stand in court as a witness against me.

On May 28, 1931, they took us from Jaffa Prison to the central courtroom, located on the opposite side of the prison from Saraya Square. A Muslim judge, 'Aziz Bey al-Dawoudi, and a Jewish judge, Adon Shalosh, presided over the trial. The third, an English judge, who usually mediates between the two Palestinian judges, recused himself from this case, so as not to be accused of colonial prejudice.

Najati Sidqi in the middle, with his brother Ahmad and his father.

The lawyer defending Mahmoud and me was a Jewish socialist. This was either because the Arab lawyers refused to defend us under pressure from the security services, or because they had a weak sense of lawyerly duty.

The trial began with a routine question, "Are you guilty?" I answered, "No."

Then, the public prosecutor proceeded to deliver the indictment, limiting it to three points: first, possession of secret leaflets; secondly, belonging to an illegal party, including forging a passport (a charge directed against me only); thirdly, calling for the social order to be overthrown by force.

The public prosecutor set about elucidating these points. He read the text of the leaflet that was planted in my room, which called on the peasants to resist the usurpers of the land. Then, he attacked the Party as an agent of a forcign country.

Here I objected, saying to the two judges, "It is not permissible to drag the Soviet Union into a local case, and entangle us with international issues!"

He told me to be quiet. The public prosecutor continued his argument that we were a group bent on destruction and sabotage, and we must be removed from society for the longest period permitted by the Penal Code.

Then he raised the issue of my participation in the Profintern conference, and submitted to the court a copy of *The Times of London*, which had published a report saying that the delegate of the Palestinian Communist Party, whose name was "Comrade Sa'adi," had delivered a speech at the conference. Then he turned to me and said, "This is Comrade Sa'adi—this is the person who traveled to Moscow with a forged passport, and returned with it to Palestine via Qantara, deceiving the British border officer; we have summoned him to hear his testimony as well."

The court proceeded to hear the statements of the witnesses. Mr. Rex and his colleague, the Jewish officer Adon Shlomo, came first and told the court how they raided us in Jerusalem, and how they found secret leaflets in our room in Jaffa. They assured the court that we were not ordinary party members but dangerous leaders. Then Rex spoke to Judge 'Aziz al-Dawoudi and said, "We call the prosecution witness Ahmad Sidqi, the brother of defendant Najati Sidqi."

Everyone turned to look at poor, weak Ahmad, who had tasted imprisonment, humiliation, beatings, and persecution. So he advanced to the witness stand and took the oath, and started saying the things that he had been instructed to say: He was my brother and loved me, except that he pitied me for throwing myself into the arms of destructive movements, and he had always urged and advised me to withdraw from the Party, but I had not listened to his advice because of my stubbornness and intransigence.

The judge asked him, "Were you forced to testify?"

He replied, "No, I present this testimony voluntarily. My only goal is to shorten my brother's sentence!"

Then the court heard the testimony of the British officer who had interrogated me at the Qantara station at night, after my return from the Profintern conference. He stood at the witness stand, took the oath, and said, "Yes, this particular suspect was the one whom I interrogated in Qantara at night, when he was carrying a passport that I suspected was forged; however, I could not arrest him at that time."

The judge said, "Perhaps he is not the one who passed through Qantara."

The officer replied, "It is him. They conducted an identification among a number of prisoners. I picked him out from a lineup of suspects."

The judge directed the question to me and said, "What do you say to the officer's testimony?"

I said, "How long ago did this incident take place, according to the officer?"

The officer said, "Almost six months ago."

I said, "How can an officer remember the face of a traveler who passed by him at night, six months ago, when we know that dozens of passengers pass through Qantara Station every day?"

The judge intervened: "But the officer says he verified it was you during a lineup in prison."

I said, "It is easy to make such an identification—the security guards surreptitiously directed the officer to where I was standing, so he came and pointed to me."

The judge then asked me, "Did you leave the country this year?"

I said, "No."

The judge then said, "The charge of possessing a forged passport is dropped from the accused and he is acquitted of it. He is charged with possessing inflammatory leaflets and affiliation with an illegal association. Let him and his companion be tried on these two charges, according to article such-and-such of the Penal Code."

Then the discussion revolved around the leaflets that the detectives had planted in our room. We denied any knowledge of them, and we denied that they were ours.

The judge's response was that these leaflets were physical evidence; therefore, we could not prove our innocence.

Then he asked me, "Are you affiliated with a secret society called the Palestinian Communist Party?"

I said, "Yes."

Here the court made a racket. So did our lawyer.

The judge asked pointedly, "So you admit that you are one of the leaders of this party?"

I said, "Yes."

The noise intensified among the audience, and the judge banged his gavel, asking the audience to remain silent.

Then the defense lawyer got up and said, "The court has no evidence against my client and his colleague—who has remained silent—other than this confession. Accordingly, I ask the esteemed court to take this frank and bold approach into consideration, and to make its ruling very lenient."

The session was adjourned for deliberation between the two judges for a quarter of an hour, then they entered the courtroom again, and the bailiff shouted, "Rise!"

'Aziz Bey al-Dawoudi read out the following decision: "The Central Court, convened in Jaffa, May 28, 1931, considered the case of the two defendants, Najati Sidqi and Mahmoud al-Mughrabi, and confirmed, with physical evidence related to their possession of secret publications, and with the frank confession of the defendants, that they belong to an illegal association and are part of the leadership of said association, which adheres to destructive principles, intending to pit workers and peasants against capitalists and landlords, and to undermine the traditional social order with armed force. Therefore, we sentence them to imprisonment for a full two years, including time served, open to appeal."

After the verdict was issued, the guards decided to transfer us to Jerusalem Central Prison by train, not by car, fearing that our comrades would intercept these cars on Bab al-Wad Road and release us. On the train, an English guard sat next to me, and when we passed a group of peasants working in the field, the Englishman looked out the window and said to me, "Look, those are your friends!" Then he turned around and said, "I say this seriously, not as a joke."

The train arrived at the Jerusalem station in the evening, so we could take the prison car from there. To our great surprise, a huge army truck packed with heavily armed British soldiers came to accompany our car to Jerusalem Central Prison.

CENTRAL PRISON IN THE RUSSIAN COMPOUND

In the year 1860, the Russians built a religious, cultural and political center on a piece of land located to the north of the Jerusalem Wall, which the people of the country knew as al-Muskubiya, the Russian Compound. Russian Orthodox pilgrims, who came to the Holy Land in large numbers, came to this spot and found all the facilities for care, comfort, and protection.

On this parcel of land, there are several stately stone buildings, which the Russians used for various purposes until the British occupied the country in 1917. The British laid their hands on these Russian properties and used them to serve their colonial goals. Here is a description of it in the two eras:

The Russian Compound has a southern entrance that leads directly to the Russian Hospital, which became the government hospital during the Mandate era. Next to it are the House of Reception (which continued to serve that purpose), the Administrative Office of the Russians (now the Department of

Justice), the Russian Consulate (now the Courts), the House of Priests and the House of Women (which remained there later), and the House of the Russian Nobles (which became the police department, the C.I.D. or Crime Investigation Department).

In the middle of the Russian Compound is a large church built in the beautiful Russian ecclesiastical style, with seven domes covered in lead, known as Svyataya Troitsa, the Holy Trinity. There is also a smaller church known as the Church of Alexander Nevsky (1220-1263 AD), named after the famous Russian leader, conqueror of Sweden and Denmark, liberator of the Russians from the Tatar yoke, and one of the saints of the Russian Church. To the east of these two churches is the hostel for female Russian pilgrims, which became the Central Prison under the Mandate. Outside the wall on the northern side of the Russian Compound, there is a building built by the Imperial Orthodox Palestine Society, which was directly sponsored by the Tsar's family in 1887, chosen as a base for religious, educational and political activity in order to "save the Holy Land" from the Ottoman Sultanate.

So a person who is sent to the Central Prison, the former home of ordinary Russian pilgrims, crosses the Russian Compound in about a hundred meters starting from the courthouse and passes a barbed wire barrier, then ascends a ramp until he reaches another barrier, then walks along a ramp until he reaches *another* barbed-wire barrier, then stands in front of a small door made of iron bars. He lowers his head as a sign of submission and humiliation before walking through the door to find himself in the hands of his jailers. These jailers carry out routine prison procedures, such as registration, giving the prisoner his prison number, shaving the prisoner's head, making the prisoner put on a blue uniform (if he is an ordinary prisoner), or simply registering him (if he is detained or imprisoned for political reasons). Then, the jailers lead him to the convicts' room if he is already a convict, or to the detainees' room if he is merely detained before trial.

In his first week in prison, a prisoner feels that he is the most miserable creature on the face of the earth, deprived of freedom, of the sun, of family, friends and loved ones, and even people in general, of eating the food he desires and wearing the clothes he loves. But as soon as he enters the second week, his eyesight becomes accustomed to his new surroundings and to his monotonous daily life: getting up at 7 am, making the bed, cleaning the room, emptying and washing out the latrine buckets, and eating the morning meal consisting of tea and a piece of bread with cheese or a little oil, then walking around the prison yard (or for ordinary prisoners, going to work outside the prison), then returning to the rooms, telling each other stories about anything and everything, and reading only religious and literary books. They eat a one-bowl lunch consisting of lentils, or onions with a slice of meat, then they rest until afternoon, followed by an outing to the prison yard and a bowl of dinner. Lights are turned off at eight in the evening, and conversations take place in low voices. The prisoner's day ends by falling asleep to the guards' footsteps and the clatter of their keys.

Life in prison was tedious, and we only found psychological relief with the arrival of new prisoners who brought news of the outside world. One day, a prisoner from Tulkarm came to the prison for medical treatment. He had committed an honor killing, and was sentenced to hard labor for fifteen years, which he was to spend in the 'Atlit detention center. This prisoner told us while we were in the prison yard that the convicts in 'Atlit were expecting us to be transferred there to break rocks. The convicts also competed to guess which barrack we would be detained at, with the intention of honoring and welcoming us when we arrived. However, the guards informed them that the authorities would not place us among them so as not to influence them ideologically, and that we would spend our sentence in isolation in the Jerusalem Central Prison.

From what this prisoner told us about the 'Atlit prison, the one in charge there was an English Sergeant named Duff, who was tall, obese, and had a fierce temper. He liked to ask four prisoners, every morning, to carry him on a palanquin and move him around the quarries, with a blackthorn whip in his hand, and he would stop wherever he wanted. Then, he would loudly shout in Arabic, "Who's a tough guy?!" If one of the prisoners had a fiery disposition, he would say, "I'm a tough guy." Duff would get down from the palanquin and whip him. But the prisoners usually distanced themselves from his provocations and paid his words no heed.

ABU JILDA AND AL-'ARMIT

In prison, we met two men who kept the Mandate government busy for a long time with guerrilla warfare—they were Abu Jilda and al-'Armit.[15]

These two peasants formed a band to fight the Mandatory State. Their situation was not unlike many of the bands of insurgents scattered in the country, which were mostly composed of peasants left without land and without work.

These two revolutionaries emerged after the uprising of 1929. They organized a gang with a headquarters in the mountains to wage a guerrilla war against the British forces. Its leader Abu Jilda, a slender and short man, wanted to keep himself and his men away from accusations of being mere mischief-makers, so he wore military clothing; his shoulders were decorated with two swords and three stars. He had a long, polished sword with a gilded handle and assumed the title of "General Commander." He also appointed his colleague al-'Armit, who was a tall man, of strong build, and very powerful, as his deputy with full powers.

When the English heightened their pursuit of this gang, its members scattered all over, and Abu Jilda ended up taking refuge in Amman, asking for

15 On Abu Jilda's chronology, see Further Reading essay.

protection from King 'Abdullah. The king received him and listened to him, but was not convinced. So he handed Abu Jilda over to the British authorities, who transferred him to the Central Prison of Jerusalem. In the meantime, security services arrested his colleague al-'Armit via an informant who was a former member of the gang.

After a short detention, they were brought to the Criminal Court, which issued them a death sentence by hanging. I remember that al-'Armit's mother visited her son in prison, and he told her from behind bars, "Put a dagger in my grave so I can take my revenge on the snitch!"

One day in 1934, al-'Armit was brought to the gallows. An hour later, Abu Jilda was brought to the gallows, passing by two rows of English policemen shouting "Hip, hip, hooray!"

I should mention that the prison director, Mr. Steele, was the one who carried out the death sentences; he received five pounds for each person sentenced to death, in addition to his salary.

DETAINEE FROM CAMBRIDGE

A new political character, neither a communist nor a revolutionary peasant, was brought to the prison. He was a patriot named Wasif Kamal who had completed his studies at Cambridge University in 1931. He led a political demonstration in Nablus; there he was arrested and sent to the Central Prison.

They wanted to put him with us in our prison cell, but he refused, saying, "I am a patriot, and I want nothing to do with socialist ideological trends."

I spoke to him and he really was patriotic, not affiliated with a particular political body. He found it slightly difficult to adjust to prison; there is, after all, a difference between the dorms of Cambridge University and the cells of Jerusalem Central Prison.

There is nothing else worth mentioning about this period of imprisonment except that the stomach acid that had always plagued me, almost causing an ulcer, disappeared due to the bland prison food. I also took advantage of the spare time to improve my English, with the help of an English-Arabic dictionary composed by the Lebanese-Egyptian Shukri Antoine Tabet.

REBELLION IN THE PRISON

Life continued at this pace from the first year in prison until we decided to go on hunger strike because of the poor food quality. In addition, since the administration refused to meet our demand, we banged metal plates on the prison bars and made noise that irritated the rest of the prisoners.

We carried out this plan until the prison director, Mr. Steele, a fat man in his sixties, short and mean-looking, came and stood before the bars of our section, and said, “What do you want?”

We said, “The food sucks.”

He said, “I’ll give it a taste.”

He grabbed a bowl of onion stew, stuck his fingers into it, took out a big onion and ate it, then raised the bowl to his mouth and slurped up the remaining stew, and said, “This is delicious. Why do you refuse it?” And he left.

The next morning, we continued banging the plates on the prison bars, making a racket. The prison administration responded with an attack. The guards opened the doors, led by the prison officer, a local Sephardi Jew, and used batons to force us to sit on the floor. Then Director Steele entered the room and said to me, laughing, “Who wins this time, me or you?!”

Then the guards stood in two rows facing each other, and Steele told me, “British prison regulations require that the instigator of prison riots pass between these two rows.” The guards were commanded to beat me with their batons until I emerged from the end of the row. Then, I was taken to the government hospital in the Russian Compound.

I was in the hospital for three days. Then I was sent back to the prison, where Mahmoud and I found out we were to be transferred to the Citadel of Acre.

THE CITADEL OF ACRE

The police truck took us, accompanied by a lorry of English soldiers, to Acre via Ramallah, Bir Zeit, Nazareth, and Haifa. There we saw the hill on which Napoleon had stood; a metal hat resembling the hat of the French conqueror was mounted atop an iron pole erected on the hill. We also saw the ancient castle, which has witnessed major historical events such as the imprisonment of Prince Yusuf Shihab and his hanging by order of its governor, Ahmad Jazzar Pasha.

Moving to Acre Castle was a kind of simultaneous imprisonment and exile. They put us in a modern one-story building within the castle precinct, originally intended for foreign convicts. However, they turned it into a prison for political prisoners, and they made its yard a park for prisoners with mental illnesses. Mahmoud and I often strolled in the yard together, talking and joking with other prisoners, until one of them, named Elias, got excited and started deliriously imitating political orators, so the prison administration decided to separate our exercise time from the others'.

A Jewish corporal named Avram was responsible for us. One of his duties, when our prison door was closed, was to eavesdrop on us from under the high windows that overlooked the yard, and convey our conversations to the director of the Citadel, Mr. Pike.

It occurred to me to take advantage of Elias. He could watch Corporal Avram while strolling with his fellow inmates. I said to him, "I want to ask you a favor. When Avram closes the door and you see him standing under the windows, I want you to sing loudly: '*And I would throw myself from the window for you*'—so we'll know that Avram is eavesdropping on us."

He said, "No problem, Na'im"—that's what he used to call me.

The next day, during our siesta, I heard Elias singing: "*And I would throw myself from the window for you, O Na'im . . . And Avram is standing under the window, listening to you . . . Do you hear, Na'im . . . I would throw myself from the window for you!*"

Corporal Avram went crazy. He rushed to Mr. Pike, telling him that we had resorted to taking advantage of the mentally ill. He reported what he had heard. The director of Acre Castle ordered that people with mental illnesses be completely removed from the yard of our prison. Thus, we were rid of people whom the administration could use to harass us, themselves being free from the consequences of their words and actions.

A few days later, I learned that Elias had jumped from the bridge that extended between the moat and the castle, believing that his dead girlfriend—whom he had told us about—was calling him to meet her. He fell on his back and lost his life.

Life in the Citadel of Acre was tedious, and we spent it discussing matters both private and public until our sentence drew to an end. At the end of December 1932 we were summoned to the Citadel director's office (this was Mr. Pike, of Maltese origin). He returned our belongings to us and gave each of us half a pound, as required by prison law, so that we could manage our affairs until each of us made it home and could resume our public lives. Mahmoud traveled to Jaffa. As for me, I found my wife waiting for me, and we traveled together to Jerusalem, to live freely.

I rented a room in Jerusalem with a Christian family in the alley of the al-Aswaji School in the al-Musrara neighborhood. There I tried to rest and recuperate while being productive at the same time. So I contacted my friend Hamdi al-Husseini, and we agreed, as I mentioned previously, that I would write articles for the magazine *al-'Arab*, published in Jerusalem by 'Ajaj Noueihed, under the name "A Researcher."

We spent five months in this room, during which time we were closely watched by a Jewish detective named Rabinovich. Every morning and evening he came to the room's window on the ground floor, and holding on to its iron bars, jumped up to look at us. He always found me sitting at the table and writing.

ADMINISTRATIVE DETENTION

Labor Day, May 1, 1933, was approaching. It was the custom of the Palestinian police on the eve of this day to carry out a campaign of arrests of Party members, anticipating their participation in the May Day demonstrations, or rather they found it appropriate to arrest whomever they wanted under the Administrative Offenses Prevention Law.

Foreseeing that this could happen to me, I sent my wife to her friend's house in Jerusalem, and as for our child Dawlat, we sent her to Moscow to be safe from the troubles of our life. When the eve of Labor Day came, two detectives broke into my room, one of whom was an Arab from Beit Tahboub, and the other was the Jew, Rabinovich, who insisted on my administrative detention, just because his boss ordered it, and that I spend the night in the police station of the locality of Mea Shearim. Meanwhile, his Arab colleague tried to persuade him to leave me in my room and bring me to the center the next day. The Jewish policeman refused, rummaged through the furniture in my room, and took me to the station. The next day, I was transferred to the Kishle barracks in the Citadel of Jerusalem, where I spent two days. On the third day, I was transferred to the Central Prison, in preparation for my submission to the Administrative Court headed by the Administrative Governor of Jerusalem, Mr. Keith-Roach. This administrative tribunal was an English contrivance, by which they are able to arrest a person and subject him to surveillance and proof of presence for a whole year without any particular charge incriminating him. They justify this based on the principle that, "if you detain a person and subject him to daily surveillance, then you prevent him from committing a possible crime."

One of the farces of this court is that the governor's witnesses stand behind a screen, so that witnesses can give testimony without revealing their identity. The judge asks the witness, who may be a security officer, "What do you think of so-and-so and what do you know about him?" The witness answers with what he has been instructed, then the judge confronts the detainee with these reprimands and incriminating statements; finally, he issues his ruling based on article such-and-such of the Crime Prevention Law.

And this is what happened to me. This governor issued an administrative decision that I be subject to police surveillance for a whole year, in addition to proving my presence by reporting at the police station three times every day!

When I returned to my room after a week's detention, the landlady told me that she had canceled my monthly lease and asked me to vacate my room immediately, because she wanted to avoid problems with the government. (I now remember that I met this lady and her young daughter fifteen years later in Beirut, two miserable refugees in Bourj Hammoud, after the Jews took her house and placed it in the category of seized enemy property.)

Then I rented another room in the same locality, and every day I went to the local Mea Shearim police station to prove my presence to a British police officer, while the odious Rabinovich came every evening to the window overlooking the street, which was covered with curtains, and asked aloud, "Are you home?"

I answered, "Yes," and he said, "And who else is with you?" I answered, "I'm with my wife," and he said, "Okay. Bravo, bravo!"

Being sentenced to prove my presence three times a day was worse than staying in prison. It was absolute paralysis; the constant disgust of entering the police station and signing the book and seeing the sneering faces of the police every morning and evening.

In addition to this, the security officers wanted to annoy me by various means. For example, they instructed Jamil al-Shakir al-Husseini to demand that I pay the rent on the house that the Central Committee had rented via Joseph Barzilai in Upper al-Baqa'a, among the pine trees, which the party had been forced to vacate before paying in full. So he came to me with his two young sons and introduced himself, saying, "I am so-and-so, and I request that you pay me the remaining rent for the house in which you stayed with your companions!"

I explained that I had not rented his house, nor lived in it at all, and I asked how he could demand rent for a house that I had not lived in nor signed a lease for. He insisted that I pay; he said he would sue me in court and the police would testify in his favor!

The atmosphere became unbearable for me, especially after I met the policeman from Beit Tahboub in the street. He told me, "You do not know how to fight the British. Come to my room at the Supreme Islamic Council in Maminallah. I'll show you a terrorist project you'll love!"

Finally, the Central Committee decided to secretly leave Jerusalem and move to its new headquarters on Mount Carmel near Haifa. We carried out this plan precisely, and I moved to Haifa. Soon after that, however, the Comintern instructed me to go to Paris.

9
THE PARIS YEARS
(1933–1936)

ESCAPING SURVEILLANCE

I left Palestine with my wife in June 1933. On our way to Lebanon, in Marin near Acre, specifically in the village of al-Baisa, a villager took us across the border on two donkeys in the middle of the night. After a couple of hours we saw dim lights, and the man said, "We have arrived in French territory!"

After we had rested and eaten some food in a house in 'Alma al-Sha'ab, we continued the trip until we reached the foot of the mountains and the path leading to the city of Tyre. Here our guide told us, "My mission has ended. You'll have to find your own way to Beirut."

At this moment a villager passed by, and our guide asked him to rent us a horse to get us to Tyre.

The villager said, "I am going to Tyre myself, and I will send you a man with a donkey." We sat under a tree surrounded by rocks for about an hour until a man riding a mule appeared. He approached us; my wife was wearing a *milaya* and had covered her face with a shawl. He greeted us and said, "For one lira, this mule is yours to go to Tyre!"

I got on the mule, lifted up my wife, and we were on our way to Tyre. As soon as we reached one of the tributaries that poured into the Mediterranean, a number of gendarmes blocked our way. I immediately realized that the man who had accompanied us had told them we were fleeing from Palestine.

The corporal said, "Where is your passport?"

I showed him my passport and convinced him that the reason I was not following the official Naqoura route was that my cousin and I planned to get married despite her family's disapproval, and our marriage would take place in Beirut. The corporal asked my wife, who was veiled, "Is your cousin telling the truth?" She nodded her head in the affirmative.

Then the mule driver came close to me and whispered, "Give the Effendi three pounds!"

So I gave the gendarme three pounds—the lira was worth a lot at that time—and we continued our journey to Tyre. There, I hired a driver with a Ford that got us to Beirut.

In Beirut, I asked to be dropped off at the Sanayeh Garden entrance. There I met Nakhman Litvinsky and his wife Anyuta, by prior agreement, and they brought us to their apartment in Sanayeh. They told us they were moving to Paris. We enjoyed their hospitality for a whole week, then we continued the trip to Istanbul via the East Highway.

There we met Nakhman and his wife again, and we toured archaeological sites and the Bosphorus. It was then agreed that my wife would travel with them to Vienna while I would travel alone, as an added cautionary measure. I would meet them there at the Bristol Hotel.

I took a train to Vienna. When the train stopped at the Sofia station, my attention was caught by a shocking propaganda move: the Bulgarian royal authorities had placed a disgusting black loaf of bread in the doorway of the station, so that every traveler would see it, and they had written under it: "This is the bread that the Russians eat!"

Then the train made its way west until it stopped at Royal Belgrade Station. There, some security officers entered the train to inspect it. I was calmly sitting and reading an ordinary English magazine with a red cover, until one of them came to me and grabbed the magazine out of my hands. He found it to be an ordinary English magazine, not a leftist publication as he had suspected, so he returned it to me.

Then his boss came and began to investigate me. He spoke to me in Turkish, thinking that I was a Serb rebelling against Yugoslav rule. Soon he realized he was mistaken, so he left the carriage and the train.

The train arrived in Vienna in the early morning. I headed to the Bristol Hotel, where I met my wife, Nakhman, and Anyuta. We spent three days in Vienna, visiting the Schönbrunn Palace, the Imperial Theater, the Heldenplatz, the Pálffy Palace, the Prater amusement park, the Votive Church with its marvelous architecture, the captivating St. Stephen's Cathedral, the Opera House, and other places that capture the hearts of visitors to this immortal city.

In Vienna, my wife and I parted ways. She went to Moscow to be with our daughter Dawlat for some time. I went to Paris, where I stayed at the Mont Blanc hotel in the Latin Quarter, until I met with the Comintern representative in the French capital, Comrade Razumova, the former wife of Comrade Ma[g]yar, a prominent Comintern member. I later learned that he was purged during the Stalinist era and disappeared without a trace.

In Paris I was formally placed under the authority of Razumova, who was associated with the French Communist Party. I was transferred from the hotel to an old house near Gare du Nord in the center of Paris, not far from the headquarters of the French Communist Party. She entrusted a young Parisian woman named Suzanne with my care.

Suzanne would come to me every morning with the things I needed, lock the door for me, and come back again in the evening to inform me of the instructions she had received from Comrade Razumova. I remained in this state for about two weeks, until it was decided to issue a monthly publication in Arabic.

العدد (٢٦) — N° 26

« التحرر القومي — الحلف — وارض الفلاح! »

« السنة الثالثة » 3e ANNÉE

الشرق العربي

Mustapha el Saaïd

Directeur: M. LÉO WANNER

France : 10 francs par an.

Étranger : 15 francs par an.

Adresser les Fonds à M. René LANDAIS

170, Rue de Crimée - PARIS

مصطفى السعيد

السيدة ليو فانر

L'ORIENT ARABE - JOURNAL MENSUEL

PARIS DÉCEMBRE 1935. LE NUMERO EN FRANCE 50 CENT.

متفرقات

السلطة لم تغير سلوكها

مصر الثائرة والمشاكل الدولية

تدافع عن بلادنا العربية كشعوب حرة مستقلة لا كعبيد

Front page of the Paris-based newspaper Arab East *naming the editor as "Mustapha el Saaïd," December 1935*

AL-SHARQ AL-'ARABI NEWSPAPER

We named this publication *al-Sharq al-'Arabi* (*The Arab East*) a monthly newspaper edited by Mustapha el Omari, a pseudonym I took for myself. Its director was a communist Frenchman who did not know a word of Arabic. Then we found the only Arabic printing press in Paris, and we employed a French typesetter who set the Arabic letters by sight. This printing press had previously issued some publications in Arabic on various occasions.

Then we made a show of renting an office for the newspaper in one of the branches of Ghabta Street, supervised by Suzanne.[16] After my wife returned from visiting our daughter Dawlat, our residence in the Paris suburb of Clamart became the real office, where I edited the newspaper, packed it, and prepared it for shipment to North Africa and Arab countries, receiving letters, newspapers, and magazines in return. The first issue of the newspaper was published in September 1933.

16 We were unable to determine what Sidqi meant by Ghabta Street. The paper's masthead shows it registered at 170, rue de Crimée. —Trans.

The goal of this Arabic newspaper was to call for anticolonialism in the Arab world, support national independence movements, and support every movement that aimed at social reform among the toiling masses. The newspaper focused on defending the Arabs of North Africa; supported the Constitutional Action Party in Tunisia and the Association of Algerian Muslim Ulema; launched campaigns against the Mandate state and Zionism in Palestine; demanded the independence of Syria and Lebanon; challenged the policy of "divide and rule" in Iraq; and backed the struggle of the Wafd Party in Egypt.

The newspaper was distributed secretly in the Arab world, usually hidden inside French newspapers. Readers eagerly grabbed the newspaper. They wrote to us and sent their articles and comments to us despite the severe censorship the paper faced in France and in the occupied Arab countries.

As soon as the first issue was issued, the French security services went looking for the owners of this newspaper, including its editorial board and managers. One day I was surprised by a security officer who entered the newspaper's office. He found me there with the secretary, Suzanne, and he looked at me smiling, and I smiled blandly back at him. He introduced himself to me as an investigator and told us that his mission was to identify the office of this new newspaper. He said nothing more and left after memorizing my features and clothes. After this visit, we decided to stay away from the office completely. The first thing I did was replace my clothes, my hat, and my coat, because they were a significant part of my appearance. Even if the investigator's impression of me changed by more than half, my facial features and skin color still remained unchanged. Fortunately, my facial features alone were not sufficient for the investigator to identify me, especially since there were thousands of Middle Easterners in Paris who shared my facial features and skin color.

As for me, I knew the inspector and had memorized his appearance completely in turn: short, round-faced, full-bodied, wearing a black coat and a black bowler hat. Once I encountered him on the subway platform and he smiled at me, so I looked at him in surprise and continued on my way. Then I saw that he had a squad of fellow officers with him. I hurried to enter the metro car. Fortunately, the train door closed and the train got underway before they reached it.

In another instance, I met him as I was leaving a movie theater with a girl who looked like Suzanne. He came forward with his assistants, but he suddenly turned back and said to them, "It's not her." He thought I wasn't the one he was looking for, and he hesitated to arrest an innocent person. The last time I saw him was in the suburb of Clamart, where I was staying; he bowed his head, smiling, as if he wanted to see my reaction. I merely looked at him all confused and annoyed. He was finally convinced that the person he had seen in the newspaper office had vanished without a trace.

When the security services failed to uncover the editor of the newspaper, they tried another trick. They sent a tall, handsome detective to the newspaper's office. He courted Suzanne, inviting her to dinner or the cinema. She rejected him with a French girl's tact, saying that she was engaged and was not looking for a second suitor.

There was a strange attempt to find out my residential address in Paris through the Arab world. Someone sent me a letter from Cairo asking me to send him any of the electricity receipts for my house in Paris, so that he would know the difference in the electrical prices between Paris and Cairo! I ignored his request and threw his letter in the trash.

After these attempts all failed, the French security services decided to question the director in charge of the Arabic newspaper. The director said that he was responsible for the newspaper but did not actually know Arabic. Instead, its editors translated the most important items for him and he approved them. He told them that he was French and enjoyed all his political rights, and that the constitution gave him the right to speak, write, and demonstrate.

When the security services found no legal justification for interrogating or arresting the man, they left him alone. They kept pursuing Suzanne, but to no avail. The newspaper continued to be published monthly until the early

Sidqi in Paris, 1934 (l) and 1935 (r)

summer of 1936, when it was banned by a special decree of the French Prime Minister, Monsieur Pierre Laval (1883-1945). This French prime minister cooperated with the Nazis during World War II, and after the war ended, he was sentenced to death in absentia. When they came to arrest him, he tried to commit suicide by shooting himself, but survived. So he carried his wounds to La Santé Prison in Paris, where they put him up against a wall and executed him by firing squad.

10
RETURNING TO MOSCOW
(1936)

ADVENTURE ON THE TRAIN

Comrade Razumova told me, after the *al-Sharq al-'Arabi* newspaper had been banned, that I should go to Moscow to discuss my next missions.

I was taken to the Soviet capital by train through Germany and Poland. This trip involved a terrible risk. The comrades in Paris provided me with a fake Palestinian passport that belonged to an Arab tradesman with an ethnically ambiguous name. When the train approached Berlin, the inspectors entered, accompanied by Gestapo men. At the time, Nazism was rampant in Germany, and the Nazis were preparing to perpetrate massacres in their own and neighboring countries.

After they examined my passport and found out which country I was going to, they started exchanging looks of inquiry and surprise, and I heard them asking in German, "*Arabische . . . Muhammedanische . . . Palästinensischer Jude?*" That is: is he an Arab, a Muslim, or a Palestinian Jew? I betrayed no confusion or annoyance. I remained seated, as if it was absolutely not my concern. Then they whispered among themselves and gave me back my passport.

Fifteen minutes later, a beautiful German girl entered the compartment, sat right in front of me, and proceeded to speak to me. Our conversation went as follows:

"Does the mister speak German?"

"No . . . I speak English."

She said in English, "I am also fluent in this language. What is your nationality?"

"An Arab from Palestine."

"Are you a tourist?"

"No. Merchant."

"You'll stop in Berlin, of course?"

"No. Just passing through."

"Why don't you stop in Berlin? This is a beautiful capital. You will find all the goods you are interested in. It has parks, many amusement parks. Take this opportunity and stop in Berlin, and I will become your guide."

I said, "Thank you very much, Miss. It's very kind of you, but I have to carry on with my business travel."

She said, "And where are you going?"

I said, "Moscow."

She said, "Oh, and what Russian products do you sell?"

I said, "Timber, fish, fur, and so on."

At this moment, the train entered the Berlin station, while the German girl urged me to visit the German capital and I endlessly apologized to her. And she left the train.

I deduced that this girl was an agent of the Nazi security service, and through her they wanted to know if I was going to stop in Berlin on an assignment. They realized, however, that I had no interest in Berlin, or even in any part of Germany. I remained under their watch until the train left the German border and entered Poland.

This trip caused me a lot of stress. Simply passing through Nazi Germany, regardless of the passport I carried, was a terrible gamble for which Razumova was undoubtedly primarily responsible, and the French comrades to a lesser extent.

DISCUSSION IN THE COMINTERN

In Moscow I met Khalid Bakdash, and we stayed in the Lux Hotel on Tverskoy Street (today's Gorky Street). We debated the future of the Arab world. He clung to Stalin's point of view, which called Arab unity a reactionary slogan, while I took a more pragmatic perspective: the Arab peoples shared some historical conditions, so they had common objectives and a common future. Bakdash's adherence to his point of view proved his blind obedience to Stalin's teachings and his instinctive feeling that Arab unity threatened the interests of national minorities, including his own Kurdish minority.

We referred the matter to Comrade Georgi Dimitrov, the head of the Comintern Organization at the time, in the presence of comrade Manuilsky, head of the eastern section of the organization; leader Mao Zedong (at that time he was forty-three years old and on a visit to Moscow); Mahmoud al-Mughrabi; and a Soviet Armenian named Galdjan. I defended my opinion on the issue of Arab unity. I said, trying to convince Dimitrov, that the situation of the Arab peoples is fundamentally different from that of the peoples of Yugoslavia, for example. Arabs are descended from a shared origin, and they share a single language, land, economy, culture, history, and liberation movement. Dimitrov was not convinced because he was influenced by the separatist situation in the Balkans and that region's diversity of nationalities, languages, creeds, and cultures.

The Chinese leader intervened and supported my point of view based on one main point, namely that Arab unity is a unifying force in resisting colonialism, sidestepping any other impulses represented in Arab nationalism, the historical conquests of the Arabs, or the spread of Islam.

In truth, those points were not the real focus. Most of what I was aiming at was proper political guidance within the framework of the Arab national movement, to keep the Communists from being isolated from the ranks of the Arab peoples in their efforts to gain independence and the rule of social justice.

Manuilsky was impressed by my defense of my stance, jokingly telling me in Russian, "It appears that we have awakened the patriotism in you!" And Galdjan commented, "You are a worthy debater."

The next day, Manuilsky summoned me to his office, with Bakdash present, and said to me, "You will travel to Tashkent, the capital of Uzbekistan, to see the Soviet Union's approach to resolving the national issue." As soon as Bakdash heard this, he insisted to Manuilsky, "I want to accompany Comrade Sa'adi on this trip!" Manuilsky replied, "As you wish."

TO TASHKENT

The road to Tashkent was long, tiring and boring. By the old Russian train, the journey took a whole week, day and night. The main stations on the route were Moscow, Ryazan, Kobyshev, Uralsk, and then Tashkent. The travelers were military men, farmers, civil servants, and peoples of the east of the Soviet Union who passed the time by drinking vodka, wine, or tea, and singing and playing the balalaika (a triangular musical instrument strummed with the fingers) or the harmonium.

While we were in the train cafeteria, one of the drunk peasant travelers said to me, "What country do you two come from?"

I said, "From an Arab country." "Oh," he said, scratching his head, "and what are you doing here?" I said, "We are on a visit of acquaintance and friendship."

He blinked, shook his head in disbelief, picked at his beard, and said, "I know what you touristing types are after."

Something strange happened to me on the train. I met a group of Red Army officers traveling from Kobyshev to Uralsk. We began to exchange general and political news, then we downed glasses of vodka. The alcohol had begun to go to my head, but I was fifty percent sober. One of the Russian officers leaned over to me and asked me in Russian, "Who are you? Who sent you? What is your mission? Tell me the truth: who are you two working for?!"

In a drunken voice I replied, "We are Arabs, sent by the Comintern. Our mission is to visit Tashkent. We work for world revolution!"

Here, the officer realized that he was in the wrong and stopped asking questions. And when morning came, the group of officers had left the train.

The journey to Tashkent by train is breathtaking but unvarying. One can see only a wasteland (the desert of Central Asia), and feel nothing but bone-chilling frost. The only relief is when the train stops at a station to resupply water and fuel, and to provide travelers with boiling water for tea. Every station has water tanks that are constantly boiling.

Finally, we arrived in Tashkent, the capital of Uzbekistan, in mid-July 1936, and stayed at the Mir Hotel. The following day, a messenger came to us from the Public Relations Office and drew up a plan for us to visit the capital. We started with a visit to the most prominent personalities of the Republic of Uzbekistan at the time: Yuldash Akhunbabaev, the President of the Republic; Akmal Ikramov, the head of the party; and Fayzulla Xo'jayev, the Prime Minister.

The President of the Republic was a man over seventy years of age, tall, soft-spoken, kind-hearted. The Presidency was a symbolic administrative position. The head of the party, Ikramov, was a man in his fifties, not too overweight, nervous-tempered, medium height, stocky, talkative, and very energetic. Before the revolution and the Red Army's invasion of Turkestan, he was a prominent member of a Turkestan national party called "Hizb Jadidi."

This party is also known as "Basmachi," meaning those who gather the people's support for Turkestan's freedom and independence.

With the intensification of Bolshevik propaganda and its call to make the countries of Turkestan into Marxist Soviet republics, a conflict emerged between the new ruling power and the Jadidi (or Basmachi) party. Fierce armed battles took place between the two sides, which ended in victory for the Russians and the local Bolsheviks. The leftist Turkestan nationalist faction allied itself with the Red Russians. Fayzulla Xo'jayev was at their forefront. He then joined the Uzbek communist movement and took over the reins of the prime minister's office.

UZBEKISTAN AND BUKHARIN'S OPPOSITION

During the period when I visited Uzbekistan, the Soviet Union was swept by two waves of opposition to Stalin's politics: the left-wing opposition, led by Leon Trotsky, which I have mentioned elsewhere in this book, and the right-wing opposition, led by Nikolai Bukharin, an old researcher on Marxism who had written books on economic sciences and historical materialism. During the civil war in Russia, he was a member of the Politburo alongside Lenin, Trotsky, Stalin, and Kamenev. He was entrusted with press and propaganda affairs, and was the author of the current Soviet constitution.

Bukharin and Rykov's opposition consisted of opposition to collective farms, and reliance on small rich farmers (remnants of the previous era) known as *kulaks*—they were, in his opinion, moving towards integration into socialism. He did not fear the enrichment of bourgeois productive elements that did not pose a threat to the socialist system, did not want to rush into the field of heavy industry that produces "production machines," and wanted to revitalize the light industry that produces consumer goods.

The result was that Bukharin was expelled from the party, then arrested, tried, and executed with the Group of 21 in 1938. The charges brought against both the left and the right were: "treason; espionage; sabotage; terrorism;

collaborating with foreign countries since the beginning of the 1917 revolution; attempting to conclude secret agreements with the Nazis and the Japanese to divide the Soviet Union."

Talking about Bukharin and his opposition takes us back to Uzbekistan. The Soviet Constitution, which, as we have already mentioned, was framed by Bukharin, stipulates in Article 17 that "the freedom to secede from the Soviet Union is guaranteed to every republic in the Union."

Article 18a also stipulates that "every federal republic has the right to establish direct contacts with foreign countries, and to conclude agreements with them, diplomatic exchanges, and consular representation."

These two articles encouraged the Prime Minister of Uzbekistan, Fayzulla Xo'jayev, and the head of the Communist Party of Uzbekistan, Akmal Ikramov, to demand the realization of Article 18a, aiming to accelerate the development of Uzbekistan and open it up to the eastern and western world.

The result was that Xo'jayev and Ikramov were arrested, accused of collaborating with the Bukharin opposition, and executed along with the Group of 21. It is known that Akmal Ikramov was close to Stalin, and enjoyed his affection; despite this, Stalin did not forgive him for his slip. The ill-fated Ikramov begged his judges, "Spare my life, just exile me wherever you want!" Ikramov did not find a sympathetic ear, because that period in the country's history was a period of physical and psychological purging of every shape and type within both the party and in the army. There were storm clouds gathering in the German West and the Japanese East: the signs of World War II.

Our stay in Tashkent lasted ten days, during which we got acquainted with the city's landmarks and some of its urban and artistic aspects. We spent enjoyable evenings with Akmal Ikramov, who showed us pictures of himself and his friends having an intimate, informal get-together with Stalin in Tashkent. A photo showed Stalin wearing an Uzbek cap on his head tilted to the left, leaning on his elbow, and laughing.

We played billiards in the guest house with Ikramov and the two girls who worked in his office. We exchanged jokes and toasts. Holding a vodka shot, Ikramov said in Arabic, "Give her a purifying drink!"[17]

We visited the Tashkent Museum and looked at some Arabic manuscripts and a rare manuscript copy of the Uthmani Qur'an. We also visited the mosque of Tashkent, which had a very small number of elderly worshippers.

We wandered through the old markets of Tashkent, built from bricks in some places and elsewhere from straw-studded clay. The most important products there are colorful silks. At that time, we were in the month of fasting. It is the custom of the people to announce the breaking of the fast by blowing long trumpets from the rooftops of the houses.

We had a tour of the University of Tashkent, which was established in 1920, and which included twelve departments, from which many professionals had graduated. We also toured non-scientific and industrial institutions.

We spent an evening at the Uzbek National Theatre watching the operetta *Layla and Majnun*, based on the work of the Azerbaijani poet Mir 'Alishir Navaei, who died in 906.

They arranged a reception for us at a school outside Tashkent. We dressed in Uzbek clothes, and the students rushed to greet us, cheering and waving flags.

We were invited to lavish banquets, at which, according to their custom, they served *knafeh* before serving the savory food.

Then we visited the home of an Uzbek peasant with the intent of learning about his home. The house consisted of one room, containing a refrigerator cooled with ice sheets, a phonograph with records stacked atop it, an electric

17 A Quranic reference (Surat al-Insan) to the paradise awaiting believers after the Day of Judgement: "They will wear garments of green silk and brocade; they will be adorned with silver bracelets; their Lord will give them a pure drink." (76:21, translated by M.A.S. Abdel Haleem, 1999) —Trans.

lamp attached to a long cord hanging from the ceiling, an "apple" trestle bed that required one to climb a small three-step ladder, curtains of coarse local silk, Uzbek newspapers, and artificial flowers.

Our visit to Tashkent was, in general, a kind of vacation and entertainment, only allowing us to obtain first impressions. In ten days, we could not have conducted studies and comparisons because we were completely ignorant of what people really thought. We also knew nothing about what was going on in Ikramov and Xo'jayev's minds—whether they desired or attempted to contact the outside world according to Article 18a or secede according to Article 17 of the Soviet Constitution, knowing that this article in particular—while present in principle—cannot be achieved and implemented in real life.

When we returned from Tashkent to Moscow, Comrade Manuilsky asked me, "How was the trip?"

I said, "It was very interesting."

He said, "When you were there, did you see a difference between the Uzbek and Russian national situations?"

I said, "There is no doubt about that. The country preserves its national elements. The Uzbek character is prominent in its language, dress, and life. It is now at the crossroads between inherited antiquity and advanced modernity. Those are my initial impressions of this trip."

Manuilsky blew on his pipe and said with a smile, "*Khorosho, khorosho,*" meaning "Good, good."

11

THE SPANISH CIVIL WAR

(1936)

SURPRISE

Comrade Manuilsky called me a week after my return from Tashkent and said, "Are you following the news of the civil war that recently broke out in Spain?"

I said, "Of course, newspapers publish news about it daily, and meetings are held everywhere to support the Republicans. Also, funds are collected for the civil war in factories, schools, and every public institution."

He said, wanting to see how much attention I was paying to the Spanish issue, "Okay, and how much has been raised for the Republicans so far?"

I said, "In six days, from July 27 to August 3, 1936, they have collected 12,145,000 rubles, or the equivalent of 36,435,000 French francs, all transferred in the name of the Prime Minister of Spain, Señor Giral."

He said, "I called you here to offer you the idea of traveling to Spain to help the party there organize Arabic propaganda in Moroccan circles. You can be sure that the rise of an independence movement in Spanish Morocco today would shake the ground on which General Franco stands and decide the fate of all of North Africa."

I said, "I would be happy to carry out this mission."

He stood up, shook my hand, and said, "We will arrange for you to travel to Paris and on to Spain, and I wish you well."

HISTORICAL INTRODUCTION

Before addressing my thoughts on the Spanish Civil War, I will preface it with a brief overview of Spanish history.

During World War I, Spain took a neutral position, benefiting from trade with both warring parties. As soon as the wartime boom ended, Spanish trade deteriorated, and exorbitant taxes were imposed on business owners. Nobles and clergy were exempted from paying this tax. There were strikes and insurrections in the factories, especially in the industrial city of Barcelona, and Catalonia rose up to demand secession from Spain. Also, the Spanish state was waging a fierce war in Morocco; in 1921 it suffered a major defeat at the Battle of Annual, where thousands of Spanish soldiers were killed by the Moroccan rebels led by Prince 'Abdel Krim al-Khattabi.

The military dictatorship of General Primo de Rivera in 1923 was approved by King Alfonso XIII (1886-1941): Rivera suspended the constitution, dissolved the Cortes (that is, the parliament), and sent some free leaders into exile. As a result, resentment prevailed in the country against both the dictator and the king.

In 1931, the dictatorship established by de Rivera was overthrown, and the king agreed to restore constitutional rights. However, these developments did not satisfy the Spanish people, who demanded the abolition of the monarchy. On April 14, 1931, the Spanish monarch fled to England, and the Spanish Republic was proclaimed.

The Republic decided to abolish the old feudal method of renting land, to reconsider the tax system, to limit the power of the Church, and to prevent the army from controlling the state. It seized large parts of the vast lands owned by wealthy landowners, the royal family, and the church, and distributed them among the poor peasants. It also seized church property, confiscated the wealth of the Jesuits, and dissolved religious organizations.

These reforms incited strong opposition from those who lost their property and traditional rights (right-wing parties and clerics), while radical elements (left-wing parties) said that the state's reforms did not go far enough to reach their goals. In the 1936 elections, left-wing parties won most of the seats in the Cortes and took strict socialist measures aimed at limiting the privileges of the Church, distributing the lands of the wealthiest influential landlords to the peasants, and distributing private wealth fairly among the population.

When the Republican government felt that the conservative officers in the army were becoming restless, it hastened to demobilize a portion of the army, and transferred others to the Spanish overseas colonies. Among those who were transferred was General Francisco Franco, who was transferred to the Canary Islands.

In the meantime, the military inside Spain and its colonies, led by General Franco, began preparing to overthrow the Republican regime. On July 18, 1936, civil war broke out between the Rebels and the Republicans. It was estimated that about 90 percent of the officers and two-thirds of the Spanish army sympathized with the Rebels, who were also supported by the large landowners, churchmen, and business elite. As for the Republicans, they won the support of the remainder of the army, in addition to the "strike police" and most of the civilian population.

The civil war increased in intensity and ferocity, and a large number of middle-class leaders broke away from the bourgeois Republican parties and joined the left-wing parties (socialist, communist, anarchist, and trade unionist).

As for the Rebels, they were weakened by their disagreements over their goals. General Franco declared the establishment of a "fascist state" in Spain, and he turned to trickery to gain the sympathy of the population. He demanded the distribution of large lands to farmers, and a reduction of clergy privileges. However, these demands, in turn, sparked the resentment of the landowners and the clergy, who began to demand the return of the monarchy!

The Spanish Civil War generated within it a "civil war" between non-Spanish peoples. The Italian fascists, the German Nazis, and other nations fought on the side of the Spanish Falange, whereas Leftists, Russians, Western democrats and other peoples were fighting on the side of the Spanish Republicans. Meanwhile, some democratic countries, such as England and France, adhered to a policy of non-interference in the Spanish war, fearing that it would escalate into a general European war.

The number of foreigners who were involved in the Spanish Civil War is estimated at fifty thousand people, coming from twelve countries. Thirty thousand of them fought on the side of the Rebels, mostly Germans, Italians, and Portuguese, and twenty thousand of them fought on the side of the Loyalists, mostly Russians, English and Americans.

The civil war in Spain was ferocious and brutal, with an estimated one million victims. The overwhelming advantage was with the Rebels, due to the presence of organized forces on their side and the substantial supply of military equipment from Germany and Italy, which enabled them to take control of the western two-thirds of Spain.

In March 1938, the Rebels launched a decisive campaign across the country. Because of this, at the end of that year, the Republican capital moved from Madrid to Valencia. In January 1939, Madrid fell to the marauding forces, and with its fall the civil war in Spain ended.

The first action taken by General Franco, after taking Madrid, was to issue decrees by which he returned lands to their former owners, and also restored to the Church its possessions, influence and authority.

Spain lived under this fascist dictatorship for thirty-six years. This rule only ended with the death of General Franco on the morning of Thursday, November 20, 1975, and the return of the Bourbon royal family to Spain in the person of King Juan Carlos.

ON THE WAY TO SPAIN

At the Comintern, I was presented with an authentic Arab passport, and I returned to Paris by air on August 10, 1936. The plane stopped in Danzig, the capital of East Prussia, at about nine o'clock in the evening, and a group of bourgeois Germans of both sexes boarded it, dressed in evening clothes, fussing and giggling. I learned from my seatmate that they were on their way to a ball in Paris and would be back in Danzig in the morning.

In the French capital, I contacted qualified sources in the French Communist Party to secure a way to travel to Spain, which was ablaze with civil war. I entrusted the matter to an administrative official of the Central Committee named Richard, as Razumova had returned to Moscow permanently.

After three days in Paris, this official said to me, "Tonight you will travel from Gare de Lyon to Perpignan, which is on the Mediterranean Sea in the south of France, and there you will go to the Café Pyrénées, on the south side of the city square, and you'll ask about a person named François Orlando. Hand him this card, and he will give you instructions."

And so it was. Richard accompanied me in the evening to the railway station. He bid me farewell by saying, "Try not to get killed in Spain!"

The train raced towards the south of France, covering a distance of about 900 kilometers from Paris to Perpignan by the following day. I disembarked in a hurry and went to the address I was given, called for François, and gave him the card. He patted me on the shoulder and said, "You're driving to the Spanish border tonight, and you're not the only one going to the front line."

It was nearly one o'clock in the morning when we arrived at the Spanish town of Portbou, on the French-Spanish border. We stopped in front of one of the houses; it was shining with electric lights, and the blue, red, and green flag of the Republic was flying from it, along with the flags of the socialist, communist and anarchist parties.

We entered the house and saw a group of young men from the Republican militia, heavily armed, dressed in blue workers' uniforms and wearing black caps resembling Iraqi sidaras with a red tassel hanging from the front.

In the house, everyone was in perpetual motion; boys and girls, men and women, burning with enthusiasm. One was cleaning his weapon, another typing away on a typewriter, this one examining a passport or laissez-passer, that one coming from the battlefield to give important news, and another coming to receive instructions.

After completing the official registration process, obtaining a volunteer card and a movement card for the Republican territory, I boarded the train to Barcelona, which was crowded with volunteers going to war and their well-wishers. There was an old woman sitting next to her young son, bidding him farewell with tears pouring from her withered eyes, and a girl in the prime of her youth alone with her lover. She was speaking quietly to him, looking at him tenderly and lovingly. Then, she removed a delicate necklace from her neck and fastened it around his neck. They embraced for a long, long time, and they gradually separated, following the movement of the train that was taking off. Parents, mothers, friends and relatives: all of them came to say goodbye to the young volunteers heading to Barcelona, and from there to the battlefronts.

The train cars, inside, were like displays of wartime propaganda. Their walls were decorated with colorful images. One was a drawing of a girl wearing trousers with her sleeves rolled up, wearing a hat with a red tassel, raising the gun with her left hand above her head, and extending her right hand forward while saying: "Citizen! If you can bear arms and your country needs you, why are you not in the ranks of the militia?"

Another drawing showed copper-colored forearms, hands clasped and held high, with the words, "Strength in Unity!"

A third depicted a worker holding a gun in one hand and a trembling man with the other hand, telling him, "Looting is dishonorable, and I will punish you severely for it!"

BARCELONA TOUR

I arrived in the beautiful, luxurious, ancient city of Barcelona, the capital of Catalonia. I strolled through its wide streets, alongside which grew orange trees, also known as "Abu Sfeir." It seemed as if they were decorated with spherical red lamps. Suddenly I encountered a group of militiamen. Their chief, mistaking me for a Spaniard, came up to me and addressed me in Spanish saying, "Why aren't you in our ranks?"

I smiled and answered him in French, with the enthusiasm of youth, "I am an Arab volunteer, come to defend liberty in Madrid, Damascus in Guadalajara, Jerusalem in Córdoba, Baghdad in Toledo, Cairo in Cádiz, and Tetouan in Burgos!"[18]

A look of surprise and pleasure flashed across his face and he said, in broken French, "Are you really an Arab? You are a Moro—a Moroccan? That's impossible, the Moroccans are marching with the fascist scum! They attack our cities, pillage our homes, and assault our women."

I replied, "Those Moroccans who are walking in the footsteps of the fascist generals are insulting the Arabs and Islam with their actions. They represent only themselves, as they are deceived—deceived by the Spanish military, in association with some Moroccan leaders who have sold themselves to the devil, such as 'Abd al-Khaliq al-Tarisi."

The head of the militia was surprised by my words and started shaking his head left and right as if he did not believe what he was hearing, or as if he doubted the Arabness of the person he was addressing. To dissipate his doubt, I told him, "I am not the only Arab here. In the International Brigades there are some Arabs, and others are on the way. You can be sure that many Moroccans who sympathize with Franco will soon realize the truth, and will flee and join the Spanish Republic, and switch their support to it. They will then advocate for democracy, because their Arab civilization and historical traditions are based on the principle of consultation with the people."

18 Sidqi uses the Arabic spelling for Guadalajara: Wādī al-Hijāra (Valley of Stones). In Arabic, Cairo and Cádiz alliterate, as do Jerusalem (al-Quds) and Córdoba (al-Qurtuba). —Trans.

From their faces, it was clear that the militia chief and his comrades were delighted with my answer; we soon embraced, patting each other on the shoulders, then shaking hands, and one of them said to me, "See you at the central front, and in Toledo and its wonderful Arab palace."

I continued to walk the streets of Barcelona, amazed at what was going on in this city they called "the New York of Spain." In the air, there was an indescribable collaborative spirit, activity, enthusiasm, and high spirits. Red flags fluttered everywhere, along with the flags of the Republic. New merchandise was displayed on the sidewalks, such as caps with red tassels, buttons, stars, and laces painted in colors representing the various political parties. Maps of Spain hung on the walls along the streets, with red pins stuck into the Republican section and black pins into the Francoist section. A large audience gathered around these maps, hotly discussing the progress of the fighting.

The Plaza de Catalunya is the center of Barcelona and the heart of its commercial life. There are banks and major stores, consulates, commercial agencies, and luxury hotels. On the northern side of this square is a huge building known as the Hotel Colon. At the beginning of the fascist insurrection, it was a stronghold of the Spanish Royal Guard, then it became a fortress for rebelling fascist groups. When the people of Barcelona defeated these groups, the Catalan government issued a decree placing this hotel at the disposal of the Unified Socialist Party in Catalonia. On the facade of this building, one can see a board about twenty meters wide on which these letters are written: POS (Socialist Workers' Party), PCS (Communist Party of Spain), USC (Catalan Socialist Union), and POC (Catalan Workers' Party). After the withdrawal of the Socialist Workers Party from the Second International, these four parties agreed to unite in a popular front and join the Comintern.

I entered this Hotel Colon asking to be admitted as a foreign volunteer. As soon as I had set foot inside the main entrance, an armed guard intercepted me and asked to see my card, so I showed him the documents I had. After examining them, he said, "Who do you want to meet?" I said, "One of the union officials." He said, "I will send someone to accompany you to the third floor where the Secretary General of the Union is."

I went up to the first, second and third floors, and I was startled by what I saw: volunteers of different nationalities, slogans and instructions, revolutionary drawings of various shapes and colors randomly pasted on the walls. On every floor and corner of the United Parties Building there was hustle and bustle.

On the third floor I met the representative of the Union and introduced myself to him in French, saying, "I am an Arab volunteer. I have come today" —August 15, 1936—"from France and I am on my way to Madrid. I would like to have some information about Catalonia."

He replied warmly, "Welcome, honorable Arab volunteer! Welcome, descendant of the builders of Alhambra Palace, that marvelous Arab masterpiece! You are very welcome here. As for Catalonia, here is an overview.

"We Catalans are a self-reliant people, we have our own culture, we have our own distinctive language, and we have struggled for a long time against the Castilian masters and shed abundant blood for the sake of our national independence. But I assure you, it is impossible for the province of Catalonia to exist without inland Spain. The independence we want is internal autonomy, provided we can participate effectively in the general policy pursued by the central authorities.

"Our land is the center of large-scale industries, the cradle of the working class, and the source of their trade union movement. No wonder Catalonia preceded all the Spanish provinces in establishing political parties and trade unions. The workers of Catalonia are also distinct, in that they no sooner opened their eyes than they embraced anarchism, nourished by the teachings of Mikhail Bakunin and his successor, Prince Kropotkin.

"Our workers today have different parties that follow different theories, but they have recently united into one party, whose goal is to defeat the fascist forces by arms. I am very happy to see that this union, which I have been dreaming of all my life, has come true.

"When the Rebels tried to seize power in Catalonia—an attempt we severely suppressed—all the big industrialists, feudal lords, bankers, and other privileged people took their side, fighting the workers in the streets, shooting the masses from the windows of their palaces. The defending masses retaliated; some of the Rebels were killed, some were imprisoned, and some fled.

"When the matter was settled and relative stability was established, the Republican government saw that the large industries were devoid of capitalists. So the trade unions had to take on that role after the owners had left, betrayed their homeland, and joined the enemies; the trade unions managed their affairs through committees of workers. Accordingly, the heavy industry in Catalonia was confiscated, and the government took responsibility for production and sales.

"This situation and these measures are not at heart based in socialist theory, but rather are exceptional circumstances created by the civil war, directly caused by the big capitalists siding with the rebels. I say that it is not socialism, because the current system in Catalonia is a Republican system that, in principle, does not interfere with private ownership of industry. But expropriation then was necessary; the government did it to punish the traitors who joined the enemies of the people. Take, for example, Juan March; he is a big financier, he owns many industrial and commercial houses in Spain, Morocco, and the Balearic Islands. This man is at the forefront of those who provide the enemies of the Republic with huge sums of money; shouldn't his property be confiscated?

"And be sure that we will not touch civil commerce, nor light industry, because its owners are democratic Republicans, fighting in the ranks of the people against the junta of rebel generals.

"Today the United Socialist Party is doing everything in its power to help the central government, with our factories producing tanks, armored vehicles, artillery, and bombs. However, the anarchists in our ranks oppose this assistance to some degree, since they think that this equipment is needed only for the defense of Catalonia!"

I thanked the union representative for the information he had shared with me, and I was about to leave him when he stopped me and asked me, laughing, "Do you want to meet a young man who speaks Arabic?" I said, "With pleasure."

Moments later, a young man of about twenty joined us; he was fair-haired, laughing, and had a certain lightness to his step. The deputy of the union introduced us to each other, and the young man was very happy when he learned that I came from the countries of the Arab East as a volunteer, so he grabbed my hand and said, "Look at me carefully. Don't you see that I'm even more Arab than you—my name is even Ismail."

I learned from him that his mother was Arab and his father was Spanish; he had lived in Algeria, Morocco, and Malta, and he was preparing, as he put it, to go to the field of Castile.

THE MADRID PERIOD

I went to Madrid by train on a day when Franco's forces, the helpless Moors, and the foreign contingent of European mercenaries, including Russian officers from the remnants of the Tsarist army, were all advancing from the southernmost part of Spain to the north through the Guadalquivir Valley, and from the southwest through the town of Badajoz.

On the train I met a Spanish engineer who spoke English, and his curiosity prompted him to talk to me. When I told him I was an Arab journalist and was heading to Madrid to cover the news of the battles, he showed great interest.

He turned to his wife, who was with him, and said, "Look, a young Arab is coming from Arabia to collect news of the civil war in Spain. Isn't this a wonder?" He tried to persuade me to be fair in my articles and news and not to take sides!

In Madrid, I went to the house of the Central Committee of the Communist Party of Spain on Via Serrano. This house was previously the seat of the National Council of the Catholic Party, headed by Gil Robles. There I presented my papers, and the leaders of the [Communist] Party welcomed me, telling me that they had been advised of my coming to Madrid, and that they wished me the best in any effort I might make to remove the veil from the eyes of the Moroccan soldiers, whether in the field or in captivity.

These Spanish leaders were:

- **Dolores Ibárruri.** She was called "La Pasionaria," meaning the merciful mother. At that time she was thirty-six years old, slender, tall, her hair and eyes radiant, calm, soft-spoken, laconic, and always wearing a black Spanish dress. She was the first Spanish female worker to join the party in the thirties. She was among the Spanish delegation that represented her party at the Comintern's Seventh Congress in Moscow in 1936. She was, among other things, the symbolic leader of the global left. At the time, Dolores had a sixteen-year-old son working in a Moscow factory, and a young daughter staying at the International Children's Home in the town of Ivanovo near Moscow.
- **Jose Diaz.** The general secretary of the party, a worker from Seville, a thin man who suffered from poor health. Laconic and mild-mannered, he enjoyed the respect of his supporters and allies among the Socialists and Republicans.
- **Vicente Uribe.** Minister of Agriculture, in charge of Moroccan affairs in the party. He was Basque and had previously resided in Tetouan in Spanish Morocco; of average height, well-versed in the theory surrounding the Spanish economy, especially in agricultural affairs, slender, organized, and strict.
- **Pedro Checa.** Second Secretary of the Central Committee; bland, very thin, supervised the party's administrative affairs, gave security clearances, and went after underground fifth column groups.

- **Antonio Mije.** In charge of trade union affairs. Andalusian by birth, he also dealt with the party's financial issues. At the same time, he was a liaison officer with various party committees.
- **Emilio Hernandez.** Minister of Education; tall and very knowledgeable about science and culture.

At the time, the party's membership numbered about three hundred thousand people.

I lodged in the house of the party, and La Pasionaria treated us all with kindness and affection. She always presided at the table, serving food for us herself on the silver dishes which Gil Robles had left behind, and she spared no effort to ensure we were comfortable.

Two days after my arrival in Madrid, I was transferred to a house on Via Serrano that had been abandoned by its wealthy Rebel-affiliated owners, and I made it my headquarters. There I wrote bulletins in Arabic for the Moroccan soldiers and articles for some Spanish newspapers published in Madrid. The Spanish papers included *El Mundo Obrero*, *Claridad*, *Informaciones*, *Heraldo de Madrid*, and *Politica*. I also edited articles for some Arabic newspapers, including an article I sent to the *al-Rabita al-Sharqiyya* (*The Eastern League*) newspaper published in Beirut; its editor-in-chief, Ibrahim Haddad, published it and took the cover photo himself.

Then the Central Committee attached me to Comrade Vicente Uribe, who was Minister of Agriculture and in charge of Moroccan affairs. I took a pseudonym for myself, Mustafa Ben Jala, because I thought it had a certain Moroccan quality to it. It was also a continuation of the pseudonyms I had used in the past: Mustafa Sa'adi during my university days, and Mustapha el Omari in the *al-Sharq al-'Arabi* newspaper.

Thus I settled in Madrid, where the flames of the civil war raged on more than one front.

THE FRONTS

On July 18, 1936, General Franco announced the insurrection in Morocco, then invaded southern Spain, including Seville, Malaga, Cádiz, and the Canary Islands, while the foreign division and other forces supporting the insurrection seized Melilla and Ceuta in Moroccan territory. A third force invaded across the border from Portugal, with the consent of the Portuguese authorities, and occupied the town of Badajoz in the south.

And in this very town, the Spanish bloodbath began in its ugliest form. As soon as the Rebels secured the town, their leader ordered all the workers to gather in the bullfighting arena to hear an important statement. After they all gathered together, machine guns started shooting at them from the four sides of the arena. The Rebels' plan was to create a state of terror and panic throughout Spain and break the morale of the population. About 1,500 people were killed in this massacre.

In July of the same year, the Rebels in northern Spain took Pamplona, Zaragoza, Valladolid, and Burgos (their capital in the north). In the meantime, Italian ships landed in Cádiz and Malaga, carrying forces led by General Mancini. They planned to advance from there to Aragon, Segovia, then to Valle de Cuelgamuros and Alcalá de Henares, and encircle Madrid.

REPUBLICANS

Niceto Alcalá-Zamora was the first president of the Spanish Republic. He remained in office for six years, from 1931 to 1936. He was replaced as president of the Republic at the beginning of the Civil War by Manuel Azaña, a democratic socialist who served as Minister of Defense after the overthrow of the monarchy; he was a writer, thinker, and novelist who wrote about psychological issues. He was previously president of the Ateneo Spanish Cultural Club. During his administration, the Spanish Constitution was amended, and its first article now stated: "Spain is a republic for workers of all classes."

The prime minister at the start of the Civil War was José Giral, a chemist, left-wing republican, and close associate of President Azaña.

In September 1936, the premiership and the Ministry of Defense were entrusted to the socialist leader Largo Caballero. He brought into his cabinet three socialist ministers: the journalist Julio Álvarez del Vayo, who was assigned the Ministry of Foreign Affairs, the communist Emilio Hernandez, who was assigned the Ministry of Education, and the communist Vicente Uribe, who was assigned the Ministry of Agriculture. He entrusted the Ministry of Justice to the anarchist García Oliver.

On June 15, 1937, after Franco's forces reached the gates of Madrid, Largo Caballero withdrew with some of his ministers to Valencia, where he quarreled with the Communists over the issue of strengthening cooperation between the two parties. He and his government resigned, and a new ministry was formed, headed by Juan Negrín.

THE REPUBLICAN ARMY

- **General Asensio.** Commander of the Central Front. He planned to attack Talavera to the west of Toledo, located on the Tagus River, and liberate it from the hands of the rebels with four thousand of his men, in addition to two thousand fighters to be withdrawn from the front of Guadarrama.[19] Largo Caballero later appointed him as his deputy Prime Minister and the deputy in the Ministry of Defense.
- **Emilio Kleber.** Commander of the First International Division.
- **Pavel Lukács.** Hungarian writer, commander of the 2nd International Division.

19 Sidqi uses the Arabic spelling, Wadi al-Rama.

- **Enrique Líster.** From the Spanish province of Galicia, in the northwest of the country, commander of a Republican column in the Extremadura front.
- **Juan Modesto.** Co-captain of Enrique Líster.
- **"El Campesino."** Spanish worker, International Brigade commander.
- **Vicente Rojo.** Lieutenant Colonel and Chief of Staff of the Defense of Madrid.
- **Antonio Mije.** Military commander, member of the Traitors Committee for the Defense of Madrid, and later president of this committee.
- **José Miaja.** Military commander, member of the Committee for the Defense of Madrid.
- **Bartolomeo Gordon.** Commander of the Fifth Brigade and Victory Column of the Communist Party of Spain.
- **Durruti.** Catalan unit leader.

These leaders were communists, with the exception of the socialist Miaja and the anarchist Durruti.

The number of international battalions increased after the influx of foreign volunteers from far and wide, until there were twelve teams, divided into columns, such as the one named after Garibaldi, who fought for the freedom and unification of Italy (1807-1882); the column of Thälmann, named after the leader of the German Communist Party later killed by the Nazis; and another column named after Karl Marx. The headquarters of this international force was located in Madrid, at 63 Velazquez Avenue.

THE REBEL ARMY

There were four most prominent rebel generals.

- **General Franco.** Commander-in-Chief of Anti-Republican Forces.
- **General [José Enrique] Varela.** Franco's second-in-command. Varela is the one who said, "I will enter Madrid Square on a white horse; I will say, 'I am

here!'" It was he who announced in September 1936 that the Fascist army was attacking Madrid with five columns from five directions: from the Extremadura road, from Toledo, from Avila Guadarrama, via Segovia-Guadalajara, and with the secret column that operated within the capital, Madrid. This is how the term "fifth column" became an international term for espionage and internal political sabotage.

- **General [Juan] Yagüe.** A commander of the Spanish-Moroccan forces.
- **General Queipo de Llano.** Also known as the drunken broadcaster general.

SPANISH RADIO SERVICES

- **Radio Seville**, hosted by the Rebels. They entrusted the broadcasting of news and commentaries to the elderly general Queipo de Llano, a sharp-tongued drunkard who improvised commentaries while smoking a hookah—you could hear its clatter from the receivers. Among his comments at the time was: "A Red plane struck Seville, and the bomb fell on a man's shop and killed him. We have learned that this man was redder than the Reds themselves!" He used to broadcast this sort of commentary at nine o'clock every evening.
- **Radio Salamanca**, also affiliated with the Rebels. This station broadcast directives for the Fifth Column at a quarter to ten every evening.
- **Radio Tetouan**, which broadcast in Moroccan Arabic. On the night I listened to it, the announcer said, "We tell you, gentlemen, that Sheikh Hitler asked Göring Pasha to greet Franco Pasha with the greeting 'Peace upon you,' and that Varela Pasha hosted a dinner party for General Muhammad bin Omar, a great honor for Morocco." Then he started praising the Moroccan leader, 'Abd al-Khaliq al-Tarisi.
- **Union Radio**, which belonged to the Spanish Republic. It broadcast news, commentaries and speeches from Madrid every evening at ten o'clock. In particular, it aimed to interrupt the broadcasts from Radio Salamanca.

THE POET FEDERICO LORCA

Shortly after my arrival in Madrid, I was told that in Seville, General Varela had arrested the Spanish poet and novelist Federico García Lorca, known for his social republicanism. Varela threatened to execute him if the Republican government executed a Rebel general's son who was imprisoned in Madrid. A dialogue took place between the two parties on the radio, but the Republicans made a fatal mistake by considering the issue "a matter of principle" and executing the general's son. The next day Lorca was executed in the castle of Seville.

Lorca was a glorious poet, and a writer imbued with the lives, customs and traditions of his people. Among his plays are *Blood Wedding*, *Yerma*, and *The Spinster.*

BATTLE OF THE ALCÁZAR

The fortress of Toledo was a front in its own right. The city of Toledo was in the hands of the Republicans, while its fortress, the Alcázar, was in the hands of the Rebels. A large number of Rebels took refuge in this fort, taking along some hostages from among the workers' women and children, then closed the doors of the impenetrable Arab fortress, posted snipers on its walls, and began shooting at the fighters and the civilian population.

As for the Republicans, they surrounded the fort on all sides and set it on fire without achieving any significant results. They tried to pour petrol and glycerine through the earthen windows of the fort to set it on fire. They also brought tanks of flammable materials from Madrid on September 21, 1936, but as soon as they reached the fort, the tanks were hit by bullets and caught fire, and so the attempt failed.

José Díaz said at the time, "It would take a thousand fighters to take Fort Toledo, of which we would lose at least two hundred."

On September 28, 1936, the city of Toledo fell to the Rebels, and those besieged in the fort were freed.

GETAFE AIRPORT

On November 4, 1936, the rebels, led by the Moroccan forces, attacked the Madrid airport in Getafe; they then penetrated into the capital's garden, known as the Casa de Campo, and into the University City.

As the Moroccans approached the gates of Madrid, the Central Committee held an emergency meeting. I happened to be in the room where they planned to have the meeting; the comrades considered my presence with them an intrusion, and they told me to leave the room, as I was not a member of the committee. Vicente Uribe, however, nodded to the chamberlain, Ortega, who gently pulled me out of the room by the arm, saying, "Comrade Mustafa, your people"—by which he meant the Moors—"are at the gates of Madrid!"

The next day I met the French comrade André Marty,[20] and he said to me, "What will you do if the rebels occupy Madrid?"

I said, "What could I possibly do?"

He said, "If the fascist hordes enter Madrid, you must take refuge in the British embassy, because Britain sympathizes with the Spanish Republic, but its words hold weight on the other side. In addition, you are an Arab from the Mandates, so no doubt the United Kingdom's ambassador will take care of you!"

20 Sidqi's note: André Marty was an old French leftist. In 1918, as a naval officer on a French warship, he received orders to participate in the foreign interference in the Russian Revolution by entering the Odessa harbor and shelling the revolutionary forces there. But he defied the orders of the French fleet command, announcing instead that he and his crew were joining the Russian comrades. After preventing the interference from succeeding, Marty returned to France, where he joined the French Communist Party. In 1936 the party sent him to Spain to be its liaison to the Spanish Communist Party and to supervise the French volunteers. It is strange that no historian has paid attention to André Marty. I heard of him in Moscow in 1925 and later met him in Madrid: a substantial man, tall, in his seventh decade.

RECONNAISSANCE TRIP

The Central Committee told me that a group of International Brigade officers was heading to the Córdoba front, and that I must accompany them to this front in order to speak to the captured Moroccan soldiers and to call upon the Moroccan combatants in the area to join the Republican ranks. I was to use loudspeakers and distribute leaflets written in Moroccan Arabic.

We took the train to the city of Ciudad Real and then rode in transport cars to the town of Campo de Calatrava. There, they dropped us off at an old inn, similar to the inn in the story of Don Quixote de la Mancha. They assigned us a place to sleep in a large animal pen to protect us from air raids. As soon as we entered the pen, the stench seized our noses. We hastened to get out and take refuge somewhere else for the night, even if it meant we were exposed to an air raid.

The next morning, September 25, 1936, we were driven to the front lines in pickup trucks. As we were crossing the Sierra Morena mountains, we saw an enemy plane, so the commander ordered us to hide in the slopes until the plane moved away; if it had seen us, it would have strafed us with its machine guns.

We reached the battle lines, and those with us from the international forces joined the Republican fighters. Then one of the officers, knowing that I was an Arab, approached me and said, "Do you want to see the Moroccans?" I said, "Yes."

He led me to a solid barrier and said, "Look out through this hole." So I looked out and saw groups of Moroccans wearing turbans, ready to go into battle. So I spoke loudly through a megaphone and said, "Listen, brothers!"

They all trembled and looked intently at the barrier.

I continued, "I am an Arab like you, I come from a faraway Arab country. I advise you, my brothers, to flee from the ranks of your generals who oppress you in your homes. Come over to us, we'll strengthen and honor you, and we will pay each of you his daily allowance. And whoever does not want to fight, we will return him home, where he will find his family, his land, and his work. *Viva the Popular Front! Viva the Republic! Viva President Azaña! Viva Morocco!*"[21]

As soon as I had finished my speech and it was translated to the Rebels' leaders, the front was ablaze with all sorts of weapons. The Spanish officer pulled me back roughly and said, "What was that? Did you launch bombs from your mouth!?"

MIKHAIL KOLTSOV

After my return from the southern front, I met the correspondent of the Russian newspaper *Pravda*, Mikhail Koltsov, in Madrid. He had covered the news of the battles with his daily dispatches since August 3, 1936. I spoke to him in Russian and briefed him on my mission, and he listened to me with great interest, writing down everything I said to him. Then, he said, "I will inform *Pravda* of your mission and about the Moroccan issue." On September 20, 1936, the Soviet newspaper published Koltsov's article (written from memory) about two wounded Moroccan prisoners; he found nothing in them that was particularly terrifying. He said that the number of Moroccan soldiers who took part in the fighting was estimated at twenty thousand, and that in the past they had fought on the side of the colonialists against 'Abd al-Karim al-Khattabi, and today they were fighting on the side of Franco against the workers of Spain.

Then he described the Moroccan soldier's ability to shoot accurately and economize bullets thanks to the many battles he had fought in his mountainous

21 Sidqi transcribes the awkwardness of his attempt to speak to the Moroccans. His exhortation mixes formal and Moroccan colloquial Arabic vocabulary, giving an uneven effect something like this: "I am an Arab like you! I have come from a faraway Arab land. I advise you, my brothers, to defect from the ranks of y'all's generals (*al-jinirālāt diālkum*), who be oppressing you in your homes (*illī yazlamūnakum fī diyārkum*)."

country. He talked about the atrocities committed by the Rebels, such as killing innocent people, looting, plundering, and rape, and how they blame all of these abuses on the Moors (i.e., the Moroccans). He wrote, "Now, an attempt is being made to form a whole column of Moroccan prisoners and deserters; this work is being done by a young Arab anti-fascist named Mustafa Ben Jala." (This is pronounced Ben Khala in Spanish, and he wrote it as Ben Kala in Russian). "He invites the Rifians to seize the property of the Rebel generals in Morocco and the lands of the men of the Army of Africa. Ben Jala says in his written appeal, 'The colonizers have taken your most fertile lands from you. Isn't it madness for you to fight and shed blood for the rule of these wretched people?' These days, they find in the pockets of the fleeing and dead Moroccans the leaflets of Mustafa Ben Jala." Then Koltsov criticized the government of the Popular Front, which did not declare autonomy for the African provinces as they had done for the autonomous provinces in Spain, such as the Basque Country and Catalonia.

During my travels, I heard many complaints from Spanish soldiers on the battlefields that indicated a lack of confidence in the Moroccan soldiers. For instance, when they approached the trenches of the Moroccan forces, they would call loudly to them to join the Republican forces, so the Moroccans would raise their fists to the sky and shout "Yo estar rojo!", meaning "I am red too!" The Spaniards came up to them to shake hands, and they responded by hurling grenades at them.

When I returned to Madrid, I published an article in the left-wing Republican newspaper *Politica* about Moroccans, in which I recounted these incidents. The newspaper's editorial board published a drawing in which the Moroccan appears in the foreground, raising his fist and shouting, "Yo estar rojo!" A Rebel Spanish general stands behind him, commenting sarcastically, "If you're red, I'd rather be black!"

During the Battle of Madrid, the Moroccans attacked the University City area on the outskirts of Madrid, and some of them stormed the wing of the

Faculty of Philosophy. There, a French volunteer from the international forces met a large Moroccan soldier. They grappled each other and would not be separated; so the Frenchman extended his hand to the Moroccan's belt, snatched from it a pestle-shaped hand grenade, and hit his opponent's head with it. It exploded and killed them both.

THE STORY OF SIDI JALOUL

One morning in December 1936, a man from the Republican militia came to me and informed me that his colleagues had happened to arrest some Moroccan soldiers. He said, "Yesterday, the Rebels launched a violent attack, and their vanguards reached the central railway station. Four Moroccan soldiers sneaked into the station and rushed into the lobby, indifferent to the shells falling here and there, approached the ticket counter, and asked the cashier to exchange some foreign currency for them. As soon as he examined them, he realized that they were German marks used during World War I, with face values of 20,000 marks or 50,000 marks, distributed by General Franco's command to the Moroccan Arab volunteers, due to the lack of Spanish currency and its depreciation."

The militia man presented me with these banknotes. I took photos of them and then asked him to lead me to the place where they held the four Moroccan prisoners.

We headed to the barracks of the former Royal Guard, located near the statues of Don Quixote and Sancho Panza at the end of the Gran Vía of the Spanish capital. In a large hall of this barracks, I saw four Moroccan men lying on the ground, dusty, exhausted, and hungry. I said to them, "Peace be upon you, brothers!" They moved, tried to sit up, and looked at me imploringly. They started swarming to get close to me, hoping I might be a bearer of good news come to save them from their trouble.

I said, "Don't be alarmed, I am an Arab journalist who came to Spain to learn the truth about the civil war, and you can tell me everything that happened to you from the time you left your country until you were captured."

I had the following conversation with one of them:

"What is your name?"

"'Abd al-Qadir ibn 'Abd al-Salam."

"How old are you?"

"Thirty."

"What is the name of your town?"

"Larache."

"What is your profession?"

"Potter."

"Why did you volunteer for General Franco's forces?"

"I did not volunteer of my own accord. A police officer in Larache came and told me that I was wanted by the court. When I reached the police station, I found many of my townspeople waiting. Minutes later, they put us in a truck that carried us to the airport, where they distributed us into sections, each section consisting of thirty people, and forced us to put on military clothes, but they did not equip us with weapons. They drove us to where large planes were parked, and told us to board them. However, some of us refused to ride the 'crazy bird,' for fear of flying. They were beaten and imprisoned. The other group boarded it not knowing that they would end up on the Spanish battlefields."

"Then, what happened to you?"

"In the plane, we were packed together like sardines, one on top of another, all vomiting on each other. After two hours, the plane landed us in Jerez, Spain, where we boarded the train to Seville, and then we were taken to Salamanca, and from there to Cáceres, where we stayed for three days, during which we trained in fighting. Then we moved on to Burgos and Segovia, and from there to San Rafael. On the evening of our arrival, they took us to the Peregrinos front. The next day we fled to the ranks of the Republicans, after having spent four days without eating, wandering aimlessly through the woods."

"What kinds of propaganda against the Republic were spread among you?"

"They kept us away from politics—they just wanted us to be soldiers! However, Moroccan officers used to tell us sometimes that the Rojos"—the Reds—"were the cause of Morocco's misery. And that the Generales"—the military men—"were sent by Providence to save Morocco and its people!"

"What made you flee from Franco's ranks to the Republicans?"

My interlocutor fidgeted a little and began to think, then raised his head and said to me in a tone that revealed his instinctive naivety and blind faith:

"The night I ran away, the ghost of Sidi Jaloul came to me in a dream and said, 'My son 'Abd al-Qadir, you have to get up at once and move to the lines of the government of the Forty Verses[22] with some of your comrades whom you trust.' So I got up in a panic and carried out Sidi Jaloul's order. I woke up these three that you see here, and we entered the forests, and then we walked along the telephone lines, heading towards the Republican lands. We got lost on the road, and we spent four days with nothing to eat but wild grass. On the evening of the fourth day, we were intercepted by a group of Republican militia, and we threw down our rifles and raised our hands in surrender."

"If you saw Sidi Jaloul once again in your dream, and he said to you, 'O 'Abd al-Qadir, go back to where you came from,' what would you do?"

22 Sidqi's note: "Forty verses" was a Moroccan term for the Republic at the time. It was called by this name because they believed that those who rule it are forty deputies (نائبا), not one king.

The poor man's face reddened, and he stuttered; he did not know what to answer, and after a few seconds of bewilderment and exchanging glances with his companions, he said, "We will not return, no matter what!"

"Even if that went against the words of Sidi Jaloul?"

"Yes, even if it went against his words!"

"What is your wish now?" I asked. "Do you want to go back to Morocco, or would you rather stay here?"

"If we go back to Morocco, we will wind up in Spain again! We prefer to stay here in captivity until the war is over."

I left these poor people, promising that I'd put in a good word to ensure they were taken care of. When I was about to leave the room, 'Abd al-Qadir shouted, "Sir, sir! Look at this leaflet—they were dropped on us from planes a week ago. There are *mizyan bzaf*"—that is, very good—"words in it," and he took a neatly folded piece of paper from his turban and handed it to me. I opened it and saw a publication in Arabic as follows:

Ministry of Propaganda of the Spanish Republic

In the name of God, the Most Gracious, the Most Merciful

O Moroccan Muslim soldiers:

God and His Messenger command you not to obey those who push you to transgress, stray, and commit abominations. It is better for you to escape from the ranks of General Franco with all of your weapons. And the Government of the Republic promises you that it will secure your lives, and bring you back to your country, where your women and children are dying of hunger.

Those of you who remain with Franco will die far away from your homes and families, but as for those who come to us and surrender themselves—we will give them ten pesetas a day.

Peace be upon you.

REPUBLICAN REGULAR ARMY

I alluded in a previous section to the fact that most of the regular army was led by the Rebels, and that most of the Spanish people supported the Republicans. The Spanish people lacked regular forces, so they were forced to rely on the forces of partisan militias and on the support of international volunteers.

This was a difficult period for the Spanish Republic. While Franco marched with regular forces experienced in rural warfare, supported by Moroccan forces with experience in guerrilla warfare as well as German forces from the Panzer Division, known for its fighting prowess, and Italian forces with experience in Libya and Abyssinia—the Republicans faced them with disjointed forces inexperienced in military operations and lacking the accompanying strategic knowledge.

I remember, for example, that the Spanish people abhor sheltering in trenches, considering it an insult to their masculinity, and prefer to fight from behind a tree, or from behind a rock, or face to face with cold steel. However, this Romantic style of fighting proved useless in a war between organized armies. So it was decided to transform the Republican, socialist, communist, and anarchist militia forces into regular forces wearing official military uniforms, and to include them in the regular loyalist forces, in addition to the civil forces concerned with internal security. This was done in September 1936, and thus the militia leaders turned into regular commanders, the most prominent of whom were Emilio Kleber, Pavel Lukács, Enrique Líster, Vicente Rojo, Durruti, Antonio Mejo, and José Miaja.

THE DEFENSE OF MADRID

Air battles raged in the sky of Spain. The Soviet air forces bombed the Rebel positions, as the German and Italian air forces bombed Republican cities and positions and completely destroyed the city of Guernica. Madrid was fiercely bombarded from the air, and Rebel hordes attacked it on every side. The slogan of the Republicans was, "Fight in every street and in every house, and stand firm no matter the cost."

Madrid was almost besieged in October 1936, and then became completely besieged, with the exception of some eastern passages, on March 3, 1937. As for the Republican government, it left Madrid in November 1937 and took refuge in Valencia, then in Barcelona, leaving the matter of defending the capital to the Junta, that is, the Defense Committee led by General Miaja, Enrique Líster, and other leaders, in close cooperation with the International Brigade, which suffered heavy losses especially at the University City front.

In 1938, Franco's forces took over all of western and northern Spain, excepting Catalonia and most of Aragon, which remained in the hands of the Republicans. Madrid fell on May 19, 1939; with its fall, the last page of the Spanish Civil War was turned, leaving behind approximately a million dead.

GLOBAL CELEBRITIES

The civil war in Spain attracted many prominent thinkers, writers, and politicians, or figures who later gained prominence in those fields. They came to Spain for three reasons: to participate in the fighting, to visit briefly, or to participate in the Second International Congress of Writers for the Defense of Culture, which opened in Valencia on July 4, 1937, and moved to Madrid (which was then besieged) on July 6. Among those figures:

- **Josip Broz Tito** (1891–1980) was a party activist in his country, who was sentenced to five years in prison from 1928 to 1933. In the year 1936 he traveled to Spain as a simple volunteer, almost entirely overlooked, and joined the First International Division at 45 years of age. He participated in the Battle of Madrid, gaining great experience that benefited him in the battles to liberate Yugoslavia from the German occupation during the Second World War. He then became the President of Yugoslavia and commander-in-chief of its armed forces.

- **André Malraux** (1901–1976) traveled to China in 1925 and joined the Committee of Twelve of the Kuomintang Revolutionary Party in Canton. In 1937 he traveled to Spain, joined the Republican forces, and worked on organizing an air force of foreign volunteers. He personally served in the Republican Air Force as a machine gunner and was wounded in battle twice. The Spanish Civil War inspired him to write *La Condition Humaine* (or Man's Fate), a story of a man who died in vain to prevent the Fascists from sweeping through Spain.
- **Ernest Hemingway** (1899–1961) came to Spain on March 25, 1937. He visited the Valley of the Fallen front, in which the Republicans, led by the commanders Líster and Lukács, won a resounding victory over Mussolini's soldiers. After inspecting that front, he said, "This is the beginning of the victory over fascism." Hemingway made his headquarters in the Hotel Florida on the main street of Madrid, and from there he used to go to the battle fronts as a researcher and a student. He met the Spanish fighters and the men of the International Brigades, and he came into contact with revolutionary and peaceful villagers alike. He gained abundant information from them, which enabled him to write his famous 1940 novel *For Whom the Bell Tolls*, a novel characterized by its tension and the vigor of its protagonists, especially the fighter Pilar. Its message is: "Sacrificing freedom anywhere must result in the feeling of losing freedom everywhere." That is, whenever any party, whether Spaniard or non-Spaniard, sacrifices their freedom in any fighting, and for whatever goals, this will result in the loss of freedom for everyone. Hemingway did not find a winner or loser in Spain. Bells, in his view, toll for all!
- **George Orwell**, an Englishman, whose real name was Eric Blair, was born in India in 1903. He went to Spain in 1937, fought in the ranks of the Republicans, and was wounded. He died in London in 1950. The Spanish Civil War inspired Orwell to write a book called *Homage to Catalonia*, in which he describes an English volunteer who was badly wounded on the battle front, then had to flee and hide when he saw the militants fighting over their partisan differences in the streets of Barcelona.

- **Arthur Koestler**, a Hungarian, was born in Budapest in 1905. He worked as a journalist starting in 1928 in Berlin, Paris, Cairo and London. In 1936, *News Chronicle* sent him to Spain to cover the civil war; his articles forcefully attacked the Rebels. He later published a book in London titled *The Spanish Testament*. The Rebel general Queipo de Llano, provoked by this book, swore to execute Koestler in Malaga; Koestler was captured, tortured, and sentenced to death. Only the intervention of the British government saved him from this fate. After his release and his return to England, he wrote a new book entitled *Dialogue with Death*, in which he describes the torture he suffered in the prisons of the Spanish fascists.

THE SPANISH-MOROCCAN SOCIETY

One day, I was sitting in my office on Serrano Street when a militiaman came up to me and told me there was a beautiful Spanish girl at the front door who wanted to meet me.

I said, "What's her name, and what does she want?" He said, "Her name is Carmen, and she says she's of Arab descent." I replied, "I'll go see her."

I left my office and went downstairs to the outer door of the building, and I saw a girl in her twenties, of medium height, with white skin, black hair, and black eyes. She smiled at me and extended her hand for a handshake. "My name is Carmen," she said in French. "I am Spanish and of Arab descent."

I said, "Hello, nice to meet you."

She said, "I read an article of yours about Moroccans in the newspaper *Informaciones*, and I would be happy to speak to you about this article if possible."

I looked at her face, her expression, and her appearance, and I noticed her sincerity and innocence, so I said to her, "I hope that you will call me tomorrow to set an appointment for an interview." She seemed satisfied, wrote down my phone number, shook my hand, and went on her way.

I consulted the comrades about her and they told me, "Yesterday you met the Moroccan student 'Umar al-Wazzani, and today you met a girl of Arab descent; this is how the Arab community grows. Meet her and talk to her."

Indeed, the beautiful Carmen was a point of contact with a group of Republican Spanish youth who wanted to serve the Moroccan cause and strengthen brotherhood between the Spaniards and the Moroccans. We held meetings and agreed to establish the Spanish-Moroccan Association. We defined the objectives of this association, which were to organize battlefield propaganda in two specific directions. First, to urge Moroccan soldiers to join the Republican ranks and convince them that the Republic would give them the freedom to decide their fate. Second, to make the Spanish soldiers understand that the Moroccans were not voluntary participants in the Spanish Civil War, but rather that they had been deceived or lured to fight because of their misery and the poor living conditions resulting from Spanish colonial rule. Thus the association began its work; we set up an office for it, made a seal for it, and appointed a secretary for it, the young woman Carmen.

I did this work out of my own conviction that it would be useful. When news of the association spread in the newspapers, the Spanish comrades took note, saying that they feared the establishment of such an association. I defended my position, stressing that I could not do any fruitful work by myself, and that I had to create a movement in which the Moroccans and the Spaniards would help me together.

This association continued to work and expand until I left Spain, after which no news about it reached me. I mention here that the Spanish comrades were more theoretical than practical in their position on Moroccans and the Moroccan issue. I sensed in them, and especially in Vicente Uribe, a lack of trust in any Moroccan. I alerted them more than once to the executions of Moroccan captives. I felt in my heart that my mission was faltering, and that I had to look for a more effective and beneficial way to influence the Moroccan soldiers and the Moroccan Rif as a whole. I came up with a plan to set up a secret radio service in Algeria, broadcasting in literary Arabic and in two local dialects, Moroccan and Kabyle.

12
THE ALGERIAN PROJECT
(1936–37)

SECRET BROADCAST

At the end of December 1936, the Central Committee of the Spanish Communist Party decided to send ‘Umar al-Wazzani and me to Algiers, accompanied by a Spanish official, to establish a secret radio station there to broadcast to North Africa in general and to Spanish Morocco in particular. The broadcast aimed to target the Spanish rebels and the deceived but dangerous Moroccans accompanying the fascist advance, and then to focus on calling on Spanish Morocco to revolt against its colonial rulers.

The three of us headed to Barcelona and then to the border town of Portbou. There we parted. The Spanish official and ‘Umar al-Wazzani boarded a ship heading to Algiers, and we agreed to meet in Algiers on a specific day in a specific hotel.

In Paris I again met with Richard, who gave me a French identity card and advised me, “When you leave the ship in the port of Algiers, pay no heed to the guards, and set off with your head held high!”

I stayed in Paris for only two days. Then I traveled to Marseille and from there to Algiers. I took Richard’s advice and went straight to the hotel where we had agreed to meet.

The Spanish official had to secure the radio equipment, the engineer, and the broadcasting place in cooperation with the communist organization in Algiers. Days passed while I waited for the result of his endeavors; in the meantime, I used to go back to the Kasbah, the Islamic quarter of the city. This is a compact group of houses built on a mountain carved with staircases that ascend through narrow passages, with alleys branching off right and left, finally rising to a wide plaza where Algerians—villagers in particular—display their handicrafts and foodstuffs amidst a mixture of herds of sheep, goats, and all kinds of livestock. Here and there, one can see groups of French and foreign military men wandering around the plaza to shop and enjoy themselves.

As for the coastal neighborhoods of the city, which are inhabited by Europeans (French, Spaniards, and Italians), they are no different from the streets of Marseille: tall houses, clean roads, classy stores and restaurants, Western men with flat-brimmed hats, and elegant, attractive, playful women who combine fair skin with dark Algerian hair and eyes. Everyone jabbers in the dialects of the inhabitants of the French, Spanish, and Italian coasts.

To the south behind these neighborhoods are traditional markets staffed by Algerian Muslims who speak the local Arabic but use the French alphabet. One sees, for example, a signboard hung over the door of a *hammam*—this Arabic word is written shakily on it in Latin script. The Arabic language is completely extinct, and the people treat publications in Arabic as somehow holy. In fact, they have retained spoken and formal Arabic only due to their strong adherence to the Islamic religion, the Holy Qur'an, and the noble sayings of the Prophet. Islam alone has prevented them from losing their Arab identity.

During this time, I also visited Oran for one day only, accompanied by 'Umar al-Wazzani. It is an Algerian port with stunning views, especially from the head of the Gulf. Located 260 miles west of the capital, it has a mosque, a cathedral, two fortresses, a college, and a school. It has a reputation for trading in papyrus, iron ore, and grain. At the time, it was an important French naval base.

In Oran, ‘Umar al-Wazzani introduced me to the Secretary General of the Association of Algerian Muslim Ulema, Sheikh Muhammad al-Zahri, a man of nearly forty, tall, fair-skinned. We had a meeting in an Arab café near the Oran mosque, where he told us about the president of the association, Sheikh ‘Abd al-Hamid ibn Badis (1889-1940), and his status in the hearts of Algerians. He also told us about the association's message, which "aims to unite the ranks of Muslims in Algeria, and cares for their religious affairs and their personal well-being." It also took on the responsibility of teaching the Holy Qur'an and the Arabic language, in addition to goals of national independence that are not explicitly written in their curriculum. Sheikh Muhammad al-Zahri talked about the French authorities' persecution of this association and harassment of its president.

When I asked for his opinion on Spanish Morocco's involvement in the Spanish Civil War, he said, "We are against interfering in this war, and we oppose sending soldiers to the front—we have neither a mare nor a camel in this fight."[23]

In Oran, ‘Umar al-Wazzani informed me that he did not want to return to Algiers before the secret broadcasting project was established. Instead he had decided to travel to Tetouan to visit his family, whom he had not seen for a long time. I had no choice but to acquiesce to his wish, because although he was an Arab young man of Republican persuasion, we had no authority over him. So I bid him farewell in the hope of meeting him one day.

23 "Neither a mare nor a camel" is a common Arabic idiom, *lā nāqa wa-lā jamal*, meaning "no stake whatsoever." —Trans.

I returned to Algiers to wait for the Algerian project to be implemented. One night when I was bored, I attended a concert performed by the French Philharmonic Orchestra in the Grand Theatre, in which I listened to the Ninth Symphony, with the participation of the Grand Choir. I enjoyed listening to this wonderful work of art, and I returned to the hotel to write an article about the ninth symphony. I also set about translating the Ode to Freedom or Ode to Joy by the German poet Johann Friedrich Schiller (1759-1805), which the choir had sung at the end of the symphony.

I stayed in Algiers for about two weeks, during which we were still unable to establish the secret station. One day the Spanish official told me, "The Algerian project has failed for insurmountable technical reasons. You can go wherever you want. In my opinion, there is no point in returning to Spain, as the situation there continues to deteriorate; you'd better go home!"

PARIS . . . PARIS

I acted against the advice of the Spanish official and chose to return to Paris, thinking my move was appropriate. However, my decision led to unexpected troubles. The French party would not recognize me, saying, "You are under the authority of the Spanish party or the Comintern." Meanwhile, I was fully convinced that my mission in Spain was over and that returning there would be risky, especially since the Spanish government and most of the party organizations, politicians, and men of letters had left Madrid for Valencia, the new capital of Republican Spain. Besides, I met some leaders of the Spanish party in Paris itself. One of them asked me, "What are you doing here?"

I told him, "The Algerian project did not succeed."

"Then go back to Madrid," he said angrily.

A few days later, Khalid Bakdash passed through Paris on his way from Moscow to Beirut, and we spent Christmas Eve 1936 together. We first walked into a basement bar in the Saint-Michel district, not knowing that it was run by Colonel de La Rocque's people.[24] One of them came toward us and said in French, "I don't know whether to extend my hand to you or stab you!" We explained to him that we were just strangers bar-hopping on Christmas Eve. He was relieved to hear this and said, "Then I will extend my hand to you."

Khalid tried to persuade me to return to Spain, with Rebel forces now occupying three-quarters of the country. I explained that even with an open mind, I could not justify returning to Spain in this period of retreat and decline.

He said, "I am aware of your fears; and yet I tell you, Comrade Sa'adi, go back to Spain. If you are killed there, trust that I will not forget you, and I will write a book about you that will immortalize your memory!"

After a moment of silence he said, "If for some reason you do not travel to Spain again, you may ask the Comintern to transfer you to Beirut, where you will be at our disposal."

In the meantime, a delegation consisting of Riad Solh, 'Abdel Hamid Karami, and Robert Khalat was sent to Paris to negotiate with the French for a treaty between France and the Lebanese Republic. We visited Riad Solh at Claridge's Hotel in Rue Saint-Honoré, where he told us about his political missions. Then, we attended a meeting held by 'Abdel Hamid Karami and Robert Khalat at a Parisian club, where the Tripolitan leader spoke about the meanings of independence and patriotism. During his speech, he fixed his gaze on the horizon as if looking forward to the distant goal he was aiming for.

Khalid returned to Lebanon. As soon as he settled in Beirut, he sent Comrade Reda at the end of January 1937 to represent his party to the Central

24 Sidqi's note: Colonel François de La Rocque was an aristocratic French retired officer who established the fascist "Cross of Fire" organization in the Thirties. There were about thirty thousand members in the organization, which was supported by wealthy industrialists. It was the first French political organization to announce its hostility to the Republic and to democracy since the great French Revolution. The threat from the organization spurred the formation of the Popular Front and the election of a Chamber of Deputies with an overwhelming Socialist majority, and a rise in the number of Communist deputies from 10 to 72.

Committee of the French Communist Party. Since Comrade Reda was inexperienced in Parisian and political life, he insisted that we stay together in the same hotel near the Luxembourg Garden until a decision had been made on my behalf.

In Paris, my article on Beethoven's Ninth Symphony was approved for pub-lication. I sent it to the literary journal *al-Tali'ah*, which was supervised by the party in Beirut, and published it in the February-March 1937 issue under the title "Beethoven's Ninth Symphony." It seems that Khalid disliked the journal treating a global artistic subject with a humanist and liberating character, so he wrote Comrade Reda a letter, which I happened to see at the hotel. It said, "Comrade Sa'adi sent an article to *al-Tali'ah* magazine, in which he writes about Beethoven's Ninth Symphony. For the love of God, what is this nonsense?!"

My stay in Paris went on, but the French party still refused to acknowledge my presence, putting me in dire financial straits. Once I went to a restaurant with Comrade Reda; we had lunch together and drank wine. When the waiter came with the bill, the comrade said to me, "We'll split the bill . . . Give me six francs!"

I said, "I don't have a single franc in my pocket."

Furious, he growled, "How can you allow yourself to eat at my expense, comrade?"

After this incident, I decided to leave the hotel where Comrade Reda was staying and to avoid him as much as possible. I turned to a virtuous lady of Alsatian birth, Léo Wanner, head of the League Against Imperialism in Paris, who resided on Rue Clopin, in the district of Cardinal Lemoine. This lady sympathized with me, supported my position, provided me with every help, and prepared for me a meeting with a group of North African workers residing in Paris. At the meeting, I told the workers about the Spanish war and the miserable fate that Moroccan soldiers had met there, as Franco forced the soldiers into battle and to commit atrocities. The Republicans sought vengeance against these soldiers and seldom had mercy on them when they fell into their hands. I urged the workers to demand, in France and North Africa, the withdrawal of Moroccan forces from the Spanish front.

Léo Wanner introduced me to a man who was forty years old, of average height, sharp-sighted: "This is Mr. Habib Bourguiba, the head of the Destour Party in Tunisia." I introduced myself to him and told him I had been in Spain. He was interested in the topic and asked me to visit him at the house of the "Secours Rouge" (Red Aid) of the French Communist Party, where he was staying; he wanted to discuss Arab issues. However, this visit did not happen because I was so preoccupied with my own troubles.

My stay in Paris dragged on. My relations with the French comrades were so strained that a member of the Central Committee, someone named Georges—I think he is the head of the French party today, Georges Marchais—wanted to know where I was staying and how much I was paying. I told him that I was staying at the Marks Hotel, so he took note and started searching for the Marx Hotel. When he did not find the hotel where I was staying, he berated me: "Where did you get a hotel in Paris named for Karl Marx?" I told him, "Look for the Marks Hotel with a 'ks', not an 'x'." He swallowed and shut up.

Thus, the anger against me in Paris intensified. The main reason for this was my confrontation with the colonialist tendencies of some leaders of both the French and Spanish communist parties. I demanded the Arabization of the Algerian Communist Party, and I took stances on this topic during my stint as editor of *al-Sharq al-'Arabi*. Additionally, I had expressed my dissatisfaction with the Spanish Communist Party leaders' indifference to the murders of Moroccan soldiers, and to the Moroccan issue in general.

Finally, after a stay in Paris which lasted until April 1937, the Comintern sent instructions to pay all my debts in Paris and to provide me with a ticket to Lebanon, along with some spending money. These instructions were a shock to my enemies in Paris. One day Richard tried to provoke me in the presence of Comrade Reda, and I responded to him, saying, "If you don't stop talking right now, I'm going to throw you out!"

I got hold of myself and quickly realized that he was trying to stir me up with his insolence to cause me new troubles. A few days later I was on my way to Marseille. From there I sailed to Istanbul, and from the Haydarpaşa Station I took a train to Aleppo.

13
THE END OF THE JOURNEY
(1937–1940)

WORK IN DAMASCUS

I stayed in Aleppo for one night. The next morning, I went to Damascus and stayed temporarily at Khalid Bakdash's house in the Kurdish Quarter, then rented a furnished room on al-Halbouni Street from a widowed Armenian woman known as Madame Zohrab who earned a living by renting the room to foreign students.

The party's office was initially in an old house in an old neighborhood of Damascus. The waters of 'Ain al-Fijah flowed through there, and the house had a fountain in the courtyard. It was almost like a club that the comrades liked to frequent in the evenings after work or school.

Then the office moved to a newly-built house placed on Salihiya Street, near the Parliament, in keeping with the public status of the Syrian Communist Party during the period of the Popular Front government in France and under the guardianship of the first Syrian national government, which had arisen after the Franco-Syrian Treaty of 1936.

The first thing Khalid did when I arrived in Damascus was to direct me to the palace to meet Shukri al-Quwatli, in his capacity as the leader of the National Bloc and Minister of Finance. Khalid introduced me to him, saying, "I would like to present to your Excellency our comrade Najati Sidqi, or Comrade Sa'adi; he is a writer and journalist, who was recently in Madrid in the midst of the Spanish Civil War, and today he resides in Damascus to cooperate with us for the good of the country."

Al-Quwatli replied, "Welcome. We hope to benefit from his experience, and you, Khalid, should take care of him."

On the same day, Khalid took me to the Minister of Economy, Fayez al-Khoury, and introduced me to him, saying, "I present to your Excellency, Minister, our comrade Najati Sidqi, a graduate of Moscow University. He edited the newspaper *The Arab East*, which was published in Paris. He just returned from the civil war in Spain, and puts himself at the disposal of the Syrian national movement." Fayez al-Khoury looked at me, amazed; then he said to Khalid, "Your comrade is very welcome, even if he is overqualified. We're a group that does simple stuff, how can we compare to the civil war in Spain!"

Then, we visited Lutfi al-Haffar, the owner of *al-Insha'* newspaper, the mouthpiece of the National Bloc, and its editor-in-chief, Rashid al-Mallouhi. This visit introduced me to most of the workers in the political, literary and journalistic fields in Damascus. We used to visit them in their offices or meet them in the cafés of Damascus and exchange opinions with them about the Franco-Syrian treaty and its effectiveness, the Popular Front government in France and its impact in the Arab East, the battles against the British and Zionists in Palestine, the Italian fascist invasion of Abyssinia, German Nazism and the possibilities of a second world war fueled by Hitler and Mussolini, and Stalin's struggle against his opponents in the Soviet Union. There were conflicting views on these political issues, but everyone agreed on the principle of independence and liberation from French control by any possible means. There were even those who wished for salvation through a second world war and a Nazi fascist invasion of the Arab region.

The Arab Club in Damascus, most of whose members were educated in Germany, was showing remarkable enthusiasm for German Nazism. Meanwhile, the Syrian Social Nationalist Party saw alliance with Mussolini's Italy as the only way to freedom and independence.

There were other currents that advocated Arab unity, Islamic unity, Arab socialism, and Arab communism, whose followers expressed their principles and emotions with hand gestures representing the two global currents. The far right would spread the hand, arm firmly extended, saluting in the Roman manner; among them were some who wore Iron Shirts, i.e. shirts made of locally-made gray cloth, used in making local hemp. On the other hand, the left clenched their fists tightly, their arms also extended fully, a reference to the union and the striking hammers.

A week after my arrival in Damascus, Khalid Bakdash told me that the Central Committee of the Party had decided to entrust the Damascus party organization to me, under the supervision of Khalid himself, who considered Damascus his main base, as it was his birthplace and where he grew up.

Here are the comrades I cooperated with in Damascus:

- **Najat Qassab Hasan.** When I met him, he was an excellent student, very intelligent. He later became a lawyer, and today he is in charge of analyzing judicial and legal problems on Radio Damascus.
- **Nasha'at al-Martini.** Originally from the town of al-Bab near Aleppo, he came to Damascus to study. He was a lover of literature, and he had his thoughts on literature published in *al-Tali'ah* magazine. He was also characterized by his keen sense of observation, his daring, and even his adventurous nature. After World War II, Nasha'at moved to France and worked in the amusement park in the Pigalle district. He hired a group of enterprising Frenchmen and transported a team of Parisian artistes to New York. Then, Nasha'at returned to Paris to take control of a large number of its cabarets, and "Monsieur Martini" became the terrifying foreign boss! In 1960, while he was pushing his car with his huge body and strong muscles on the Champs-Elysées, he suffered a heart attack that led to his death. He was buried in Paris.
- **Ahmad al-Shihabi**. A young man who was impressed by the communist movement and had patriotic motives.

- **Ahmad al-'Ashi.** The son of the owner of a coffee shop in Marjah Square, a seeker of knowledge, and one of the friends of *The Arab East* newspaper.
- **Fawzi al-Za'im.** A popular worker, among the neighborhood's tough men, who was reliable and very enthusiastic about the movement.
- **Dr. Izzat al-Jundi.** A dentist in al-Salihiya neighborhood, a man of gentle manners, good-natured, romantic in attitude, and an admirer of the communist movement as a "secret society."

There were a number of other high-ranking members, including writers, students, professors, and workers, who formed the local committees of the Damascus partisan organization in Martyrs' Square, Sanjaqdar, al-Salihiya, Halbouni, Bab Tuma, al-Hamidiyeh Market, and the Kurdish Quarter.

PARTISAN WORK

My partisan work in Damascus was confined to the educational and literary spheres. Meanwhile, Khalid was in complete control of the organizational and official work, and the political leadership of the party belonged solely to him. This was because he was very concerned to maintain Stalinist-style unilateral leadership, which was consistent with the typically eastern mentality of authoritarianism and control. Khalid Bakdash introduced "eastern modifications" in some party concepts.

First, he replaced the phrase "party general secretary" with "party head," because this designation is more understood in popular circles. Its connotation is also more influential psychologically. Second, he asked members to stand up with respect and reverence every time he entered the office, given that Arabs were still operating within patriarchal customs, i.e., revering the fathers and male elders. Third, he asked the Kurdish members to be proud of their Kurdishness, to learn the Kurdish language, and to speak it in the party. Whenever he met a Kurdish party member, he said to them, "*Shawah*!", which means "bravo" in Kurdish.

Khalid's relationship with me oscillated between trust and jealousy. He trusted me because of my theoretical knowledge and practical contributions, but his jealousy was an instinct that could only be controlled by culture in its most comprehensive sense. So, for example, if he felt "annoyed" in a meeting, and I was in another room, he would shout angrily, "Where are you Sa'adi! Comrade Sa'adi, come at once!"

The comrades would then realize that he was the supreme leader, and that I was but his lowly assistant.

INCIDENT WITH THE ARMENIAN LADY

The party's relations with the authorities in Damascus worsened, both because it kept trying to make inroads with the people at the National Bloc's expense, and because of the campaigns of criticism it directed at the national government for not keeping pace with the French Popular Front in the issues of the [Franco-Syrian] Treaty and İskenderun. So, in retaliation, the national government began a crackdown against the party organizations on May 29, 1937.

In the meantime, Khalid visited me in my room in al-Halbouni at Madame Zohrab's apartment (this room was among the party's safehouses). An informant who was tracking him saw him enter the apartment, and after about half an hour he knocked on the door. Khalid looked through a window slit and saw an investigator he recognized, accompanied by the informant. He was confused and rushed to the Armenian woman, begging her to hide him, so she took him up to the kitchen attic and covered him with sacks. As for me, I remained calm, opened the door, and said, "Let me through."

The investigator said, "Who lives here?"

I said, "I'm staying here with the Armenian landlady."

He said, "What is your profession?"

I said, "A student from Beirut."

He said, "Who else is in the house other than yourself?"

I said, "No one but me."

Madame Zohrab went to the door and answered the investigator's questions. After a while, he apologized to her and walked away, scolding the informant. As for Khalid, he came down from the attic, uttering thanks and praise.

After Khalid left the house, I had to explain to Madame Zohrab what happened and clear up her doubts by making up a story for her. I told her that my colleague had participated in a student demonstration, and the police were after him; I assured her that there was no danger involved. Then, I paid my rent for three months in advance.

This incident was known simply as "Madame Zohrab's Attic"!

MAYSALUN DAY

On the twentieth of July, 1937, we held a meeting at the Party headquarters and discussed participating in a commemoration of the Battle of Maysalun (July 24, 1920), during which the fledgling Syrian army, headed by Yusuf al-'Azma, had tried to halt the French forces marching against Damascus. This Arab leader met his death at Maysalun, and the Syrian state later built him a tomb in the shape of an airplane on that site.

We decided to participate in this commemoration. We rented four trucks, filling them with comrades and friends, and headed to Maysalun on July 24, 1937. There we found a large gathering of citizens and the family of the deceased, among them a group of youth who wore the "Iron Shirts" and berets. They had occupied the right side of the tomb, so we gathered to its left. The speakers began, starting with the father of the deceased, who gave an impassioned nationalist speech. Whenever an orator finished speaking, the group on the right extended their arms in a "Roman salute," and we responded by raising our fists in the air, the proletarian salute.

I would not have been surprised by a scene like this in France or Spain or Germany, but among the hills on the Beirut-Damascus road—that made it the strangest of strange things to me.

We returned from this interesting trip singing enthusiastic anthems. I remember among them "Oh, Glorious Syria!", "My Exalted and Beautiful Homeland", and "Oh Comrades of the Mountains" by the Lebanese poet Qablan Markzal.

BALDUR VON SCHIRACH

One day in the fall of 1937, at the Damascus Airport, a Lufthansa plane from Germany landed carrying a team of Nazis, led by the Nazi Youth Führer Baldur von Schirach. Members of the Arab Club, some Nazi admirers, and other curious spectators rushed to meet them.

The next day, in al-Salihiya, I met Ms. Marie 'Aflaq, the sister of Michel 'Aflaq, at the Bakdash family restaurant. She was interested in local politics and politics in general, and she enthused to me, "Yesterday I was among those who received the leader of the Hitler Youth at the airport in Damascus!"

I said, "What is his mission?"

She said, "He and his colleagues are on a tour to get acquainted with Arab nationalist youth in the Middle East. But the authorities did not allow them to leave the airport, so they traveled on to Baghdad."

In fact, the Nazis' sudden visit to Damascus at that time caused a great stir, and caused embarrassment to the national government and the circles of the French mandate.

Eight years after that visit, the Nazis were defeated in World War II. Baldur von Schirach was arrested, brought before the Nuremberg Tribunal (1945-1946), and sentenced to life imprisonment. He would serve only fifteen years of that sentence; he was released when he was sixty years old.

BAKDASH AND 'AFLAQ

One afternoon in September 1937, we sat in al-Sharq Café in Marjah Square. 'Aflaq, Bakdash, Bitar, al-Mahairi, and others gathered to play backgammon. While we were talking, Bakdash raised the subject of the Arab newspaper,

The Arab East, which I had published in Paris. 'Aflaq stopped playing, and he wanted to know the name of its real editor. He asked the question in a slightly pointed way.

Khalid glanced at me, then said to 'Aflaq, "Here he is!"

'Aflaq was confused and apologized, saying that he did not mean offense or criticism.

I told 'Aflaq that even if *The Arab East* was lacking in some aspects, it was the only newspaper in that period that fought against colonialism and called for the freedom of the Arabs in all their countries, and it did so boldly and objectively. I also told him that I edited, reviewed, packed, and shipped the newspaper all by myself while being relentlessly pursued by the police.

After we left the café, I asked Khalid, "Why did you say 'Here he is'?"

He said, "I just wanted you to get the real Damascus treatment!"

IBN MURAD

Also in Damascus, I knew that I had a relative from the Murad family who lived in the Salihiya neighborhood. So I wanted to look for him and find his house. I went around the alleys of al-Salihiya asking about Murad's house, until a shop owner told me, "The Murad house you are looking for—it is the only one in this area—you will find at the end of that alley, so knock on the door and perhaps it will be what you are looking for."

So, I went to that house, knocked on the door, and a young man, approximately thirty-five years old, appeared. I said, "I am looking for Murad al-Yafi's house."

He said, "You are at Murad's house."

I said, "I mean Murad the Jaffan's house."

He said, "I think we have relatives in Jaffa . . . What can I do for you?"

I said, "I just want to find the family. Do you know so-and-so… and do you know so-and-so?"

He said, “Let us suppose, sir, that you have not found the house you want. In any case, let us get acquainted; please come in.”

So I took a few steps into the house of this stranger Murad, and he asked me what I was doing in Damascus. I told him that I was a student. I found out that he worked in journalism and literature, so we talked about the Damascus and Beirut press, then we talked about politics and partisanship. Both of us erred on the side of caution in expressing our opinions and points of view.

After he felt at ease with me, and was assured that I really was a student, he said, “Could I offer you some books that will benefit you as a knowledge-seeker and expand your social awareness?”

He went to his closet and took out a bunch of books and pamphlets, wrapped them in a newspaper, and gave them to me. I got up to say goodbye, and he walked me to the door and said, “I hope to see you again.”

I said, “What is your honorable name, exactly?”

He said, “My name is So-and-so Murad. Secretary-General of the Syrian Social Nationalist Party in Damascus.”

I left the house quickly, laughing at this strange visit and the paradoxes it entailed. Then, I got rid of Murad’s “gift” by throwing it into a swiftly-flowing stream that runs through one of the old Salihiya neighborhoods. After this incident, I gave up searching for family and relatives in Damascus, so as not to fall into some even worse predicament.

THE FLOODS

In the winter of 1937, heavy rains fell in Syria, which quickly caused flooding. One of these torrents ran through some villages near the capital, sweeping away boulders, livestock, houses, and people in its path. The disaster was frightening and tragic. So the Damascus party organization hastened to convene an emergency meeting, in which it made a decision to help the affected villages. We recruited a team of comrades and took a large freight truck carrying spades and shovels. We headed to the disaster sites and began demolishing houses which had been damaged by the floods.

I said to Khalid while we were watching the progress of the work, "It is truly said that the communist is a mighty destroyer!" He liked this remark and stopped the comrades from working, narrated it to them, then commented on it. He explained to them the difference between demolishing for the sake of demolishing, and demolishing for the sake of building and reconstruction!

We couldn't stop the floods. We also could do little in the rescue work. However, we did fulfill a national and humanitarian duty, and we secretly intended to win the affection of the people at the same time.

SAWT AL-SHA'AB

The first issue of *Sawt al-Sha'ab* (Voice of the People) newspaper, the mouthpiece of the party, was published in Damascus in May 1937. In the first issue, I published an article about the civil war in Spain, and I decorated it with a large photo that I had brought with me from Spain: a big, tall Moroccan soldier embracing a skinny Spanish soldier, as a sign of fraternity and reconciliation between the two peoples.

As soon as this issue of the newspaper reached Comrade Reda, the party's representative in Paris, he presented it to the leaders of the French party, who expressed their great dissatisfaction with the photo. They sent a letter of protest to Khalid Bakdash, saying, "This is a picture different from the reality of the Spanish war, as the truth is that the giant man is the Spanish soldier, and the skinny man is the Moroccan soldier!"

What kind of objection is this? That picture was from Spanish propaganda sources, and I wasn't a photographer. More importantly, the point is not the bulk of this or that soldier, but rather the human significance expressed by the image itself.

I stopped publishing articles about Spain in *Sawt al-Sha'ab*, so as not to arouse the sensitivities of the French and Spaniards, and preferred to publish

This appears to be the photo which Sidqi republished later; here it is published in Estampa (Madrid: October 24, 1936), with the caption: "Moroccan militiamen fight for the Republic."

them all in one book. At the same time, *al-Tali'ah* magazine intended to publish the manuscript of *Revolution and Sedition in Lebanon* by Yusuf Yazbek. However, the Lebanese writer was ill, and he was unable to publish that manuscript. So the editor-in-chief of the magazine, Raja Hourani, asked me to start publishing the chapters of my book on Spain in the magazine instead of Yazbek's manuscript; I agreed to do so, and the first chapter was published in June 1938.

A few days after this chapter was published, Khalid Bakdash said to me, "Wouldn't it be better if you presented to me what you want to publish about Spain and the civil war, and then I published it under my name in a book?"

I said, "But, I planned to publish the research as a series in *al-Tali'ah*." He said, "You publish these articles of yours while you are compelled to hide your name, which makes them lose their personal charm. As for me, I would publish the book under my actual name on behalf of another person, so the information I recount would be of a very personal nature."

I provided him with only a little bit of information—which is not what was published in this book—and Khalid's book was published with the title *An Arab Who Fought in Spain.* Some readers thought that Khalid was the Arab, and that he used the third person out of revolutionary humility.

Sawt al-Sha'ab newspaper continued to be published, and Khalid used it to boost his own profile, an action prohibited by communist parties all over the world. However, he aroused severe criticism when he had the audacity to publish a special issue of the newspaper on the occasion of his father's death, claiming that he was "one of the leaders of the Ghouta rebels in the fight against French colonialism in 1925."

At the time, the objectors said, "Khalid deserves to publish a special issue of the party's newspaper on the Syrian revolution, and to mention his father among its fighters. However, in choosing to publish a special issue of the party's newspaper specifically for his father, and mentioning a family member in the newspaper, he did something that completely contradicts the party's ideology. Additionally, if he wanted to choose a specific person from among the men of the Syrian revolution, he should have chosen Sultan Pasha al-Atrash as the leader and symbol of this revolution."

AL-TALI'AH MAGAZINE

In 1935, the party launched a literary and political magazine in Beirut, which was called *al-Tali'ah* (*Vanguard*). Its top editors were 'Umar Fakhoury, Yusuf Yazbek, and Qadri Qalaji.

In 1937, after opening up to the Syrian national movement, the party moved the headquarters of *al-Tali'ah* magazine to Damascus, and assigned its editor-in-chief position to Raja Hourani. This magazine, although partisan in affiliation, was Arab in its sentiments, patriotic in its approach, and progressive in its goals. *al-Tali'ah* clearly contributed to Arab thought and the Arab literary movement in the 1930s. Its discussions were sober and powerful, its writers were from the elite of all Arab countries, and it is considered an important reference for followers of intellectual and literary activity in the period of struggle against French and English colonialism and Zionism before World War II.

In this magazine I published a series of research papers, including my undergraduate thesis, "Materialist Views on the Arab National Movement, from the Unionist Coup to the Era of the National Bloc," in the issues from November 1937 to April 1938.

Raja Hourani presented it with a preface in which he said, "In this article and in the following issues, Professor Najati Sidqi tries to study and present the historical developments of the Arab national movement from a materialist point of view. Perhaps in this study, he will shed new light on the movement that, as far as we know, has not been studied by any writer from this perspective. Undoubtedly, studying history materially is the most accurate and truest lesson in the history of any country or movement. *Al-Tali'ah* thanks Professor Sidqi for his efforts, and we hope that readers will benefit as intended from these lessons."

As for the other articles on which I published in *al-Tali'ah*, they are:

1) "Beethoven's Ninth Symphony with a Translation of Schiller's Cantata."
2) "Ibn Khaldun against Idealism."
3) "Abd al-Rahman ibn Khaldun and The Material Interpretation of History."
4) "Charles Robert Darwin: His Life and Theories, and the Opinions of His Opponents."
5) "René Descartes and Mechanical Materialism."
6) "Five Months in Republican Spain"—just one chapter.
7) "The Persecution of Science and Scholars During the Dissolution of the 'Abbasid Arab State."

This last topic had a sequel, but Khalid Bakdash asked Raja Hourani not to publish it, because the subject raised "historical sensitivities," even though the research was purely academic and historical. So I was forced to publish the sequel to this research in the weekly newspaper *al-Makshouf* (Uncovered), which was published in Beirut in 1938.

In fact, Khalid's instruction to stop publishing this research in *al-Tali'ah* was the beginning of the end of the magazine's life. It seemed to Khalid that this magazine had escaped from his grip, that he had lost control over it. It seemed to have become a "liberal Arabic" magazine, while he wanted it to be "strictly partisan" in the orbit of the French Popular Front, and immersed in the Stalinist debates against right-wing and left-wing deviations. Then, he decided to cease publication of *al-Tali'ah*, and later he replaced it with *al-Tariq* (The Road) magazine. He entrusted its editor-in-chief position to the architect Antoine Tabet.[25]

With Tabet's appointment, we saw the disappearance of the names of liberal, non-partisan Arab writers, and the emergence of writers whose topics were difficult for Arab readers to digest.

WORK IN BEIRUT

The permanent central committee of the party, consisting of Khalid Bakdash, Farajallah el-Helou, and Nicola al-Shawi, decided to transfer the bulk of the party activity to Beirut. To the committee, Beirut seemed more suitable for political action after the outbreak of unrest in Syria resulting from the

25 Sidqi's note: Antoine Tabet, who came from a prominent Maronite family in Beirut, joined the Lebanese Communist Party in the 1940s. Later, in the 1960s, he became ill and was sent for treatment to Moscow, where he passed away. The Soviet architects' union arranged for his body to be placed in the central building of the Syndicates' Union, as was usually done with prominent Soviets when they died. People came to pay their respects, both those who knew him and those who did not; then his body was flown to Beirut.

intransigent French position on ratifying the Franco-Syrian treaty. The party established its headquarters and the administration of *Sawt al-Sha'ab* in a building located in front of Beirut's Grand Teatro, at the end of al-Ma'rad Street. Today, the building is the Grand Hotel.

As for me, I rented a room from a comrade, an Armenian barber, on the corner of al-Ma'rad Street. I went regularly to the party office in the mornings and afternoons, contributed to editing a daily critical column in *Sawt al-Sha'ab*, and took part in some of the work of the Party's central committee. During this period, I became acquainted with Raif Khoury, newly returned from Palestine, where he was teaching Arabic literature at the Zion School in Jerusalem; 'Umar Fakhoury, director of real estate offices in Beirut; Qadri Qalaji; Yusuf Yazbek; and other writers who supported the party. We also often met in the offices of the weekly newspaper *al-Makshouf*, owned by Sheikh Fouad Hobeish, located on the first floor of the same building as the offices of the party and *Sawt al-Sha'ab*.

On May 1, 1938, the Central Committee held a meeting in Beirut and decided to send a telegram of gratitude to the Central Committee of the French Communist Party, including a warm greeting on the occasion of International Workers' Day, gratitude for the commendable efforts made by the party to ratify the Syrian and Lebanese treaties, and other expressions of fraternal unity between the two parties. The telegram bore the signatures of Khalid Bakdash, Farajallah el-Helou, Nicola al-Shawi, and "Sa'adi" (i.e., my signature) as well.

As soon as the comrades in Paris received this telegram and saw my signature, all hell broke loose. They hurriedly sent a letter to the comrades in Beirut, declaring their indignation at the party's cooperation with me, and asking them to suspend me, i.e., neither expulsion nor cooperation.

Bakdash and his colleagues succumbed to this French communist order and began to show hostility towards me. I faced financial troubles after I was fired from *Sawt al-Sha'ab*. I sought to earn a living by freelancing in the Lebanese press without clashing with the comrades.

One day I met the writer and novelist Tawfiq Yusuf 'Awwad, who at that time was the editor-in-chief of *an-Nahar* newspaper. I met him in Fish Square (today it is Riad Solh Square). He commended me on my long-term research into the Arab national movement and told me, "You have clarified in your research the real causes of the Arab issue, uncovered the material factors in this issue, and explained aspects that were previously vague and ambiguous." Then he said, "What are you doing these days?"

I said, "I'm looking for a job in journalism."

He said, "You are a materialist analyst, so why don't you become the economics editor of *an-Nahar* newspaper?"

And so it was. I joined the *an-Nahar* staff headed by its owner, Gebran Tueni, when its offices were above al-'Ajami Restaurant, at the entrance to Fakhry Bey Market. The staff included colleagues Tawfiq Youssef 'Awwad, editor-in-chief; Louis al-Hajj, managing editor; Kamel Mroué, foreign policy editor; Hanna Ghosn, domestic policy editor; and me, the editor of the weekly economics page. In addition to this editing job, I also edited *al-Jumhur* magazine for its owner, Michel Abi Shahla; its office was in the building of the Savoy Hotel in al-Burj Square.

After the outbreak of World War II, I joined the staff of the *al-Marahil al-Musawwara* magazine, which is affiliated with the French newspaper *L'Orient*, owned by Gabriel Khabbaz. This illustrated magazine was the first of its kind. Its staff's photos appeared in the first issue issued on January 22, 1940: Yusuf Yazbek, Dr. Nicolas Fayyad, 'Abdallah Saleh, 'Umar Fakhoury, Michel Trad, Qadri Qalaji, Fouad Haddad, Najati Sidqi, Fadel Saeed Akl, Muhammad al-Naqqash, and Robert Abella.

At this stage, I had to define my political position on current events without being bound by anyone else's opinion. The non-aggression pact concluded between Hitler and Stalin on August 21, 1939, seemed to me to be a spurious agreement, intended to buy time. I condemned it, while other comrades welcomed it as a decisive step towards a rapprochement between international communism and German National Socialism.

Then I started publishing articles in the *al-Marahil al-Musawwara* magazine on the topic of Islam and Nazism, with the intention of pitting the Muslim world against Nazism and fascism. I later collected these articles in a book entitled *Islamic Traditions and Nazi Principles: Are They Compatible? A Social, Political, and Religious Study* (Dar Al-Kashf, Beirut, 1940).

As soon as I finished publishing these articles, ʻAzmi al-Nashshashibi, the press attaché at the British Embassy in Beirut, contacted me and told me, "This research of yours serves the cause of the Allies and contributes to repelling the Nazis from Arab countries, in addition to defending democratic freedoms. What do you think about translating it into English and publishing it as a book?"

I said, "I don't mind, but who will translate it?"

He said, "I think the best person to translate it into English is Ameen Rihani."

I said, "There is no doubt that if Ameen Rihani agrees to translate the book, it would give the book special importance. However, commissioning the great Lebanese writer to translate the book would not be cheap."

He said, "We will take care of the translation and printing costs, with full rights to you."

I said, "Alright, then. I will discuss the matter with Ameen Rihani."

I took advantage of Rihani's visit to Michel Abi Shahla, in the office of *al-Jumhur* magazine. They had returned with a Lebanese press delegation from a visit to Spanish Morocco, at the invitation of General Franco. I showed him the Arabic version of my book, and on behalf of ʻAzmi al-Nashashshibi, I offered it to him for translation. He said, after examining the book in detail,

"This book is worthy of translation . . . but I cannot do it because I am tired from traveling, and my health requires me to rest."

After a little silence, he smiled and said, "What are you expecting from writing this book in Arabic and translating it into English?"

I said jokingly, "To get a medal!"

He said, laughing, "Yeah, you need medals? And don't forget that the Germans treat 'Heil Hitler' just like the Muslims do 'God is Great'!"

I learned later that the book was translated into English and printed in London. Its translation was directed by Sir Hassan Suhrawardy, India's delegate to the British royal court. I received one copy of the English edition. As for the Arabic edition, it is kept in the American University Library in Beirut filed under "Sidqi, Najati."

I will mention on this occasion that after the publication of this book I received a card from the French High Commissioner, Monsieur Gabriel Puaux: "To Mr. Najati Sidqi. With thanks and congratulations for his book, which gives the soul happiness and hope. Beirut, June 15, 1940."

I also received a note from the British consul-general in Beirut, stating, "Mr. G. Havard thanks Mr. Najati Sidqi for the gift of a copy of his book with its committed dedicatory text! Beirut, May 5, 1940."

On July 7, 1940, *The Orient* newspaper published an article about the book, its value in relation to its topic, and the method of its scientific and objective treatment.

My position on Nazism angered the comrades in Lebanon. They considered my reliance on Islamic texts in confronting Nazism to contradict the Party's policy, so they decided to expel me from their ranks. They announced this decision in a secret gelatin-printed party newspaper.

The policy that the Party followed during World War II was the beginning of a tragedy for it, its members, and its leaders, as the Mandate authorities considered them enemies of the Allies and global democracy. The authorities suspended all operations of the party's newspaper, *Sawt al-Sha'ab*, chased down the people responsible for it, and forced them to disappear; those of them who were arrested were imprisoned in the Miye ou Miye detention center in Sidon. They did not realize the great mistake they had made until it was too late—that is, after Nazi forces swept across the Soviet border in 1941. At that point they declared their readiness to join the French army in defense of freedom and democracy.

I have hidden this phase of my political life for almost thirty-seven years, and I omitted it from the study about me that the late Ya'qoub al-Oudat (also known by his pen name, al-Badawi al-Mulaththam, the Veiled Bedouin) published in *al-Adib* magazine on May 1, 1968.

As for the second phase of my intellectual life, it has consisted of literature and writing: translation, broadcast journalism, and writing radio programs, plays, and short stories. Some of this work has been published in thirteen books kept in the American University Library in Beirut.

Beirut, January 1, 1976

THE TIMELINE

GLOBAL EVENTS

JULY 1908
The Committee of Union and Progress stages a coup in the Ottoman Empire and gains power.

AUGUST 1914
World War I breaks out.

JUNE 1916
The Arab Revolt begins in the Hijaz.

FEBRUARY 1917
The Tsarist regime in Russia falls; a transitional government takes power.

SEPTEMBER 1917
The transitional government in Russia falls to a Bolshevik coup.

THE SIDQI FAMILY

MAY 15, 1905
Najati Sidqi is born in Jerusalem, in Ottoman-ruled Palestine. He has an older brother Ahmad (1903–1965). They eventually have a younger sister, Fikriyya (1919–1979).

NOVEMBER 2, 1917
The British government issues the Balfour Declaration, stating that Britain would "view with favor" the establishment of a Jewish homeland in Palestine.

OCTOBER 30, 1918
The Ottoman Empire agrees to the Armistice of Mudros with Great Britain.

1919
Najati accompanies his father to the Hashemite war against the Ibn Sa'ud dynasty in the Hijaz.

MARCH 8, 1920–JULY 25, 1920
The Arab Kingdom of Syria ruled by the Hashemite king Faisal bin Hussein declares independence but is quickly crushed by French forces imposing the Mandate in Syria.

1921
The Communist University of the Toilers of the East (KUTV) is established in Moscow. It remains open until 1935.

MAY 1, 1921
The Jaffa Riots break out: a clash between socialist and communist groups within the Jewish immigrant community in Jaffa escalates into broader intercommunal violence.

JULY 1921
The Profintern (Red International of Trade Unions) is established in Moscow as a Communist counterweight to the social-democratic Amsterdam-based International Federation of Trade Unions. The Profintern lasts until 1937.

APRIL 3, 1922
Iosif Dzhugashvili Stalin becomes General Secretary of the USSR.

1923
The leftist opposition within Poalei Zion applies to join the Comintern, is accepted, and takes on the name "the Communist Party of Palestine."

SEPTEMBER 1923
Bulgarian communists attempt to stage a revolution and fail; some flee to the USSR. Sidqi will meet some of them in Odessa.

1923
Najati works in the Jerusalem post office, where he comes into contact with communist activists.

LATE 1924
Najati is offered a scholarship to Moscow, inducted into the Communist Party of Palestine, and elected to the Youth Central Committee.

16 SEPTEMBER 1925
Najati leaves for Moscow.

FROM 1925 TO 1929 *he studies at KUTV under the pseudonym "Mustafa Sa'adi," soon joined by his older brother Ahmad ("Saul" or "Shaul").*

FEBRUARY 1929
Leon Trotsky is exiled from the USSR.

FEBRUARY 1929
Najati hands in his thesis on the evolution of the Arab nationalist movement. Afterwards, he returns to Palestine and joins the Palestinian Communist Party's Central Committee.

1929
Najati begins a relationship with fellow PCP member Lotka Lorberbaum, an immigrant from Poland also born in 1905. They marry in late 1929.

AUGUST 23–29, 1929
The 1929 Palestine Riots (known as "the Hebron Massacre" or "the Events of 1929" in Israeli memory, and "the Buraq Uprising" in Palestinian memory) kill 133 Jews and at least 116 Arabs.

OCTOBER 1929
The Great Depression begins, intensifying economic, social, and political tensions around the world.

NOVEMBER 7, 1929
Stalin announces the end of the New Economic Policy, marking a sharp turn back towards state control of the Soviet economy.

DECEMBER 27, 1929
Stalin announces a policy of "liquidating the kulaks as a class," beginning a campaign of deportation, starvation, and state violence.

MARCH 17, 1930
Najat and Lotka's eldest child, a daughter named Dawlieh (later called Dawlat or Dulia) is born at Rothschild Hospital in Jerusalem, Palestine.

1930
Najati and another Party member are sent to the Profintern conference in Leningrad. They travel via Marseilles, Paris, and Berlin. After his return, Najati is appointed to the PCP Central Committee.

FEBRUARY 2, 1931
Najati is caught and detained without charges.

MAY 28, 1931
He is finally put on trial. His brother Ahmad testifies against him. Convicted of belonging to the PCP, he is imprisoned by the British until 1932, first in Jerusalem Central Prison, then in the Citadel of Acre.

OCTOBER 5, 1931
Lotka Lorberbaum Sidqi is arrested in a police raid. Her trial later that year receives sensational coverage in Palestine's Hebrew press. While both parents are in prison, their daughter Dawlieh is sent to a children's home in the Soviet Union.

LATE 1932
Najati is released from prison.

JANUARY 30, 1933
Hitler becomes Chancellor of Germany.

MAY 1, 1933
Najati is placed in administrative detention in the Citadel of Jerusalem for one week. Afterwards, a judge orders that he be subjected to surveillance for one year.

SEPTEMBER 1933
Najati moves to Paris, where he begins publishing a clandestine monthly communist newspaper, The Arab East*.*

OCTOBER 13–29 1933
The 1933 Palestine riots (in Hebrew "the Events of 1933") begin with the British police's violent repression of a Palestinian protest in Jaffa and continue for two weeks, with clashes between Palestinian protesters and British police. In total, 26 Arabs and one policeman are killed.

APRIL 19, 1936
The Arab Revolt in Palestine begins with a general strike of Arab workers. The revolt continues for three years, resulting in the deaths of about 5,000 Arabs, about 500 Jews, and 262 British soldiers.

EARLY SUMMER 1936
Najati's paper The Arab East *is banned by a special decree of the French government.*

JULY 17, 1936
The Spanish Civil War begins with the revolt of the Spanish army in Morocco under General Francisco Franco.

AUGUST 19, 1936
Stalin's Great Purge begins. In the next two years, the Purge will claim at least 600,000 victims.

JUNE 1936
Lotka, using a Comintern-provided fake passport, travels across Nazi Germany to the USSR. She lives in Moscow's Lux Hotel with Dawlieh, seeking to either obtain Soviet citizenship or leave the USSR with the child; both requests are denied. She finally leaves alone in February 1939.

SUMMER 1936
Najati is called to Moscow. He travels there by train across Nazi Germany. From Moscow, he goes with Syrian communist Khaled Bakdash to Tashkent to view Soviet efforts to "resolve the nationalities problem" within the USSR's borders. There, he meets Uzbekistan Communist Party officials Fayzulla Xo'jayev and Akmal Ikramov.

When he returns from Tashkent, he is dispatched to the Spanish Civil War.

AUGUST–DECEMBER, 1936
Najati travels through Paris to Republican Spain. He visits the front, writes pamphlets directed to the Moroccan soldiers fighting for Franco, and interviews captured Moroccan troops.

LATE DECEMBER 1936
Najati is sent to Algeria to establish a radio station intended to broadcast into Spanish-held Morocco; this effort fails.

1936–1937
Najati spends time in France, in mounting debt, as he waits for new instructions from the Comintern.

1937
The Comintern sends Najati to Syria to work with Khaled Bakdash, a partnership fraught with tensions.

MARCH 1938
The "Trial of the Twenty-One," a show trial intended to eliminate the Right opposition within the USSR, takes place. Opposition leaders Nikolai Bukharin and Alexei Rykov are executed, as are Uzbek politicians Fayzulla Xo'jayev and Akmal Ikramov, with whom Najati Sidqi had joked and drunk vodka in Tashkent.

NOVEMBER 17, 1938
Stalin turns against the main perpetrators of the Great Purge, Genrikh Yagoda and Nikolai Yezhov. Both are executed for their supposedly unauthorized excesses. The Purge ends.

FEBRUARY 1939
Lotka drops off Dawlieh at the Interdom children's home in Ivanovo, Russia, before traveling back to the Middle East. Najati and Lotka reunite in Jaffa later that year.

APRIL 1, 1939
The Spanish Civil War ends in a Nationalist victory.

AUGUST 21, 1939
The Soviet Union and Nazi Germany sign a non-aggression pact.

AUGUST 21, 1939
Najati bitterly criticizes the Soviet-Nazi non-aggression pact in a series of articles later published as a book, Islamic Traditions and Nazi Principles: Are They Compatible? *(1940). This criticism leads to his expulsion from the Communist Party.*

AUGUST 26, 1939
The Arab Revolt in Palestine ends, accompanied by the British White Paper of 1939 promising some limits to Jewish immigration to Palestine.

SEPTEMBER 1, 1939
World War II begins with the Nazi invasion of Poland.

AUGUST 20, 1940
A Soviet secret police agent assassinates Leon Trotsky, in exile in Mexico.

1940
Najati returns to Jerusalem and begins working for Britain's Near East Broadcasting Station there. He remains in Palestine until shortly before the Nakba of 1948.

JANUARY 23, 1941
Said Sidki, Najati and Lotka's son, is born in Palestine.

MAY 15, 1945
Hind Sidki, Najati and Lotka's daughter, is born in Palestine.

SEPTEMBER 2, 1945
World War II ends with Japan's surrender.

Najati focuses on Russian literature, publishing short Arabic books introducing and translating Pushkin (1945) and Chekhov (1947).

1946
The Red Cross reconnects Najati and Lotka with Dawlieh. They correspond actively, but their attempts to reunite do not succeed.

SEPTEMBER 3, 1947
The UN issues a Partition Plan for Palestine.

NOVEMBER 30, 1947–MAY 14, 1948
The 1947-1948 civil war in Mandatory Palestine breaks out. During the civil war and the subsequent Arab-Israeli War, Zionist militias expel approximately 750,000 Palestinians, a mass displacement known in Arabic as the Nakba, or Catastrophe.

MAY 14, 1948
The State of Israel declares independence. The 1948 Arab-Israeli War begins; the Nakba continues.

EARLY MAY 1948
Near East Broadcasting moves to Cyprus. The Sidqi family moves with it, living in Limassol until 1950. Najati and Lotka never return to Palestine.

Displaced from Jerusalem by the Nakba, Najati's brother Ahmad and sister Fikriyya stay in Palestine and live in Ramallah for the rest of their lives.

1950
Najati moves to Beirut and works in journalism and literature until 1976. The family lives as refugees with support from the United Nations Relief and Works Agency for Palestine Refugees in the Near East (UNRWA).

1958
The 1958 Lebanon Crisis breaks out.

APRIL 13, 1975
The Lebanese Civil War begins.

1956
Dawlieh, now called Dawlat in Arabic and Dulia in Russian, is allowed to visit her family in Beirut for the first time. She decides not to stay.

1963
Said Sidki moves to the United States to study mathematics.

APRIL 1976
Fleeing the Lebanese Civil War, Hind and her family move with Najati and Lotka to Athens, Greece. Najati carries the just-completed manuscript of this memoir.

NOVEMBER 17, 1979
Najati Sidqi dies in Athens, Greece, at the age of 74.

SUGGESTIONS FOR FURTHER READING

Najati Sidqi is a generous memoirist; writing in an age before the Internet, he offers his reader capsule histories, biographical portraits, and analyses of many key players and events. For those who want more context and detail to understand the memoir, or who need a jumping-off point for further research, here is a non-exhaustive list of places to start. We begin by offering general background on Sidqi's story and then proceed chapter by chapter.

GENERAL BACKGROUND ON SIDQI

The publication of Najati Sidqi's memoir in Arabic, edited and introduced by Palestinian poet Hanna Abu Hanna in Beirut (Institute for Palestine Studies, 2001), provoked a wave of scholarly interest in Sidqi. For overall background on Sidqi, see Salim Tamari's "The Enigmatic Jerusalem Bolshevik," a review essay published with some translation excerpts in the *Journal of Palestine Studies* (32:2, pp. 79-94) in 2003, and revised for Tamari's book *Mountain against the Sea: Essays on Palestinian Society and Culture* (University of California Press, 2009). We have consulted those excerpts, translated by Joseph Massad, in preparing our own translation.

An accessible introduction to the Palestinian Communist Party is Joel Beinin's essay "A Century after Its Founding, the Israeli Communist Party Is at a Crossroads" (*+972 Magazine*, July 28, 2023). For academic sources, see

Musa Budeiri, *The Palestine Communist Party 1919-1948: Arab and Jew in the Struggle for Internationalism* (Haymarket Books, 2010); and Zachary Lockman, *Comrades and Enemies: Arab and Jewish Workers in Palestine, 1906-1948* (University of California Press, 1996). For Budeiri's 1970s interview with Sidqi, see Musa Budeiri, "Interview: Najati Sidqi and the Arabisation of Palestinian Communism," *Birzeit Research Review,* no. 2 (Winter 1985/86). Budeiri has also published a collection of essays and sources in Arabic: *Shuyūʿīyūn fī Filasṭīn: shaẓāyā tārīkh mansī* [Communists in Palestine: Fragments of a Forgotten History] (Muwāṭin, 2013). On Communist organizing in Syria and Lebanon, see Tareq Y. Ismael and Jacqueline S. Ismael, *The Communist Movement in Syria and Lebanon* (University Press of Florida, 1998). For other sources, see Budeiri's annotated reading list: "Essential Readings on the Left in Mandate Palestine (by Musa Budeiri)," *Jadaliyya, https://www.jadaliyya.com/Details/41513.*

Irritated by the propaganda term "Islamofascism" and the discourse around the infamous photo of Grand Mufti of Jerusalam Hajj Amin Al-Husseini sitting with Adolf Hitler in 1941, many scholars have seized on Najati Sidqi as a beacon of Arab anti-Nazism. See Mustafa Kabha, "A Bold Voice Raised Above the Raging Waves: Palestinian Intellectual Najati Sidqi and His Battle with Nazi Doctrine at the Time of World War II," in *The Holocaust and the Nakba: A New Grammar of Trauma and History*, ed. Bashir Bashir and Amos Goldberg (Columbia University Press, 2018), 154–72; and Israel Gershoni, "Why the Muslims Must Fight against Nazi Germany: Muḥammad Najātī Ṣidqī's Plea," *Die Welt Des Islams* 52, no. 3/4 (2012): 471–98. See also John Broich, "Did the Muslim World Really Fall for Hitler?," *Slate*, March 13, 2017. In French, Gilbert Achcar discusses Najati Sidqi's antifascism in his book *Les Arabes et la Shoah: La guerre israélo-arabe dans les récits* (Actes Sud, 2009).

After Sidqi left the Communist Party in 1940, he earned a living as a journalist, short story writer, and literary translator. A useful Arabic study of his literary work is Ibrahim Abu Hashhash, *Najātī Ṣidqī: ḥayātuhu wa-adabuhu, 1905-1979* [The Life and Literature of Najati Sidqi] (Palestinian Academic Society for the Study of International Affairs, 1990). A more recent study is Mona As'ad, *Najati Sidqi: Al-adīb wa-al-mufakkir al-siyāsi* [Najati Sidqi, Litterateur and Political Thinker] (Palestinian Center for Research and Strategic Studies, 2008).

Finally, the heartfelt experimental documentary *You Come from Far Away* (2018), directed by Egyptian filmmaker Amal Ramsis, foregrounds the Sidqi family and includes extensive interviews with Sidqi's eldest daughter Dawlieh/Dulia/Dawlat Saadi (1930-2018) in Moscow; it has won awards at festivals but has not been publicly distributed.

1. IN JERUSALEM

Sidqi paints a colorful picture of diverse Jewish migrants in pre-1948 Palestine, a population known as the *yishuv*, or "settlement." The Zionist migration to Palestine in the early interwar period encountered several previous waves of migrants as well as a significant pre-Zionist Jewish population, called "the Old Yishuv." While the Old Yishuv is often understood as a more monolithic group contrasted with the newer arrivals, recent work points to a diverse community. See Yair Wallach, "Rethinking the *Yishuv*: Late-Ottoman Palestine's Jewish Communities Revisited" (*Journal of Modern Jewish Studies*, 16, no. 2, 2017). On linguistic diversity among Jewish immigrants, see Liora R. Halperin, *Babel in Zion* (Yale University Press, 2015). Sidqi describes the Ashkenazi Jews as having come from Austria (*al-Namsa*); we have silently corrected this to Germany.

By 1948 the dominant strand of the Zionist movement was Labor Zionism, which mixed socialist attention to working-class interests with Zionism. On the differing Zionist socialist approaches to the Palestinian Arabs, see Yosef Gorni, "Zionist Socialism and the Arab Question, 1918-1930," in *Middle Eastern Studies*, 13:1 (Jan. 1977).

On what Sidqi terms the Jaffa Uprising of 1921 (now best known as the Jaffa Riots), among other issues in this early period, see Jeffrey Auerbach, "Before the Mandate: British Rule in Palestine, 1920-1922" (*Israel Studies* 26:3, Fall 2021). There was also an official British investigation of the events, the Haycraft Commission.

2. ON THE ROAD TO MOSCOW

Starting in this chapter, and at many subsequent points in Sidqi's journeys, he struggles with the complex process of evading border police. The irritation of this process was not an accident: fear of Communist infiltration was central to the maintenance of the border regime. See Burak Sayım, "The Communist International, Forged Passports and the Interwar Border Regimes in the Middle East" (*History Workshop Journal* 98, Autumn 2024).

3. THE STALINIST KUTV UNIVERSITY

Our translation splits up Sidqi's long third chapter, dividing his description of the Communist University of the Toilers of the East (KUTV) from his memories of mingling with Russian and Soviet people outside the university. Here are some specific notes on his memories of Moscow as well as general background.

KUTV, active from 1921 to 1938, was both a wellspring of anticolonial internationalism and a tool of Soviet public diplomacy in what was later called the Global South. It was officially closed in 1938, as Stalin's purges decimated its student body and faculty. The purge seriously weakened Soviet links to third–world anti-colonial movements, and these connections would only re-form at their former scale after Stalin's death; by this time the Soviet Union had lost its centrality to anti-colonial activism. A snapshot of this vanished lifeworld is Brigitte Studer, *The Transnational World of the Cominternians* (Palgrave Macmillan, 2015). However, it focuses mainly on Europeans, making no mention of Arab Cominternians.

KUTV's "Arab" section at first comprised mainly Jewish students from Palestine. For an analysis of its development and profiles of many of Sidqi's classmates, see Masha Kirasirova, *The Eastern International: Arabs, Central Asians, and Jews in the Soviet Union's Anticolonial Empire,* especially chapters 2 and 3 (Oxford University Press, 2024); and Kirasirova's essay "The 'East' as a Category of Bolshevik Ideology and Comintern Administration: The Arab Section of the Communist University of the Toilers of the East," *Kritika: Explorations in Russian and Eurasian History* 18:1 (2017), pages 7–34. On the Egyptian comrades, see also Rami Ginat, *A History of Egyptian Communism: Jews and Their Compatriots in Quest of Revolution* (Lynne Rienner, 2011). Sidqi's acquaintance Nazim Hikmet, later a leading Turkish poet, wrote his own memoiristic novel featuring his time at KUTV: *Life's Good, Brother* (Persea Books, 2013). The emotional history of KUTV is beautifully explored in Elizabeth McGuire, *Red at Heart: How Chinese Communists Fell in Love with the Russian Revolution* (Oxford University Press, 2018).

In criticizing his comrade's article for the wall newspaper, Sidqi thoughtlessly employs the term *galiata*, from Egyptian Arabic. Masha Kirasirova explains (in "The 'East' as a Category"): "The word *galiata* is usually used to describe tactless or tasteless behavior, usually not writing, so [this] does seem like a misuse of the term. The root of the word also originally meant the fatty residue of fermented milk, making it one of many idiomatic expressions that compare people's personalities to heavy, rotting things."

Sidqi's brief account of his meeting with the pampered aesthete Vijaya Lakshmi Pandit, whom he tersely describes as "Jawaharlal Nehru's sister," belies her historical significance: she later became the first female president of the UN General Assembly and was India's most important diplomat in the immediate post-Independence period. See her memoir, *The Scope of Happiness: A Personal Memoir* (Speaking Tiger, 2018).

The street children's song Sidqi quotes was well known at the time. We have translated the version he remembered. A more common version goes:

So I'll die, I'll die
They will bury me.
And no one will know
Where my grave is.
And no one will know
Where my grave is.

To my grave
No one will come, you know
Only in early spring
The nightingale will sing.
Only in early spring
The nightingale will sing.

The badboy Russian poet Sergei Yesenin (1895-1925) died in a Leningrad hotel room, not a rural bog. On his tumultuous life and his relationship with Isadora Duncan, see Gordon McVay, *Esenin: A Life* (Paragon House, 1988), and the recent graphic novel by Julie Birmant and Clément Oubrerie, *Isadora*, trans. Edward Gauvin (SelfMadeHero Books, 2024). Sidqi quotes from Yesenin's 1922 poem "Yes! Now It Is Decided." Yesenin's poetry was banned for many years after his suicide. Some copycat suicides followed Yesenin's death, leading Soviet authorities to fear a wave of "Eseninism." See Dimitrii K. Ravinskii, "'Dangerous Reading' in the Soviet Era," in *Libraries and Culture* 33:1, Winter 1998.

On Syrian-born lexicographer Mikhail 'Attaya (1852-1924) and early Soviet Orientalism, see Svetlana Kirillina, "Arab Scholars in Russian Universities (19th-Early 20th Century)," *Al-Jami'ah: Journal of Islamic Studies* 44:1 (2006): 1–21. 'Attaya compiled an important Russian-Arabic dictionary in 1913, a fact Sidqi notes on page 44 of the Arabic text, where the Arabic translation of the Internationale also appears.

4. MINGLING WITH THE RUSSIANS

The Arab KUTV students who expected Soviet Russia to be a land of sexual freedom came too late: already, as Sidqi describes, the spirit of "sexual anarchy" inspired by thinkers such as Alexandra Kollontai was fading, or rather being smothered by an increasingly prudish Stalinist cultural politics. However, gaps did exist in Party control. Gregory Carleton surveys the writing and culture of the time and finds a more complex picture than either Stalinist prudishness or revolutionary hedonism: see *Sexual Revolution in Bolshevik Russia* (University of Pittsburgh Press, 2005).

In general, Soviet life in the late 1920s and 1930s was marked by an odd mix of revolutionary ideas and mundane cares. As an international student Sidqi was lucky, with access to housing and basic resources. For many Soviet urban citizens, the norm was cramped apartments and hustling for resources through personal connections and misuse of official positions—even as citizens were aware of themselves as existing in a revolutionary period and acted accordingly. For a classic social history of the urban Soviet Union during the early Stalinist period, see Sheila Fitzpatrick, *Everyday Stalinism* (Oxford University Press, 1999). A different approach, emphasizing the period's real modernization and focusing on the steel center of Magnitogorsk, is Stephen Kotkin, *Magnetic Mountain: Stalinism as a Civilization* (University of California Press, 1995).

Sidqi's experience in Russia indicated that, at least in the early Stalinist period, the removal of religion from the public sphere was not much more than skin-deep—or in the case of one priest Sidqi met, no deeper than a winter coat. On Soviet religious policies, see Victoria Smolkin, *A Sacred Space Is Never Empty* (Princeton University Press, 2018), and Sabrina Petra Ramet's earlier edited volume *Religious Policy in the Soviet Union* (Cambridge University Press, 2004).

In the section introducing Sidqi's visit to the Crimean Peninsula, Sidqi gives the official Soviet line regarding the dissolution of the region's autonomy and, though he does not mention it, the mass deportation of the Crimean

Tatars. For scholarly accounts, see Greta Lynn Uehling, *Beyond Memory: The Crimean Tatars' Deportation and Return* (Palgrave MacMillan, 2004), and Brian Williams, *The Crimean Tatars: The Diaspora Experience and the Forging of a Nation* (Brill, 2021).

5. RETURNING TO THE HOMELAND

Sidqi's extensive list of Palestinian Communist leaders from the 1920s attests to the party's diversity. Mahmoud al-Atrash al-Mughrabi, a Palestinian Arab who joined the party with Sidqi and was imprisoned alongside him, wrote a memoir, *Ṭarīq al-kifāḥ fī Filasṭīn wa-al-Mashriq al-'Arabī: mudhakkirāt al-qā'id al-shuyū'ī Maḥmūd al-Aṭrash al-Mughrabī* [The Path of Struggle in Palestine and the Arab East: The Memoirs of Communist Leader Mahmud al-Atrash al-Mughrabi] (Institute for Palestine Studies, 2015). Joseph Berger, Sidqi's Jewish colleague in the PCP, wrote a memoir about his experience in Stalin's gulag (*Shipwreck of a Generation*, Harvill, 1971). Further information is available in Musa Budeiri's extensive work on the party, including his *The Palestine Communist Party: Arab and Jew in the Struggle for Internationalism*, cited above. For Budeiri's Arabic-language interviews with early Palestinian Communists including Sidqi, see Musa Budeiri, *Shuyū'iyūn fī Filasṭīn: shaẓāyā tārīkh mansī* [Communists in Palestine: Fragments of A Forgotten History] (Muwatin, 2013).

Sidqi's exposure to Soviet popular culture seems to have continued significantly after his time at KUTV. The film about homeless children that Sidqi summarizes in Chapter 3 appears to be *Putyovka v Zhizn'* (Road to Life), a 1931 Soviet film directed by Nikolai Ekk. The first film with sound made in the Soviet Union, it won an award at the 1932 Venice International Film Festival. However, Sidqi could not have seen it while at KUTV in 1924-29. Later, in Chapter 4, he quotes a joke featuring President Herbert Hoover, who would serve as U.S. President from 1929 to 1933, and Neville Chamberlain, who would become Britain's Prime Minister only in 1937. This suggests either that Sidqi changed the names or that he remained in touch with Soviet cultural touchstones—including edgy political jokes—through contacts in Paris or elsewhere. It is possible that he saw *Road to Life* during his visit to the Profintern Conference, when it would have been recently released (see next chapter).

6. THE PROFINTERN CONFERENCE

On the Profintern, or Red International of Labor Unions, see Reiner Tosstorff, *The Red International of Labour Unions* (trans. Ben Fowkes; Brill, 2016). Regarding the main issues facing the labor movement in Palestine, see Zachary Lockman, *Comrades and Enemies*, cited above.

Sidqi's several passages through Germany give us snapshots of the steadily decaying political situation in the Weimar Republic. For a detailed history of the Weimar Republic, see Frank McDonough, *The Weimar Years: Rise and Fall 1918-1933* (Apollo, 2024). Street fighting in the period is explored in Dirk Schumann's *Political Violence in the Weimar Republic, 1918-1933* (Berghahn Books, 2009).

7. THE PARTY'S MAIN ISSUES

The intercommunal violence of 1929 not only tore through Palestine but divided the global left. Sidqi, following the Communist Party's line and probably his own viewpoint, describes the events as an uprising or revolution (*thawra*). Other Arabic sources call it the Buraq Uprising, because the initial spark of violence was a conflict over access to the Western Wall site, known to Muslims as the Buraq Wall. Israeli official historiography refers to these events as simply "the events" (*me'oraot*), and the British called them the "Western Wall Riots." For a detailed history based on both Hebrew and Arabic sources, see Hillel Cohen, *Year Zero of the Arab-Israeli Conflict 1929* (University of Chicago Press, 2015). For an argument that the riots sharpened communal boundaries in Palestine, to which Sidqi's own experience also attests, see Alex Winder, "The 'Western Wall' Riots of 1929: Religious Boundaries and

Communal Violence," in *Journal of Palestine Studies*, 42:1 (Autumn 2012). The official British report of the violence was produced by the Shaw Commission of 1930 (Report of the Commission on the Palestine Disturbances of August, 1929) and stressed the role of growing Jewish immigration combined with the Zionist movement's massive land purchases undertaken. On the rural land crisis of this period, see Charles Anderson, "The British Mandate and the Crisis of Palestinian Landlessness, 1929-1936" (*Middle Eastern Studies* 54:2, 2018).

In Haifa, Sidqi worked with 'Izz al-Din al-Qassam, who became among the best-known early Palestinian insurgents. Among the many works on this figure, see Mark Sanagan, "Teacher, Preacher, Soldier, Martyr: Rethinking 'Izz al-Dīn al-Qassām" (*Die Welt des Islams* 53:3-4, 2013), which summarizes existing historiography and presents a new interpretation of al-Qassam's identity and aims.

8. ON THE WAY TO PRISON

Najati Sidqi's experience in British prison was by no means unique. Imprisonment was the primary tool the British wielded in controlling rebellion in Palestine, and some British policing tactics were later adopted by the Israeli state, such as the use of administrative detention (especially in the Occupied Territories). Emergency ordinances issued during the Mandate remain in force to this day. On British policing policy in Mandatory Palestine, see John Knight, "Securing Zion? Policing in British Palestine, 1917-1939" (*European Review of History* 18:4, 2011). See also Matthew Hughes, "A British 'Foreign Legion'? The British Police in Mandate Palestine" (*Middle Eastern Studies* 49:5, 2013). Hughes describes the romantic self-image of the British force in Palestine, in contrast to the brutal tactics it employed.

Regarding highwayman-turned-folk hero Abu Jilda, see Alex Winder, "Abu Jilda, Anti-Imperial Antihero" in *The Routledge Handbook of the Middle East Mandates* (Routledge, 2015). Sidqi's account of getting acquainted with Abu

Jilda's story in prison in 1930-1931 is implausible, since Abu Jilda's activities began in 1933 and ended with his execution in 1934.

9. THE PARIS YEARS

For much of the second half of his revolutionary career, Sidqi's home base was Paris. Paris was not only an imperial metropole but a well-known center for anti-imperial activism. See Michael Goebel, *Anti-Imperial Metropolis: Interwar Paris and the Seeds of Third World Nationalism* (Cambridge University Press, 2015). This book also discusses Sidqi's friend and colleague Léo Wanner.

The newspaper Sidqi published from Paris, *The Arab East*, bore the address 170 rue de Crimée, not Ghabta Street; we have not been able to locate a Ghabta Street; it may be a typo.

10. RETURNING TO MOSCOW

The Soviet Union, as in Sidqi's account, used its "enlightened" policies towards internal non-Russian minorities as a model for its anti-colonial empire. The umbrella term for this is Soviet "nationalities policy," and these policies had a long-term effect on the courses of ethnic formation and ethnic conflict in the post-Soviet space. For a classic account of the Soviet approach to its many nationalities, see Terry Martin, *The Affirmative Action Empire: Nations and Nationalism in the Soviet Union, 1923-1939* (Cornell University Press, 2001); see also Ronald Suny and Terry Martin's edited volume *State of Nations: Empire and Nation-Making in the Age of Lenin and Stalin* (Oxford University Press, 2001) and Masha Kirasirova's recent work on the Soviet Union's "internal East," *The Eastern International*, cited above. Ongoing work by historian Roy Bar Sadeh explores how Soviet nationalities policy ramified into (and was somewhat shaped by) developments in South Asia and the Middle East.

The Jadidi Party in Central Asia during the Russian Civil War did not call itself Basmachi, which means "bandit"; this derogatory term was applied to them by the Soviet (and before them, Tsarist) forces which suppressed them.

On Jadidism, see Adeeb Khalid, *The Politics of Muslim Cultural Reform: Jadidism in Central Asia* (University of California Press, 1999). For the formation of Uzbekistan and Uzbek identity in the early Soviet period, see Adeeb Khalid, *Making Uzbekistan: Nation, Empire, and Revolution in the Early USSR* (Cornell University Press, 2019). For the Soviet approach to Islam in Central Asia, see Eren Tasar, *Soviet and Muslim* (Oxford University Press, 2017).

In this section, Sidqi also describes the Stalinist purges, which many historians have studied. For descriptions of the effect of these purges on international activists in the Soviet Union in particular, see William J. Chase, *Enemies within the Gates?: The Comintern and the Stalinist Repression* (Yale University Press, 2001).

11. THE SPANISH CIVIL WAR

Moroccan conscripts' participation on the Rebel side in the Spanish Civil War has become notorious and deeply embedded in the popular memory of the war: the famous Republican song "No Pasaran" begins by referencing "los Moros que trajó Franco"—the Moors Franco brought over—announcing that as long as one militiaman lives, "the Moors will not pass." For an account of Moroccan involvement in the Spanish civil war, see Ali Al Tuma, *Guns, Culture, and Moors: Racial Perceptions, Cultural Impact and the Moroccan Participation in the Spanish Civil War (1936-1939)* (Routledge, 2018).

But there were Arabs on both sides, as Sidqi's story attests. A new Spanish account of anti-Fascist Moroccan fighters is *Moros contra Franco: El Antifascismo y la Guerra Civil Española en el Mundo Arabe* [Moors against Franco: Antifascism and the Spanish Civil War in the Arab World] by Marc Almodóvar and Andreu Rosés (Verso Libros, 2025). For a Palestinian historical novel about 'Ali 'Abd al-Khaliq (*alias* Ibrahimov), Sidqi's fellow Communist who served in the International Brigades, see Husayn Yasin, *'Alī, qiṣṣat rajul mustaqīm* (Al-Ru'ah, 2017).

For a more general account of the Republican experience of the war, see Helen Graham, *The Spanish Republic at War, 1936-1939* (Cambridge University Press, 2002). Death tolls and accounts of atrocities perpetrated during the civil war are hugely contested. For example, Sidqi, in his account of the Badajoz Massacre, cites a number of 1,500 dead. This is in the approximate center of modern estimates, which range from 500 to 4,000, though most estimates are on the higher end. See Paul Preston, *The Spanish Civil War: Reaction, Revolutions & Revenge* (Harper Perennial, 2006). Because the Nationalists won the civil war, no investigation was conducted into the massacre. A still bigger-picture analysis is Nir Arielli, *From Byron to Bin Laden: A History of Foreign War Volunteers* (Harvard University Press, 2018).

Sidqi's wartime service has fascinated Spanish-language scholars. Nieves Paradela analyzes his memoir in the last chapter of her book *El otro laberinto español: viajeros árabes a España entre el s. XVII y 1936* [The Other Spanish Labyrinth: Arab Travelers to Spain from the 17th Century to 1936], (Ediciones de la Universidad Autónoma de Madrid, 1993). Later she translates his Spanish Civil War chapter into Spanish: see "Recuerdos de Un Comunista Palestino en La Guerra de España" [Recollections of a Palestinian Communist in the Spanish War], *Nación Árabe* 18:51 (2004), 137–52; in the same magazine, see Salvador Bofarull's essay, "Brigadistas Árabes en la Guerra de España: Combatientes por la República" [Arab Brigade Members in the Spanish War: Combatants for the Republic], *Nación Árabe* 18:52 (2004), 121–34. Fascinating photos from the period, including the one that later got Sidqi in trouble, appear in Moroccan historian Abdelatif Ben Salem's chapter "Nayati Sidqi, un internacional palestino en el Madrid de la Guerra" [Najati Sidqi: A Palestinian International in Wartime Madrid] in *De Maŷrit a Madrid: Madrid y los árabes, del siglo IX al siglo XXI* [Madrid and the Arabs from the 9th Century to the 21st], edited by Daniel Gil-Benumeya (Casa Árabe/Lunwerg 2011).

Sidqi's own Spanish-language publications during the war were collected in *Mundo Obrero*, the still-active newspaper of the Spanish Communist Party, while Sidqi's experiences were published in Arabic under Khalid Bakdash's name in *al-'Arab wa-al-ḥarb al-ahlīya fī Isbāniyā* [The Arabs and the Civil War in Spain] (Damascus, 1937).

12. THE ALGERIAN PROJECT

On the role of radio in the complex soundscape of 1930s Algeria, see Rebecca P. Scales, *Radio and the Politics of Sound in Interwar France, 1921–1939* (Cambridge University Press, 2016).

After his failed broadcasting project in Algeria, Najati Sidqi returned to France to find a situation of growing complexity. Spurred by the rising threat of fascism, the Comintern encouraged the Communists and Socialists of France to form a Popular Front, which won a narrow victory in the elections of 1936 and held power until 1938, implementing a range of social and economic reforms. Julian Jackson has chronicled this experience in *The Popular Front in France: Defending Democracy, 1934-1938* (Cambridge University Press, 1990). But the threat of violent reaction inside France was also growing, as attested by Sidqi's experience in a pub sympathetic to the Croix de Feu on Christmas Eve. This rightist movement, which began as a World War I veterans' organization, became a leading force on the French far right, participating in the February 1934 riots that brought down a left-wing government. See Robert J. Soucy, "French Fascism and the Croix de Feu: A Dissenting Interpretation," *Journal of Modern History,* 26:1 (Jan 1991); and William D. Irvine, "Fascism in France and the Strange Case of the Croix de Feu," *The Journal of Modern History*, 63:2 (June 1991).

13. THE END OF THE JOURNEY

During the period of Sidqi's stay in Syria, the country was on the eve of independence and in the process of negotiating the Franco-Syrian Treaty, which would define relations between the colonizer and its former mandate after independence. The treaty would have returned Alawite and Druze areas to Syria after the Mandate's partial partition of the country, but negotiations ultimately broke down, with the French legislature refusing to ratify the treaty. Syria did not gain full independence until mid-World War II. For a history of this period, see Philip Shukry Khoury, *Syria and the French Mandate: The Politics of Arab Nationalism, 1920-1945* (Princeton University Press, 1987).

During the 1930s and 1940s, as Sidqi chronicles, alliance with the rising powers of Fascist Italy and Nazi Germany was not beyond the pale for some anti-colonial activists in the Middle East, who saw in Fascism a possible ally to drive the French and British from their region. Regarding right-wing nationalism in Syria and the ambiguous relations between right-wing nationalists and the Nazi regime in Germany, see Götz Nordbruch, *Nazism in Syria and Lebanon: The Ambivalence of the German Option, 1933-1945* (Routledge, 2008). And see also the edited volume *Arab Responses to Fascism and Nazism* (University of Texas Press, 2014), which criticizes the common misconception that the Arab mainstream during the leadup to World War II was pro-Nazi. For Sidqi's own role as an exemplar of Arab antifascism, see the works by Mustafa Kabha and Israel Gershoni cited at the start of this essay.

The binational PCP split after 1948; following the Soviet line, the Israeli Communist Party accepted Partition and the establishment of the Israeli state. The later history of the party after Sidqi's sidelining, including its acceptance of partition and a two-state solution, is explored in Joel Beinin, *Was the Red Flag Flying There? Marxist Politics and the Arab-Israeli Conflict in Eqypt and Israel 1948-1965* (University of California Press, 1990). However, the Communists remained one of the few non-Zionist options on the Israeli political scene for decades after the Nakba. On the fate of the broader Arab communist movement after Sidqi parted ways with it, including the Syrian Communist Party under Khalid Bakdash, see Laure Guirguis, ed., *The Arab Lefts: Histories and Legacies, 1950s-1970s* (Edinburgh University Press, 2020).

As this essay has shown, Najati Sidqi's eventful life intersected with many key moments and movements of twentieth-century Palestinian, Arab, and global history. His memoir requires some contextual knowledge to understand, and it contains some gaps and minor factual errors, but it is a unique resource that has enriched many different research projects and can inspire many more. The reading suggestions in this essay have aimed to illuminate Sidqi's reminiscences, making them more accessible without explaining them away. We hope his story and our bibliographic suggestions have provoked curiosities that will lead to deeper exploration across many fields and disciplines—perhaps the best way to honor the wide-ranging curiosity and restless intellect of Najati Sidqi himself.

INDEX

NOTE: *Page numbers in italics indicate figures. Najati Sidqi's fellow KUTV students, nursing students, and Comintern members are glossed as such.*

The following abbreviations have been used:

Najati Sidqi's name has been abbreviated to **NS**

Communist Party members are glossed with their party abbreviation:

***Communist Party in Lebanon and Syria*—CPLS**

***French Communist Party*—FCP**

***Palestinian Communist Party*—PCP**

***Spanish Communist Party*—SCP**

A

S

T

www.ingramcontent.com/pod-product-compliance
Lightning Source LLC
Jackson TN
JSHW080254101025
92324JS00002B/107

* 9 7 8 1 4 7 7 3 3 3 2 2 8 *